D1281153

Please remember that this is a library book,
and that it belongs only temporarily to each
person who uses it. Be considerate. Do
not write in this, or any, library book.

A World Without Words

THE SOCIAL CONSTRUCTION OF

CHILDREN BORN DEAF AND BLIND

David Goode   *Foreword by Irving Kenneth Zola*

 TEMPLE UNIVERSITY PRESS | PHILADELPHIA

Temple University Press, Philadelphia 19122
Copyright © 1994 by Temple University. All rights reserved
Published 1994
Printed in the United States of America

⊗ The paper used in this publication meets the minimum
requirements of American National Standard for Information
Sciences—Permanence of Paper for Printed Library Materials,
ANSI Z39.48–1984

Library of Congress Cataloging-in-Publication Data
Goode, David, 1948–
A world without words : social construction of children born deaf
and blind / David Goode ; foreword by Irving Kenneth Zola.
    p.   cm. — (Health, society, and policy)
Includes index.
ISBN 1–56639–215–2. — ISBN 1–56639–216–0 (pbk.)
1. Blind-deaf children—United States—Case studies.   2. Rubella
in pregnancy—Complications—United States—Case studies.
I. Title.   II. Series.
HV1597.G66   1994
362.4′1′083—dc20   93–51038

*To my family, the Goodes, Guzmans, Fingerhuts, and
Makarons, who were hardworking housepainters, tailors,
seamstresses, candy store and Laundromat owners,
and who dreamt of educated and respected children and
grandchildren. Their aspirations and efforts live,
I believe, in these pages.*

AND

*To all persons who cannot use language
to tell their own story.*

CONTENTS

vii

FOREWORD

■ I HAVE FOLLOWED David Goode's work since the mid 1970s. In particular I identify with his struggle and persistence in publishing unusual research. Like him I collected data on a set of experiences (in my case, a village in the Netherlands inhabited solely by people with disabilities) deemed so esoteric that it would have little relevance beyond its geographical confines. Like him I saw the material published in a book over a decade later. And like him (after many formal rejections) I found editors at Temple University Press who recognized that such a manuscript occupied a special niche and deserved publication. My book was *Missing Pieces*, and they tell me it is selling better in 1993 than it did in 1982. *A World Without Words*, however, "pushes the envelope" in far more multifaceted ways.

In the 1960s a ubiquitous poster states, "If you do not understand my silences . . ." It meant to honor and respect the time when there are no words to express our feelings, when, as often stated, "words fail us." It has taken nearly three decades for this humane insight to penetrate social analysis. For whether it be in therapy or in theories of the formal organization of society and culture, we have overstressed the essentialness of spoken speech. It has even snuck into many formal educational and social policies. Ask people identified with deaf culture to describe their efforts to get sign language accepted as meeting their schools' language requirements or even designated as an essential social service and a legitimate, if not preferred, mode of communication (see the play or movie *Children of a Lesser God*).

ix

In *A World Without Words* David Goode has focused our attention on an even more socially rejected and psychologically devalued group of people—not only deaf but blind and essentially alingual. His research is based on children born with rubella syndrome, which caused not only these disabilities but in addition central nervous system damage, including cerebral palsy, mental retardation, orthopedic and cardiovascular sequelae. For the most part, such children are permanently institutionalized and are perceived as having untestable (and thus no real) intelligence and no self-help skills and as requiring round-the-clock supervision and care. The skills they "may" be able to be taught are generally so labor-intensive and the results so uneven and frustrating that most professional personnel eventually "burn out." Goode's book revolves around two young girls, Christina and Bianca, and their immediate support systems—in Christina's case, David Goode himself, and in Bianca's, her immediate family—who did *not* give up on them. What David and Bianca's family had to do to communicate is clearly not everyone's "cup of tea." To others, the effort may not be worth the trouble. But anyone that reads this book cannot but acknowledge that there is "a meaningful quality of life" in individuals that have historically been called and treated as "things" and "animals."

Goode's work is also a methodological tour de force—a treatise stimulated by the work of his mentors Harold Garfinkel and Melvin Pollner—in the perspectives of ethnomethodology too often regarded arcane. His work took time, years as both a direct-service provider and participant-observer on the ward where Christina was "housed" and almost a year doing in-home ethnography in the household where Bianca "lived." Without drowning the reader in the dense details of his observation, Goode gives the essence of its intense method and the insights it can yield. This work ranks with the study by Garfinkel of the insider view of sex-role change in his now classic *Studies in Ethnomethodology*. Invisible to the clinical lens, Goode has delineated a picture of Christina's and Bianca's "lived experience" despite others' doubt that they were living anything. His conclusion is stated gently. "She [Christina] was not dissimilar to other humans. She differed primarily in the forms in which these needs were met and in her inability to express these symbolically with acceptable language or postural formats."

Each chapter challenges our thinking in a different way. Building first on the case studies of Christina and Bianca, Goode continually raises deeper questions about the social construction of human communication and language. Still later he reflects on what all of this tells about our willingness, if not our ability (that is, with current concepts and methods), to understand the lived experiences of others, especially children.

I am sure that at the time this book and my foreword are printed, the controversy about "facilitated communication"—where "a usually normal adult physically assists a person with a disability to use a typewriter or word processor"—will still not be resolved. To those of us trained, perhaps overtrained, in positivistic methods, Goode's call for acknowledgment of "biographical specificity" presents troublesome dilemmas. For he argues that what he has found *re* Christina and Bianca, as well as the successes of much of facilitated communications, is not easily replicated. In fact, the successes are the product of just the two (or, in Bianca's case, several) people's involvement in intense long-term interaction. In short, the tremendous repertoire of communicative acts are not particularly observable to anyone else. That "you had to be there and for a long time" may not satisfy the traditional canons and methods of science. On the other hand, that does not per se make their claims untrue.

At the end of the book, Goode thus leaves us with a challenge and an invitation. It will take an enormous amount of dedication and systematic and often *in situ* research on communication networks actually to document the body's lexicon and forms of making meaning of everyday existence. If we do, one day we may actually be able "to write the language of the body" and "to know it in a more comprehensive and critical way." Goode's work is certainly a step along this road.

Irving Kenneth Zola

ACKNOWLEDGMENTS

■ OVER THE TWENTY years since the fieldwork for this book began in 1973 as part of my dissertation research, a great number of people have contributed to it in various ways. Within the text I refer to the ethnomethodologists in California who were instrumental in guiding my education as a graduate student and supervised the collection and initial analysis of data reported in this book. Foremost among these were Harold Garfinkel and Melvin Pollner, with whom I spent very many hours discussing these materials on a professional and personal level. It was Garfinkel who first served the "sweet poison" of ethnomethodology; he and Pollner shared in guiding its ingestion during graduate school. Other members of my dissertation committee at UCLA—Robert Edgerton, Robert Emerson, Warren TenHouten, and Mike McGuire—played important roles supervising the research. Manny Schegloff, at UCLA, and Aaron Cicourel, at the University of California at La Jolla, afforded me good ethnomethodological advice, as did Carlos Castaneda, Garfinkel's most famous student. Although not officially on the committee, Herbert Grossman, a senior pediatric neurologist at the UCLA Medical Center, also supported me as if he were a member of the dissertation committee. Finally, two senior graduate students in anthropology, Sylvia Bercovici and Donald Sutherland, psychologically and physically bolstered me during the times when graduate school and the dissertation process was personally overwhelming. Their friendship and intimate involvement in this research was, in the deepest of ways, part of its history and social construction.

After this initial period, there were many ethnomethodologists and sociologists who, through their review of my work and their encouragement, helped me to see it to this conclusion. The editor of the series, Irving Zola, was incredibly supportive; without his personal and professional backing for the past ten years, this book would probably not be in the reader's hands. Jerry Jacobs, Steve Taylor, and Bob Bogdan, at Syracuse University, and George Psathas, Jeff Coulter, Mike Lynch, and David Helm, at Boston University, were tremendously encouraging, as was Fran Waksler, at Wheelock College, and Gary Woodill, at Ryerson Polytechnic Institute. Marten Soder, Lars Kebbon, and Britta and Bo Hannestrand of the University of Uppsala, Sweden, Alain Coulon of the University of Paris, France, Ulla Beth Larrsen of the University of Linkoping, Sweden, Ernst and Gugu Kristofferson of LEV in Copenhagen, Denmark, and Phil Davies of the Oxford Rehabilitation Research Unit in England provided me with opportunities to lecture abroad on these materials, to keep them alive by updating and reformulating many of my ideas, and to get feedback from scholars with different educational perspectives. In retrospect, I see how important these opportunities were for the development of this book.

There have been many people in the field of human services and human services research who encouraged me to pursue this book. I especially want to acknowledge Burton Blatt, Bengt Nirje, Oliver Sacks and Wolf Wolfensberger, who reacted enthusiastically to earlier articles. George Tarjan, Sterling Garrard, Gershon Berkson, Ted Tjossem, Al Roehrer, and others were supportive of these studies and their publication in the disabilities field.

More recently there have also been several writers whose positive reactions served as literary fuel for the fire. Most important was Donna Williams, a writer who herself has a disability (autism), who worked professionally with children who were deaf and blind, and who corroborated my interpretations of the world of these children. The great clinical writer, Oliver Sacks, sent me several letters about the importance of this work for the human sciences, and in 1990 we had a lengthy conversation that probably was the single most important incident in motivating me to try to publish this research. Jim Swan, an English professor at SUNY-Buffalo, helped immensely through his detailed and penetrating readings of earlier articles, as well as chapters in this book.

Thanks also to my editor, Janet Francendese, who persevered and (finally) was successful, to Keith Monley for his excellent copy editing, and to the staff at Temple University Press for their excellent and timely work on this project.

I especially recognize and appreciate the many years of support of my wife, Diane, and son, Peter. They endured me and my stubbornness regarding this book and were the *sine qua non* of this writing.

Last, I acknowledge the children, parents, siblings, staff, physicians, sociologists, and others who were "subjects" in this research. It is upon the existential reality of our shared lives that any possibility of writing or reflection rests. We collectively made the events reported in these pages, which attempt truthfully to report and explicate our work together.

A World Without Words

Introduction

1

Who then . . . tells a finer tale than any of us? Silence does. And where does one read a deeper tale than upon the most perfectly printed page of the most precious book? Upon the blank page. When a royal and galant pen, in the moment of its highest inspiration, has written down its tale with the rarest of ink of all—where, then, may one read a still deeper, sweeter, merrier and more cruel tale than that? Upon the blank page.

—Isaac Dinesen, "The Blank Page," Last Tales

■ WHEN I FIRST read these lines by Isac Dinesen, I thought first of all the children and adults I have known who were born deaf-blind, did not develop any formal language, and are without any words to tell their own stories. This is a book about these people. I then thought of "ethnomethodology" because I am a practicing "ethnomethodologist," a form of sociology specifically concerned with the description and describability of the world and with the relation between text and worldly events. It should be of no surprise to the reader, then, that in a book about persons who use no words, by a scientist who looks critically at the use of words as descriptions of the world, one of the central preoccupations is whether writing can at all capture the world of the children and adults I studied—a world, as the book's title announces, without words. It was a particularly personal moment to find this text by Dinesen; it resonates so strongly with these parts of my life and with the central methodological problem of this book—how to use formal language to tell the story of persons themselves without formal language. Obviously, the fact

1

that this book exists indicates that I have worked out *some* sort of response to this methodological question, albeit one that might not satisfy the reader. But I am getting ahead of myself, and there is ample space to explore this and other issues concerning the world of children born deaf-blind.

Within these pages the reader will find an ethnomethodological examination of the lives of children who were born with rubella syndrome in the 1960s. Prenatal exposure to rubella, or German measles, sometimes caused children to be born with rubella syndrome (see Chapter 2 for a more complete description)—deaf and blind, often with mental retardation and a host of other disabilities. As children and adults, these persons have had very complex medical problems, multiple disabilities, and extremely limited development in many areas of life. They have been some of the most extraordinary persons I have ever seen, both in the positive and negative senses of "extraordinary." They have been incredibly challenging "clients" in human services, complex and demanding children in families, and particularly fascinating sons or daughters, or friends, for those who have known them intimately. The "rubella children" of the 1960s have been this, and much more. This is the reason I did not reject the idea of writing about them—they are so incredibly interesting, as well as incredibly misunderstood.

The purpose of this introduction is not to develop an overarching logic to this book, or even to summarize its arguments. It has too many arguments, and not all of them are consistent. (This is often the case with phenomenological studies, but I would maintain that all such studies are in a phenomenological sense true, or veridical, to the phenomena under consideration.) Instead, I will try to provide the reader with the lay of the land through brief descriptions of the chapters, after first discussing some historical elements of the writing.

I conducted the research reported within these pages in the 1970s while I was a graduate student at UCLA; the central chapters are based on articles that I published in journals and books and presented as papers over the past fifteen years. The material is substantially different now, having been reworked and rethought.

There are opposite ways to interpret this time lag and rewriting process. On the one hand, the material has had time to mature, since now a forty-six-year-old can reconsider what he wrote in his late twenties, with the benefit of the additional personal and professional experience. In this text I have allowed myself the liberty of a "deep reconsideration." Of course, I have preserved the scientific data, the field notes, in the same way that one would preserve statistical data or any other kind of scientific data. None of these were rewritten or changed in any way other than to correct typographical or grammatical errors. But I have allowed myself every opportunity to reconsider the meaning of these data, since I do not feel that the original interpretations were necessarily correct or complete, and I find no contradiction in a phenomenologically based, inductive scientific approach to reconsidering their meaning now.

On the other hand, it can be rightly argued that the data and their interpretation were freshest in my mind when I wrote them in the late 1970s, and that their re-presentation now is bound to distort them in some fundamental way or to lose the essence that made the work alive then. After all, fifteen years is a very long time to complete a writing project. And in fifteen years won't memory and changes in values and attitudes cause one to distort what the original research was? I think that these are reasonable questions, and I do not have ready answers to them that are likely to satisfy even the less skeptical of my readers. But I can share with you my thoughts about the fifteen-year gap between the completion of the research and publication of this book.

I tried to publish a book-length version of this work around 1980, and for many years I lamented that I was unsuccessful. I no longer do, at least for myself. I wish for the children with rubella syndrome, who have lived very difficult lives, that the book had been published back then. It might have helped them a little, although I seriously doubt that it would have made any great difference in their lives. Academic books simply are not the stuff by which human service systems change. As a writer and merchant of ideas, I value books, but I also have no illusion about their power to change systems. In both career and scientific terms, I must admit that this current text, a text with which I am likely to be academically associated, is much deeper and more mature than the one I presented in 1979. I can also say that I have very consciously, in recasting this material, avoided playing too fast and loose with that original work. I have attempted in substance and style to preserve what made it alive and meaningful for me then, although I have not remained faithful to all of the ways I initially thought about my data and experiences. That is, again, because I have learned something since I originally wrote the field notes and articles.

Thus, there are qualities to this work their are undeniably the result of the length of time it has been in progress. At some points in the text I appear to be arguing what today seems obvious; so I will point out that the reader needs to remember that the data was collected in 1976. Some of the substantive discussions in the data (for example, whether the children really had a viewpoint on things, or thoughts about things at all) are somewhat dated. But these are still relevant in a historical way; the sentiments expressed in them still survive in today's human service system, though they are perhaps less openly expressed. These kinds of data are also valuable because the dynamics of the social construction of the children I studied are very much still pertinent and important phenomena about which those in the field of sociology and disability know far too little. I must also admit that the reactions of very knowledgeable others, including writers, professionals in the field, and persons with disabilities all over the world, have helped me to reach the conclusion that this material is still timely and significant to the field. Finally, I can say that in reading these chapters I still feel the same sort of excitement I felt when I first considered these data; for me the data, and the issues they raise, are still very real, vibrant, and alive.

The following is a brief overview of the chapters.

In Chapter 2 I present a study of a child who lived on a ward in a state hospital for persons with mental retardation. The chapter presents this child's "social construction" within the world of the hospital, and my own attempts to socially reconstruct her and to appreciate this child's experience of the world. The chapter documents these attempts and my reflections upon them.

Chapter 3 examines the communication between a child with deaf-blindness and no formal language and her parents. It is an empirical inquiry into the nature of their human communication and understanding and is organized into three sections. First, there is a brief overview of ethnomethodological observations of mainstream social science research methodology and the relevance of this critique to clinical and behavioral research on families with retarded members. Second, the details of the ethnomethodological study of communication practices in the family are provided. Third, some implications of the study are briefly discussed.

Chapter 4 considers the possibility of understanding between children with deaf-blindness and without language and adults who can see and hear and who use language. The two communicative networks examined in Chapters 2 and 3 are reconsidered in order to ask of them, how was intersubjectivity achieved within these networks and what is the significance of such achievement for our understanding of human communication and language? Phenomenological and ethnomethodological literature is used to anchor the recommendations of these studies in previous formulations of similar issues.

The purpose of Chapter 5 is to explore and explicate, from an ethnomethodological perspective, the logic of researchers' construction and analysis of data in their work as researchers. Because I was involved in disability research, I drew exemplary material from this domain, but my arguments are equally applicable to other forms of inquiry. The chapter attempts to portray the varieties of social research practices in the construction of data. As a secondary matter, I view the construction of these forms of data with particular reference to their relation to practices and "facts" of everyday life of persons with disabilities and their families. This chapter is important in the book's overall conception because it analyzes in some detail many of the methodological issues only briefly explored in the case-study materials presented in earlier chapters. It also provides an opportunity for me to turn the ethnomethodological light upon my own work, something that is difficult, though not inappropriate, to do while attempting to display a part of the everyday social world through observation and interpretation of field data.

Chapter 6 describes the significance of these studies to the concept of kids' culture, socialization, developmental theory, and adult-child interaction generally.

The concluding offers an update on the population and some discussion of how these studies bear upon currently topical issues in the field of disability, such as quality of life and facilitated communication.

A
World
Without
Words

2

And with what simplicity they ignore words, the signs with which objects prostitute themselves. They experiment with blindness, deafness, paralysis, olefactory anaesthesia, paradisaical mental silence, and if they are nevertheless obliged to see, hear or smell, they refrain from organizing their impressions into disciplined companies, thus from the very start avoiding the temptations of self-delusion . . . ; the idiot is a born democrat who does not deprive objects of the freedom that must someday be restored to them willy-nilly. . . . God bless . . . this being pampered by the blissful present, who revels in his awareness of his sense organs; he is the hero of the here and now, foster brother of objects, our masters.

—*Gyorgy Konrad,* The Caseworker

■ BETWEEN 1973 AND 1976 I conducted participant-observation research on a state hospital ward for children born deaf-blind who were diagnosed as profoundly mentally retarded and who had failed to develop any formal language. Many of these children were born with rubella syndrome, a viral embryopathy that causes some of the most severe disabilities we have ever seen in children. They were some of the most complex and interesting children I have ever been privileged to have met.

In doing this research I had no specific a priori theoretical or methodological issues; rather, these concerns emerged during the course of the study. I was confident that the ward was an extremely interesting place, but did not know what my involvement with ward personnel or residents would come to in the long run.[1] My primary motivation, as I perceived it at the time, was a genuine fascination with the interaction between children who were congenitally deaf-blind and without formal language and adults who heard, saw, and spoke normally. I must confess that as a senior graduate student I had read enough sociology to understand that sociologists assigned language a critical role in the organization of social relations and human behavior. Thus, I realized at the time that I had stumbled upon a society in which shared formal language could not play such a function, and perhaps this realization represented a general research motivation. In the end the research covered many topics, not all of which are written about in this volume or were related specifically to language. This chapter presents one extremely important aspect of that work—my attempts to understand and describe the phenomenal and experiential world of a particular child who resided on this ward.[2]

■ THE SOCIAL CONSTRUCTION OF CHILDREN WITH RUBELLA SYNDROME

Many things about this ward and its inhabitants were fascinating; it was initially notable that these children lived in a "total institution," with all the segregation, regimentation, and harshness described by Goffman (1961) and later openly documented by the news media in the era of "deinstitutionalization" during the 1970s and 1980s. They lived very socially circumscribed lives, interacting essentially with only two kinds of persons (two "statuses" in their society, to use sociological language), namely, the clinical professional and the ward and school "direct-care" staff. Despite this relative social homogeneity, there existed in this simplified and cut-off world of the state institution considerable open disagreement about how to interpret the actions and behaviors of the deaf-and-blind children. Indeed, there were frequent and readily observable disagreements about the specific (in)capacities and social "identities" of individual children (see Goode 1985). Given the relative smallness of the hospital society, with only three statuses (the third being "patient"), the existence of "multiple identities" for children with such profound mental retardation and severe multiple disabilities was a notable and interesting research finding.

I very quickly became aware of this "multiple identity" phenomenon through participation in discussions with direct-care staff during which the clinical assessments of particular children by certain professional clinical staff (all M.D. or Ph.D.) were seriously questioned. Cynical and derogatory remarks were passed, such as "That doctor does not know the first thing about Dawn" or "He sees him once every six months for ten minutes and then thinks he can tell me what I should do with him; I take care of him every day!" Such remarks were signposts for what turned out to be a sociologically interesting phenomenon, and held great import for these children with deaf-blindness.

These disagreements signified what Garfinkel described as the "organizationally incarnate" character of the children. This generic concept refers the reader to the way all objects and people are constructions of and participants in the immediate circumstances in which they are found (or in which they find themselves). These deaf-blind children were socially constructed in the sense that their very bodies and actions were given life, form, and meaning through immediate social relations and practices that surrounded them and in which they participated. When the organization of immediate social relations with the child differed radically—for example, the long-term, subjective, and intimate knowledge of a child's daily life experienced by a direct-care worker on the ward compared to the short-term, objective, and

nonintimate knowledge of a child characteristic of a clinical relation—perception of that child reflected the differences in these
relations. "Who" a child was taken to be and "what" he or she
could do would be perceived in ways that reflected these substantial interactional differences. In other words, children were
assigned multiple and, to a large degree, conflicting identities
that reflected differences in the microsociology of face-to-face relations with the children. Doctors saw these children through
the organization of doctors' work with them, and direct-care staff
experienced the children through the organization of their custodial and teaching work with them.

Thus, on the ward there were two different "versions" of these
children—clinical and custodial, if you will—and each reflected
the very practical relation and tasks required by these very different forms of social connectedness. Clinicians looked at these
children through the eyes of medicine (or development psychology, speech pathology, or what have you), and it is no surprise
that in their view these were the "lowest functioning" children
in the hospital, with very few human qualities and little progno-
sis for improvement. Indeed, they were "so" retarded and disabled (see below, description of rubella syndrome) that it was very
difficult to treat them or examine them as patients at all. If doctors' work is primarily to diagnose and cure, these children were
terrible partners for them in such work—hard to diagnose, difficult to treat, and impossible to cure. Since I had the opportunity
to observe children in clinical situations, I was able to appreciate
how frustrated and impotent physicians felt in their professional
work with the deaf-blind children. There was no such thing as
"curing" someone with rubella syndrome. Such an idea is well
beyond any medical technology we can even imagine. Add to this
that their medical conditions are often so complex that regular
health care would be problematic even if they were "good" cooperative patients.[3] Thus, the childrens' pejorative clinical identities
emerged as "figures" against the "ground" of the clinical/medical

enterprise. Unfortunately for these children, it was the viewpoint of the professional staff about them that was reflected in their official habilitation program (called then an Individual Educational Plan, or IEP). The "medical model" was dominant at the hospital during this period, and it was the clinical identity of these children that was their "official" identity.

The direct-care staff,[4] on the other hand, saw these children in terms of their day-to-day, long-term involvement with them. They were charged not with clinical diagnosis and cure but with custodial care of the children, with teaching them basic living skills; and to do this the staff had to be with them for substantial periods of time each day. Thus, the staff knew these children intimately and well, but, as with the clinicians, it was their practical routine work with the children that formed the basis for the children's identities, perceived and remarked-upon characteristics, and competencies and incompetencies. The practices involved in direct caring and teaching provided ward staff the "frames" within which deaf-blind children were encountered (or it was against this "ground" that the "figures" of the children emerged). Thus, on the ward the children were talked about as "cooperative" or "aggressive," as a "soiler" or "masturbator," "spoiled," and so forth, that is, in terms relevant to what a direct-care worker might actually have to do with the child day in, day out. The staff were charged with the basic teaching programs, and because the children had very few basic skills (even walking and eating were somewhat problematic in many cases), the staff were involved with endless teaching/correcting encounters with them. Working with many of these children at once was hard, even impossible at times. Sometimes one did *so much* teaching and correcting that it was almost comical (since I initially spent five months on the ward acting in the role of a direct-care staff person, I can speak about this with some authority). It was as if you were in a preprogrammed dance sequence in a movie, moving from one child to the next without time to think or shift gears.

"Too many kids to fix, too few people, too little time"—our work motto. Work with the same difficult-to-reach children, same place, five days a week, was, however, essentially unfunny. It "burnt out" *many* of the staff during my stay on the ward; that is, people quit or transferred out of the unit because they could not take the job anymore. While a couple of the staff remained with the program during the period I was involved, I observed several generations of staff come and go. The really competent persons who had the skills and the will to stay with the program were, without exception, offered better, higher-paying positions elsewhere in the hospital. Those without a commitment to work with deaf-blind children ended up leaving or were laterally transferred.

Both clinicians and direct-care staff were engaged in some practical form of "social construction" of the children with rubella syndrome, producing radically differing identities for them. From my observations it appeared that the direct-care staff ultimately had more reliable and concrete knowledge about the children than the professional, clinical staff, despite the fact that the clinical identity of the children was the official one. Indeed, if I wanted to know what a particular child might see, hear, and understand, I began by talking to the direct-care worker most familiar with that child. I did not read the clinical file. These, I eventually understood, were filled with inaccurate assessments (for the reasons described above). The staff, on the other hand, knew from long-term, intimate observation what children could and could not do and were generally more accurate in their assessments (which is not to imply they were completely accurate or did not have a particular slant on the children). Programs for the children were devised exclusively by professional staff without consultation at *all* with the ward staff. This is a general problem in human services in which decision making is left in the hands of professionals.

Thus, the childrens' lives were dominated by these two versions of who they were: "socially constructed" as bad patients on the one hand and difficult custodial objects/students on the other. While one version of these children (that of the direct-care staff) had more detail and accuracy than the other, neither version had seriously considered that these children were first and foremost children like other children, or that they might have their own version of who they were. That is, what was absent from this little society, as opposed to "normal" society, were social representations (utterances, for example, or collective action or activity) on the part of the children themselves and representing the childrens' perspectives about things, including themselves. This was true, in part, because of the childrens' alinguality, multiple sensory disabilities, and institutionalization. As a consequence of their powerlessness to define their own situation, their lives on the ward resembled those of animals in training. The areas, contents, and form of their "Individualized Educational Plan" (formulated by professional staff and enacted by direct-care staff) in *no way* took the childrens' own ideas and goals into consideration. The children generally could not understand the motivation behind most of the habilitation and educational work; it remained largely extrinsic to their own ideas about and enterprises in life. When I pointed this out to some of the professional staff, I was told that "such children have no ideas or goals"—an incredible and dehumanizing statement. The reader may also appreciate why the project I chose, the description of the experiential world of one of the children, was so critical.

Dehumanization for the expressed purpose of humanization, something all too common in many human services, was made most clear to me early in my stay on the ward when I first assisted the children eating lunch. Eating was done en masse, each child sitting in a particular seat in a large lunch room. Bibs were tied around their necks and draped on the table, and a plastic tray was put on the bib. In this way children who were messy eaters would not soil their clothes, and dropped food would fall onto the bib. This was the logic, although this arrangement failed that logic as often as it succeeded; children managed to cover themselves and their clothes with food nonetheless. All children ate in this fashion. One child held a fork in one hand, while her noneating hand rested squarely on the top of her head in an uncomfortable-looking "prisoner of war" fashion. I observed this for about fifteen to twenty minutes before I asked why her hand was on top of her head. It seemed such an uncomfortable and unnatural position. I was told the following unbelievable story. She had been a "food groper and stealer," meaning that she used to grab food with her left hand while eating with her right. To stop this unacceptable behavior she had been given aversive stimulation in the form of electric shocks. At first she was put in a straight jacket wired with accelerometers (devices that detect movement and send an electric impulse). As a result, Kim—that was her name—got a shock when she grabbed for the food. But she also got a shock when she pulled back from the food; she thus went into immediate experimental neurosis, shocking herself continuously! The next procedure employed a cattle gun and allowed the experimenter to dole out the shock at will. It proved effective—she learned not to put her left hand on the table—and what I was observing was the result of that procedure.

This treatment most clearly illustrates what I mean by "animal training." You can ask all sorts of serious questions about Kim's treatment. First, the use of electric shock is highly questionable as a clinical technique. Second, whose problem is it that Kim steals food? If a ten-year-old child is hungry, why not give her or him more food? Third, why all the concern with how the children eat in the first place, that they not use their hands and instead use utensils? The "party line" on this from ward staff was that by eating "normally" they would look more normal and be more accepted by others in the society. About this, one had to ask whether it was socially unacceptable for children, or even adults, with deaf-blindness to eat with their hands and, most important, if so, whose problem that was. Today, in hindsight, I would say the problem was really society's, not the deaf-blind childrens'. At the time of the study a different logic prevailed.

The act of eating, for a child with deaf-blindness, would naturally, without instruction, consist in eating with the hands; this included a variety of techniques of manipulating and touching food as well as transporting it to the mouth. One got a sense that many of the children really resented having to use a fork or spoon. They failed to grasp the "logic" to it when all they had to do was grab the food. I also think it was important for the children to touch the food—it was part of what they wanted to do when eating, to feel the food with their hands. One could imagine how this need to touch the food they ate would be a natural and logical outgrowth of their being deaf and blind. They also sniffed and smelled their food intensely when they could, and looked at it in a studied fashion with whatever vision remained.

This "behavior modification," the use of aversive or positive reinforcement to mold behavior, came to represent for me the way in which the childrens' own ways of being human, their own choices and preferences, were totally ignored in the programs designed for them. Indeed, in Kim's case, a sensible and logical behavior was brutally, and perhaps permanently, extinguished. Such program goals and methods substantiated the observation that most professionals did not believe that children like Kim operated from a vlid perspective or had ideas about things worth examining.

A year of intensive ethnographic observation and videotaping on the ward told me this view was demonstrably incorrect. I had massive amounts of observational data indicating very active mental processes in the children, as well as complex forms of social participation and relatedness. While it might be true that these mental and social activities of the children were not reflected in their clinical assessments, they were nonetheless observable aspects of their everyday life on the ward. When I presented some of these field notes and ideas at a research rounds at the hospital, I was passed anonymous notes from several researchers in attendance advising me to "see a psychiatrist," so unthinkable was the idea that such children might have their own perspective on things and that we ought to be interested in that perspective (one has to remember that this was in the early 1970s).

The ward staff were less skeptical about my observations. In fact, when I shared this line of thinking with them, they were generally enthusiastic in their response, if for no other reason than the fact that my analysis of the situation was antimedical and participated in a certain ground-up distaste for medical professionals at the hospital. But their support was more than this. When I told ward staff that I thought many of these children were "smart" in their own way, many of them were quick to agree and to cite evidence to this effect for particular children. I told them I was interested in finding out more about how these "kids" perceived things. I said that we should be more interested in what the children want and should listen to the childrens' choices and goals. The direct-care staff were generally supportive of these ideas because, I believe, their long-term and intimate involvement allowed them to see the same things that I had recorded in my observations. And while their jobs with the children, as described above, rarely provided opportunities for them to discuss the children in this way, to formulate them as "smart," they were still able to observe the same phenomena that I had. They also appreciated how understanding "where a child was coming from" was an integral part of helping that child to realize "program goals."

It was thus generally with the direct-care staff's blessing, and with the research staff's disbelief, that I began a research enterprise aimed specifically at retrieving the phenomenal and experiential world of a particular child with rubella syndrome residing on the ward. Apart from the scientific and methodological issues involved, the reader may now have a sense of why this project was so important for these children. It's aim was to discover and make known precisely what was missing from their lives and what made these lives appear to be like those of animals. In my way of thinking at the time, as well as that of several of the staff members, it was an opportunity to socially reconstruct these children in a fashion truer to their actual human qualities and capabilities, invisible though these be to the clinical lens. Establishing an understanding (intersubjectivity) *with* the children in their "own terms" would be significant not only for our understanding *of* them but for our efforts at teaching and socializing. While the intellectual issues involved were intriguing (see Chapter 4), there was far more at stake in this enterprise than academic knowledge.

■ ACHIEVING INTERSUBJECTIVITY WITH CHRISTINA

Ordinarily we take it for granted that we live in an intersubjective world, a world whose physical, social, and psychological aspects are communicated and shared with reasonable accuracy. Yet on this ward there were in a sense two "worlds": one shared by myself and the staff (normal perceivers) and another inhabited by the residents. Indeed, by the very differences in our sense organs, the residents were living and acting in a different perceptual place than I—one in which the reception of audiovisual stimuli had been degraded as a result of a prenatal viral infection. It was decided that only intimate and persistent interactional contact with the residents would likely enable me to enter into their world. A major obstacle to such a task was the variation in perceptual abilities displayed by particular residents: they did not inhabit a deaf-blind world at large; rather, each exhibited a specific configuration of perceptual/cognitive skills and deficiencies. Consequently, I decided to concentrate on a nine-year-old female resident, Christina (Chris), and to spend a number of daily cycles (twenty-four-hour periods or longer) with her, sharing "average days" in her "ordinary life." In addition to naturalistic observation of her behavior, I employed videotaping and viewing of normal ward routines and other interactional procedures ("mimicking" and "passive obedience").

My relatively long-term involvement with Chris gave me access to observational data unavailable to medical practitioners, who would see her during relatively short, structured, and "nonordinary" medical examinations. From our interactions and my observations over a period of a few months, I gathered the following information about her perceptual, motor, behavior, and language abilities (see also Goode 1974a, 1974b, 1975b).

MEDICAL AND BEHAVIORAL PROFILE

Medical examination records, developmental assessments, and interviews with the child's mother were used to construct a medical-behavioral profile.

During Chris's prenatal existence, she (as a fetus) was subject to an "attack" of a virulent and destructive cyclical virus known as rubella, or German measles. During the second or third week of pregnancy, the rubella virus entered her mother's bloodstream and attacked the sensitive, rapidly multiplying cells of the embryo (rubella embryopathy), causing damage in the forms of hemorrhage, brain lesions, lysis damage to the cochlea, cataract, and so on. As a result, Chris was born with a severe syndrome of multihandicaps (rubella syndrome) whose sequelae included bilateral cataracts, congenital heart disease (patent ductus and stenosis), functional deafness (the "intactness" of Chris's hearing mechanism has never been established), clinical microcephaly, central nervous system damage (a low-grade diffuse encephalopathy), abnormal behavior patterns, and severe developmental retardation. The degree and nature of Chris's multihandicaps had been difficult to assess, since medical procedures for making such determinations were usually designed for normally perceiving and communicating persons (see Goode 1974a). At the age of five, Chris was diagnosed as legally blind, legally deaf, and mentally retarded and was placed in a state hospital for the retarded.[5]

Vision. Chris was able to orient visually to large objects in her path and would normally "fend" against these by using her right arm. She was also able to inspect objects at a very close range and was observed to eat by bringing the spoon to her right ("good") eye to a distance of perhaps one to two inches for the apparent purpose of inspecting the food's color and consistency. Chris's visual acuity varied considerably depending on such factors as setting, emotional state, motivation, and quality of visual stimulus. In close face-to-face presentation, she sometimes seemed to be studying my physiognomy.

Hearing. Chris's auditory acuity also seemed to vary considerably. When motivated, she seemed to be able to orient herself to the sound of my guitar being played at a considerable distance from her, and in a number of "natural experiments" she was observed to "home in" on this sound from distances of more than twenty feet. She loved sound stimulation of all types—especially music, with its regular rhythms and variety of frequencies. She attended to my singing to her or speaking to her in her ear (she used her right ear more than her left and would maneuver herself so that she could turn this ear toward the sound stimulus). It was difficult to assess the amount or quality of sound she was receiving, but several clinicians concurred with my belief that she received a variety of sounds but had problems in "processing" the sound as normal hearers do.

Touch. Chris was extremely touch oriented. She used her tongue as her primary organ for perception whenever possible and would lick anything within her reach. I learned to conceive of this activity as Chris's way of asking, What is it? although I also observed repetitive licking of smooth surfaces (apparently for purposes of sensory gratification). Chris was "ticklish," and her usual response to being touched all over her body was laughter (sometimes, as her teacher noted, this laughter might have been defensive—that is, an effort to curtail interaction rather than to participate fully in it). Although she could easily distinguish between textures by touching objects with her hands, her sense of heat and cold seemed depressed relative to mine.

Autosensory Stimulation. Light and sound for Chris were often a matter of self-gratification and self-stimulation, that is, compared with normal youngsters her age. She exhibited many autostimulatory behaviors, including "finger-flicking" (autophotic behavior), repetitive licking of smooth surfaces (autotactual behavior), and rocking and head swinging (autokinesthetic behaviors). We developed a number of games (described below) based upon her pursuit of perceptual gratification. But Chris's use of her senses was not purely autostimulatory. She also used them in goal-directed activities (for example, finding a toy, building up some objects so that she could climb on them and get her ear closer to the radio in the day room, looking for the ward door, fending against objects, finding the guitar sound). The autostimulatory use of her senses was, however, a characteristic and conspicuous feature of her behavior.

Gross Motor Behavior. Chris enjoyed gross body activities of all kinds and was in this regard a fairly active deaf-blind child. She enjoyed interacting with me by having me pull her up while she simultaneously grasped my neck with her arms and my waist with her legs. From this position rather common to parent and child, she would engage in a variety of head-swinging and head-rocking movements. Often I would bounce her and throw her into the air, and she seemed to enjoy her helplessness—

abandoning herself to the sensations these activities provided for her. During such activities she would rub her genitals against me (something that was not promoted but also not punished). Chris also characteristically rocked her body to music and in auto-photic reactions to strong light sources (such as an overhead fluorescent light). In a life described as one of "scattered achieve-ments," Chris's most significant ones were in the areas of gross body interaction and in her use of touch.

Self-Help Skills. At the time of my study Chris was untrained in areas of self-maintenance other than eating. Urination and defe-cation "accidents" often occurred during the course of data col-lection (and in a gesture of good faith vis-à-vis the staff and Chris, I took care of these). Chris was unable to dress or bathe without assistance or to walk without supervision. Teaching such skills to people who are congenitally deaf-blind and retarded is a very time-consuming and difficult enterprise, and given the paucity of staff in general and trained staff in particular, Chris had never mastered these skills. Of course, she could engage in elaborate behavior schemes in order to gratify herself (she could get up without any cue, go to the music room, and let herself in), but she could not master the skills and rationale behind procedures of toileting and dressing. By hospital regulations these matters were usually taken care of as a matter of routine. Chris was cleaned and dressed whether she participated voluntarily or re-sisted violently.

Communicating Skills. Chris did not seem to share any aware-ness of what a linguistic symbol was. However, this is not to say that she did not regularly communicate with me and with the staff. To communicate her wishes, she liked gross physical ac-tions that relied heavily on "background expectancies" (Garfinkel 1967)—for example, walking into the dining area and sitting at her table ("I'm hungry") or going to the ward and waiting ("I want to go out"). She also used gross body movements to indicate that I should continue or cease some of our activities (for example, grabbing my arm and simulating a strumming movement apparently to indicate her desire that I continue playing guitar, or pushing me away to indicate her wish to terminate interaction). At one point her language teacher claimed to have gotten her to say the word "more," and I have seen her use the gestural symbol (Signing Exact English symbol) for "more" when I vigorously structured the activity and coaxed her. It is doubtful that Chris's grasp of the symbolic character of these actions resembled my own. At the time, Chris could receive a modified version of the food sign but had not been seen to use the sign expressively.

General Behavior Summary. When I was present in the research setting and interacting with her, Chris appeared to possess an inquisitive and active intelligence, housed in an extremely flawed body. She was oriented toward getting physical and perceptual satisfaction in any way she could. She displayed her dissatisfaction and liked to have things "her own way." She actively pursued contact with adults and was socially sophisticated relative to her development in other areas. At an educational conference at the hospital, one administrator commented on her ability to "wrap me around her little finger," and in some sense this observation was true. Granting all the difficulties in making a determination of this kind, it was my own conclusion that Chris's primary problems stemmed from her lack of intact visual and auditory fields upon which we build our systems of symbolic communication and organize our practical interactional activities. She had never had an intact model for her behavior and did not understand what Schutz (1970) called our "recipes," "motivational relevancies," or courses of rational activity. This is not to say that Chris was an acultural being, only that in many areas of her life the actions and skills manifested by "normal" cultural members were not evident.

MEETING CHRIS ON HER "OWN GROUNDS"

As described above, the staff's job—its institutional rationale and its concomitant "purposes at hand" (maintenance and teaching the children)—was directly related to the particular features they formulated about the residents. I came to understand that I could take advantage of my institutional position (my not having that job and being charged with maintenance and teaching) to pursue particularly interesting lines of research. I could deconstruct the staff's construction of certain of the residents' behaviors as retarded (that is, as faulted) to discover the logical underpinnings behind the residents' system of practical reasoning—a system that produced behavior displays as faulted. By doing this I hoped that I might also be able to unmask some of the skills the children exhibited--skills that the remedial stance of the staff was "hiding." This enterprise would entail establishing an understanding of and with the residents on a somewhat different basis from that of the staff. Basically, I wanted to try and understand things from the child's perspective.

I had inspiration in formulating the task to myself from the journals of Jean Itard, the French educator who took up the habilitation of the Wild Boy, Victoire of Aveyron.[6] I wanted to avoid—as Jean Itard failed to do with Victoire—seeing the children as tabulae rasae, acultural beings who needed cultural repair work done on them. Although they were culturally deficient, to make them seeable and describable in only those terms was to ignore a whole storehouse of skills that they had developed but that were not specifically cultural achievements. Commenting upon Itard's dismal failure to habilitate or teach Victoire, Mannoni (1972) rightly noted that if Itard had accompanied Victoire in living in the Caune Woods (where Victoire had survived for seven or eight years as a youngster), Itard's storehouse of cultural knowledge would have been quite beside the point. Stripped naked, battling the elements, Itard would have *had to learn from Victoire in order to survive* (the woods creatures' "purpose at hand"). In that setting an understanding of Victoire's world, using only the stock of knowledge at hand in eighteenth-century French culture, would have been maladaptive. Metaphorically speaking, I decided to "go to the woods." To make this journey I had to locate where I was (see Chapter 6 for a more complete discussion of Itard and Victoire).

Self-Examinations. Although I saw my task as establishing inter-subjectivity (a mutually recognized mutual understanding, or a mutually recognized interiority to a same world) with Chris, there was also an awareness that this would not be at all easy to do and that "I"—my "seeing, hearing, speaking self"—would inhibit achievement of the task. I wanted a dialogue to begin between us but in her "own terms." The problem was how to recognize what her "own terms" were. And there was this ever-growing awareness that I was in a very real sense the greatest obstacle to being interior to Chris's world. It is thus interesting to note, as the title to this section implies, that a regular part of my work with Chris was thus work on and about myself. I sought by a series of exercises to "clear myself out of the way." I began a series of experiments in simulating deaf-blindness in my own life, a serious course of dream analysis, and critical reflection on my own writings about Chris. These particular self-examinations were crucial to my work with Chris but really did not involve her directly.

First, I attempted to approximate her perceptual environment by the simultaneous use of ear stops and blindfolds. I discovered that I was quick to make the necessary adaptations to the features of the visual-auditory world I already took for granted. This is not to say that the blindfolds and ear plugs did not cause me a lot of trouble, that they did not render me essentially helpless without the aid of a sighted or hearing person. Rather, the cognitive categories I already had learned allowed me to be deaf and blind in a fashion that bore little resemblance to the *congenital* deaf-blindness of the residents. They were congenitally deaf-blind and knew no other condition; I was adventitiously deaf-blind and contained in my memory the full array of knowledge and experience that had been mine while seeing and hearing. For example, when I tried to eat my meal while "deaf-blind," I realized that what I was trying to do while eating was to produce that course of events that I already understood to be "mealtime" through my participation in the hearing, seeing, and speaking culture. The "meal" was already in my head, so to speak, and the deaf-blindness only posed technical problems to me in trying to produce it deaf-blindly.

This was not at all the kind of deaf-blindness that the children experienced, since the "meal" was not in their heads at all. Thus, while they ate, they would finger and feel their food, sniff the food, examine it carefully with their residual vision—things that I did not do and for which I had no particular motivation while experiencing my temporary deaf-blind meal.

This is not to say that temporary, simulated deaf-blindness was not useful in some ways to help identify with Christina and the other children. Some features of their experience were made evident to me, such as the relative danger of a world that is unpredictable or unanticipatable. Relying primarily on the kinesthetic sense and sense of smell makes the experiential world relatively "thin," immediate, unpredictable, and therefore dangerous. This is especially true when other moving bodies are present. In a sense, one's world is collapsed to one's immediate bodily space, unless through familiarity with the environment one "knows" that the room one sits in is so large, with such and such furniture. Without such familiarity the world of deaf-blind people is severely and dangerously collapsed onto themselves. This was easy to learn in my simulations through all the accidents and broken objects in my home. My poor wife and cats had to suffer these indignities, but the lesson to me was clear.

Not only was the relatively unseeable and hearable world dangerous to me, I was also dangerous to it. I also found that being
deaf-blind made achieving the simplest things sometimes difficult and that I became frustrated and short-tempered. I had an
uneasy relation to my surroundings, which I think had something to do with the way Chris and other children on the ward
experienced their surroundings. And while the differences between the ways we were deaf and blind were obvious and crucial
to my understanding of Chris, the deaf-blind simulations did
allow me to identify with some aspects of the her situation.

Another piece of self-examination that I was called upon to do
in order to identify with Chris and her experiential world was on
the emotional level. It would be accurate to say that almost all
persons who worked on the ward were emotionally moved on
some level when working with these children.[7] I was particularly
involved with Christina, and as time progressed, these emotions
became powerful influences on the course of the research. Without such powerful emotions I seriously doubt that I would have
undertaken many of the things I did for Christina's sake. At the
same time, these emotions were dangerous influences on how I
saw Chris and my relationship with her. I felt them to be both
necessary and dangerous to the task of gaining interiority to
Chris's world.

Their danger was marked for me clearly in two recurring
dreams, the windows to our emotional lives. One was a seemingly benign and strange dream in which Christina and Huey are
being married as adults.[8] They are talking to me, talking being a
common thing that parents and others report in their dreams
involving deaf-blind children, and thanking me for saving both of
them, for teaching them to speak, and for helping them to get
together and get married. I am in the emotional role of savior in
the dream and "feel" this emotional pressure to accept their
thanks gratefully and without egotism. This dream was experienced by me basically as fun.

The other dream that recurred was not at all pleasant. It involved a combination of frightening events and auditory and visual symbols. In this dream I see a small point of light off in a black sky. This small dot begins to grow in size as a crescendo of loud "stringlike" sounds gets louder and louder. At a certain point the dot becomes visible as a black-and-white picture of Christina's face inside a bull's-eye. As the face gets incredibly large and blots out the visual field entirely, the music becomes unbearably loud. I am overwhelmingly afraid and angry and hit the face (in fact, I "front punch" it—a karate technique). The face then returns back to the black sky, and the music subsides, and I usually awaken. This dream was recurrent and caused me to awaken in sweats. Perhaps as a way to reduce its real emotional stress, I would refer to it as my "pow Alice right to the moon" dream—a reference to Jackie Gleason's television comedy show *The Honeymooners*. The dream nevertheless was a "marked dream." Because it was recurrent and accompanied by these powerful emotions, it announced itself to me as important in my work with Chris.

I felt I had to understand both these dreams in order to allow myself to be in Chris's world. I came to understand after some time that these dreams represented different parts of my emotional self's reaction to Chris. One part of me (empathy and compassion) wanted to save Chris and make her like me. Another part of me (fear, hate, and perhaps sympathy) wanted her literally off the face of the earth. What I came to understand about these emotions was that they were *my* emotions, not Chris's. Chris neither wanted to be saved from her "condition" nor wanted to leave the earth because her existence was so unbearably horrible. Those were *my* reactions to Chris, reactions that I believe I had to make clear to myself, not thereby to purge myself of them, something that I never really did, but to allow myself to understand my reactions to Chris, my way of emotionally constructing her life for myself. I realized that I had to distinguish between this and how Chris experienced her own world if I was to have any chance of understanding Chris in her own terms.[9]

This separation of the helper's self-interests from those of the person being helped is really a general problem in human services of all types; the helper is able to help the person needing the help only insofar as the helper understands and can separate out his or her own self-interests in the helping situation. While this is not at all a new or profound idea, I did not know it at the time, and I had to have these matters made clear to me—to clear myself out of the way and let Christina speak.

Finally, there was a self-directed exercise that was very valuable in removing myself as an obstacle to seeing Christina—a critical examination of my own writings about her. One thing that I clearly observed was that Chris did not share outsiders' perspectives toward her world and actions. I thought I could begin my task of willing suspension of belief by attempting to separate the valuative (my reactions) from the descriptive (her experience of doing something) in my accounts of Chris's actions. This looking back at my own evaluative characterizations of Chris can be seen in the following field notes:

Watching Chris walk, I saw clearly that her arm movements were spastic, her gait wide, and her movements and balance awkward. She also did not seem to walk purposively— that is, she would walk a few steps, stop, bend over or stare into the sun, run, twist around, laugh, sit down, get up, walk, and so forth. She seemed to enjoy the physical sensations involved in her admittedly "abnormal" techniques for ambulation. While it is clear that she does not walk correctly, it is equally clear that it is only incorrect with respect to the dominant seer-hearer culture's version of walking—a version, by virture of her impaired sensors, almost inaccessible to her. Most important, while watching her, we were prompted to ask ourselves, Who is getting more from the

activity of walking, Chris or us? It is no great cognitive accomplishment, no mystery, no great analytic task to watch
her walk (eat, play, excrete, and so on) and to find her actions "faulted," "wrong," "abnormal," and so forth. Any
competent cultural "member" (Garfinkel and Sacks 1970) —
that is, anyone who understands the rational and socially
sanctioned set of activities for which "walking" (eating,
playing, excreting) is an appropriate name—could and
would find Chris's walking abnormal. The question is, how
should we evaluate what we see? Is it wrong to act abnor-
mally, and does one's detection of abnormal behavior require that remedial work be done upon the child to correct
the observed flaws? These questions seem particularly important when asked with regard to persons who, in very
obvious ways, do not share the perceptual-cognitive world
that occasions normal walking.

Evaluations seemed inextricably involved in my simple descriptions, my direct experience of Chris's behavior. To find a
"way out" of these evaluations embedded in experience, I had to
turn not to a cognitive reshuffling of categories but to a change
in my practical activities with the residents. In other words, a
suspension of belief could emerge only if I reorganized the material, concrete interaction that Chris and I produced.

Even with what I had learned from these critical examinations
of myself, there was still no simple technology by which I could
accomplish my purpose, and any procedures would have to be
accompanied by a crossing over from one "world" to another.
My work with Chris was rarely a simple progression, and at times
it seemed impossible to bridge this gap and the consciousness
interior to each world. At certain moments it was as if my own
reality were thrust into relief by Chris's, and I started to see that
my world was a collection of perceptual biological mechanisms
accompanied by rules for their use. My eyes and ears, once I

had been socialized to use them "correctly," provided me with a relatively coherent gestalt of experience, experience based upon these seeing-hearing beliefs and practices. These were the gifts of my family and their forefathers and allowed me to produce a stock of practical knowledge about my life world. But this body of knowledge had taken on a *sui generis* character, an existence of its own that I had to take into account. I had had no control over this learning how to see and hear reality, since the activities I had been taught were the same activities by which the knowledge was "validated." The knowledge was Castaneda's "description"; it was a "perceptual bubble" (von Uexkull 1934) in which I was trapped. What I consciously experienced was a natural language accounting of phenomenon, reified but kept alive by the activities that constituted my phenomenology. I had been taught the work of making this "reality," this bubble of perception, not the work of unmaking it. Yet it was a bubble I had to burst in order to discover Chris's "own terms."

Interactional Procedures. I felt I could use certain interactional procedures (changes in my purposes at hand) in order to gain an experiential basis for the kind of understanding I sought. I tried to focus my thinking on this new goal; achieving this understanding was to be my new purpose at hand with Chris. I stopped trying to remedy the "obvious" faults I perceived in Chris and tried instead to intuit, while interacting with her, what purposiveness or rationality her activities might have had from her perspective. My first major change in interactional strategy was to allow Chris to organize activities for both of us by "remaining *obediently passive.*" On the first occasion I did this, she organized the following activity for us:

Activity no. 1, or "*MMmmm . . . mmm . . . K . . . h.*" Chris maneuvered me in such a way that she was lying on my lap, face up, and had me place my hand on her face. She held my hand so that my palm was on her mouth and my index finger was on her right ("good") eye. She then indicated to me, by picking my finger up and letting it fall on her eye repeatedly that she wanted me to tap on her eyelid, smiling and laughing when I voluntarily took over this work as my own. (She had also "shown me," by moving my body, that she wanted me to speak in her ear and flick my fingers across her good eye.) While I tapped Chris's eye, she licked and sniffed my palm occasionally and softly hummed seemingly melodic sounds. We did this for about ten or fifteen minutes.

I named this activity by the sound Chris produced while doing it, in order to remind myself, even in the reading of my own material, that my purpose was to burst the "bubble." To do this consistently I could not *properly* code my sensory experience of the activity into a natural language (as Chris apparently could not do), because the "bubble" and the "language" were so intimately related that to sort one from the other would have been a practical impossibility. Thus, in my first encounter with Chris's desired form of interactional activity, I became aware that in my writing about the activity I necessarily transformed it into something she could not possibly have intended in her own organization of it. The description I sought to suspend belief in was itself imbedded in the very language I used to formulate my attempt. I realized that my *enterprise was a standing contradiction,* but I was willing to let this be, since to do otherwise would have meant to abandon all attempts to communicate to others what I was discovering. I was in much the same position as the anthropologist trying to code a native's language into the anthropologist's tongue. I was like Carlos Castaneda trying to speak of the world of the sorcerer by employing the language of the laity—admittedly the "old" language left much to be desired in terms of its descriptive power in the "new" world, but it was for him, as it was for me, the only language available.[10]

An interesting example of the use of natural language categories in "making sense" of the residents was the staff's use of the
category "play." Resident-initiated activities were considered by
the staff "play" activities and not particularly relevant to their
purposes at hand. Usually these activities merited a smile from
the staff or an utterance such as "Cute." There was an interesting
parallel between the staff's approach to these and Itard's approach to his walks in the woods with Victorie (seen by Itard as
play periods and not relevant to his teaching of the boy except
insofar as the walks provided Victoire with relief from the stress
of the pedagogical situation). It was not as if Chris hadn't played
with ward staff before I arrived on the ward. It was a question of
how they, normal seer-hearers, interpreted and categorized her
actions and what consequences these interpretations had in formulating her as a social object. Chris quickly expanded our repertoire of activities to include many varieties of bodily exchange
and perceptual play. Patterns of the activities were constantly
being refined and varied, sometimes in very subtle ways. These
activities consisted of *gross body interaction*—swinging, jumping, rocking, running—and generally long-term and repetitive
perceptual playing. They also included volitional participation in
the activities of perception in order to achieve gratification—for
example, having me play with her light reception (as above), singing and jumping from a baritone to falsetto range (which de-
lighted her), or putting my fingers in her ears rhythmically to
"stop" sound. When I began to cooperate with her in such pursuits, they sometimes culminated in Chris's reaching peak periods of excitement. Occasionally, these peaks would result in her
urinating and defecating.

I found music a possible avenue into Chris's world. She was a
musical person, deeply and genuinely enjoying listening to, and
even making, music. Because of her keen appreciation of music,
and because I was also a musical person, Chris and I engaged in
many musical explorations. I would often use these to teach

Chris, observing her carefully during such sessions. I introduced Chris to a small toy electric organ and observed the following:

> Chris would place her left hand on the keys of the organ that produced the lower-frequency sounds. She would then engage in two related sets of body movements. One was to move her head and body in a rhythmic rocking motion that took her right (good) ear closer to and farther from the organ sound source. The other set of movements involved her leaning her head back to face the overhead light and swiveling it back and forth, from side to side, while vibrating her lips as little children imitate motorcycle sounds but without the vocal component). In both sets of body movements there was an obvious rhythmic quality—like that of seer-hearers when they are engrossed in the activity of keeping beat to music. In Chris's case, however, there was no clearly discernible beat to the droning sounds she was producing by holding the organ keys down.

My initial encounter with these behaviors, as with Chris's brand of walking, was characterized by my engaging in the "vulgarly available" (Harold Garfinkel, personal communication, 1974). I "naturally" saw that these behaviors were obstacles I would have to overcome in my pedagogical enterprise (my initial purpose at hand)—a pedagogy designed to make Chris attend to sound in the "right" way. It was in this "rightness" that my evaluations of Chris resided. Once I gave up this remedial stance toward Chris, her alternative treatment of light, sound, and tactile stimulation took on a rational and even intelligent quality. I stopped trying to teach her, and began to let her teach me.

> I decided to *mimic her actions* in order to gain more direct access to what such activities were providing her. I used wax ear stops (placed more securely in the left ear, since Chris has a "better" right ear than left ear) and gauzed my

left eye with a single layer of lightweight gauze to simulate the scar tissue that covers Chris's left eye. I began to imitate Chris's behaviors at the organ. While the procedure had its obvious inadequacies with respect to my gaining access to Chris's experience of these activities, I did learn a number of interesting things in this way.

In both sets of body movements *the motion of the head itself gave the experienced sound a beatlike quality, and this was uniquely present by virtue of performing those movements.* In adapting to deficient eyes and ears and their resultant degraded perceptual fields, Chris had developed a way of "doing" hearing so as to make any long-term and reliable sound source available as a source of music. For example, when Chris was wearing her hearing aid, I would sometimes find her engaging in similar kinds of body movements, even though there was no hearable sound source in the room. This became a clue for me that Chris was probably getting "white sound" (feedback) from her hearing aid. I knew that Chris was able, when presented with appropriately amplified music, to keep "accurate" beat to that music in the fashion described above. I had also found Chris keeping completely inappropriate beat to music while listening to a small transistor radio with low amplification and a small speaker with poor bass quality. Put simply, when beat was not a "hearable" feature of the mechanically given sound stimulus, Chris had learned to endow her experience of that sound with that quality.

Rolling the head on the shoulders (the other set of body movements Chris engaged in) was a difficult, uncomfortable practice for me to mimic because Chris's neck muscles were suppler and looser than my own. Nevertheless, I discovered that Chris's head rolling provided not only for a beat to the music (which in its performance it does) but also for what one observer called a "light show," By "light show" I mean that the head rolling, which Chris performed with her head leaned back and her eyes facing the overhead fluorescent light, provided the following overall effect: alternative musical beats, occurring when the head was accelerating from one extreme position to the other, were culminated when the head came to rest in either light stimulation (when the head rested on the left shoulder, thus directing her good eye toward the light) or a lack of light stimulation (when the head rested on the right shoulder, thus interposing her nose between the light source and her good right eye). Chris was providing her otherwise impoverished perceptual field with a richness her eyes and ears could not give her. She accomplished this by the use of her available and intact bodily resources—her good eye, her nose, her muscles, and her skeletal frame. I was, and still am, struck by the inventiveness in this activity.

Another excerpt from field notes illustrates how I was able to look at music making together less judgmentally and thereby could better understand Chris's world. This was written after a particularly interesting teaching session with Chris (Goode 1974a). I was trying to demonstrate the use of various music-making toys vis-à-vis the "familiarizing" procedures described by Robbins (1963).

Chris demonstrated skill in "alternative object readings." By this I mean that Chris's inability to grasp the intentional meaning and activities for which "triangle" or "rattle" are appropriate glosses—that is, "rattle" or "triangle" as members' glosses for the practices entailed in recognizing, picking up, and shaking a rattle to make rattle sounds or banging a metal triangle with a metal bar to produce triangle sounds—allowed her to constitute a rattle as an object that could provide for her a number of alternative experiences. Initially, our play sessions consisted in precisely my

attempting to provide for her the "proper" cultural for-
mula—that object X is a rattle and is to be used (in satisfaction of the criteria of a rational course of action) in such
and such ways. After demonstrating the rattle's use to her
by placing it in her hand and placing her hand within my
own and then engaging in the appropriate shaking motion,
I would hand her the rattle. Although such demonstrations
were successful in that Chris would, without assistance,
hold and shake the rattle appropriately (for ten seconds or
so), she invariably brought the rattle to her right (good) eye
or mouthed it. She would bring it within two inches of her
eye with the apparent purpose of determining what it
could visually supply for her (parts of the rattle were metal
and reflected the fluorescent light in the room). This visual
examination would be of short duration (less than fifteen
seconds). Of the longest duration, often lasting till I would
interrupt her somewhat intense involvement, was her use
of the rattle as an object from which she could obtain various forms of stimulation in and about the mouth. Parts of
the rattle were employed as tongue thumper or lip
thumper, licked inside and outside the mouth, rubbed
against the front teeth, banged against the front teeth,
pushed against the cheek, and so on. Characteristically,
when Chris was through with or had exhausted the immediately present and interesting possibilities of the rattle, she
would drop it with no concern as to where it fell, its break-
ability, or its future uses. While such actions posed "problems" with regard to teaching Chris to use objects
appropriately (similar behavior was observed with regard to
many objects), I had to ask myself, Who is getting maximum
mileage out of that rattle? Is it we, who use it singularly and
for specific purposes, or Chris, who uses it in a variety of
ways? Let's put it another way: the meaning of Chris's not
knowing how to use a rattle is problematic. Her not know-

ing disqualifies her from membership in the category of persons who know how to use a rattle. However, it also *qualifies* her as a member of a category of persons who, by virtue of their not knowing how to use a rattle, do things with it that are inaccessible to persons who "know" its proper use. The superordinate ranking of our use of the rattle, on the basis that we realize its intended purpose by our actions, constitutes the "ground" for the pejorative statement "Chris does not use the rattle appropriately."

It is quite reasonable, given Chris's deficient eyes and ears, that she should place rattles or triangles or paper or fingers in her mouth. The tactility of the relatively sensitive tissue of the lips and tongue, as well as the ability of the teeth to conduct vibration, makes her mouth the organ around which she can successfully organize reliable perceptual activities. Her adaptations to her perceptual handicaps have allowed her to become an "expert" in the use of the mouth as an organ of primary perception (something like the use of the mouth by infants). From this perspective, her behavior is available to normal seer-hearers as an alternative set of mouth-perceptual practices against which our mouth perceptions are deficient versions of her more active pursuits. Yet most of her mouthings are inaccessible to the competent cultural member. Chris will put almost anything into her mouth that does not frighten her. For example, she will not mouth a lit match, does not like toothpaste or a toothbrush, but would undoubtedly try to lick a broken piece of glass or the porcelain parts of toilets if given an opportunity to do so. I was unable to adopt this stance toward objects, unable to overcome the culturally engrained notion that "something bad" would happen to me were I to lick a window, the floor, and so on.

My initial reading of these observations provided me with two general categories of findings. One concerned the reasoning embedded in my (and the staff's) "fault-finding procedures" with the residents," and one concerned the rationality or purposiveness (from Chris's point of view) behind these same behaviors.[11] It was not as if Chris's behaviors, or the meaning ascribed to them, existed apart from the procedures and circumstances by and in which she was apprehended. *Her behaviors were "rational" to me, "faulted" to the staff.* This multifacetedness of Chris was an important finding. As a material object, Chris's "horizons" were open. Like her rattle, she could be seen filled with the possibility of multiple interpretation, or she could be discovered to be singularly "dumb."

With regard to Chris's purposiveness, she was basically self-seeking, hedonistic, and amoral in her interactions. She would often rub her genitals against me or pantomime her (our?) recognized "behavior display" to denote a rocking or swinging activity. She did not seem to care whether I was getting pleasure from the activity. Instead, she focused on structuring the interaction so that she could get as much of what, I believe, she inwardly perceived as "good feelings," though I really don't "know" what these words index in terms of her experience. This seemed quite understandable to me, since, in terms of her life on the ward, Chris did not live a life particularly filled with gratification — especially when she was interacting with others. However, left to herself, she was quick to provide herself, through varieties of autostimulatory behaviors, with experiences she apparently enjoyed. Generally she occupied a powerless and frustrating position in many of her interactions and did not have the cognitive equipment (concepts, language, logic) through which she could rationalize (understand) her experience. She could only accept or reject, and on rare occasions "puzzle." She did not have the physical ability to aggress or, for that matter, even to defend herself against "attack." Compliance with sometimes not understood pulls and pushes from the staff was characteristic of daily life. When the staff could not force compliance (for example, when her language teacher could not get her to make the sound "Mmmm"), she seemed to sit in a sort of dull passivity. Other times she seemed to be puzzling—that is, trying to "code" what it was I was trying to do into some understanding or feeling she could deal with, what a program administrator called her interior "language" system. Generally, when she initiated interaction, it was to seek as much pleasure as she could, however she could. We often index such a behavior pattern by the term "infantile," but Chris was no infant. She was nine years old and had lived long enough to have gained some sophistication in achieving her pleasure-seeking ends.

Within the limits of hospital routine, I cooperated with her in achieving her goals. I became a sort of "superplaymate," perhaps (with the possible exception of her father) the only one in her life she had ever had (there were many references in field notes of myself as Chris's superplaymate). Although there were a number of sympathetic and loving custodians and teachers in her life, the institutional definition of their relations with Chris prevented them from simply cooperating with her. From time to time I observed activities in which the staff's role was precisely to be Chris's playmate (for example), when it was hot out and they would sprinkle the residents with a hose, or when they took the residents to the pool to "swim"), and on these occasions the staff and residents seemed to enjoy themselves immensely. But the staff did *not* see, just as Itard had not seen in his work with Victoire, "play" sessions as pedagogically relevant to their work with the children. By the end of my stay on the ward, I had become a little sad about the way in which the institutional and medical "contexting" of the children seemed to victimize the staff as well as the children.[12]

By interacting with Christina, by looking carefully at my own investments in the way I socially constructed her, I discovered in Chris the "internal contradictions" by which she was propelled into relations with others and by which she could be *particularly distinguished* from other social beings (Mao 1971). Christina, like all other human beings, was a collection of unique contradictions, including those embedded within her deaf-blindness and stupidity. One power of using descriptive method in sociological research is the ability to capture a sense of these contradictions and paradoxes inherent in social life. I believe this was evident in the concluding remarks on Chris's rattle activities.

Perhaps the most interesting feature of Chris's mouth-perceptual practices is the way she can be seen as both wise and deficient in how she constitutes objects and experiences the world. I described her alternative object reading of the rattle and noted how she used the rattle for three general purposes: what she could make seeable with it, what she could make hearable with it, and what she could provide tactually with it. I claimed that her not grasping the intentional meaning of the object allowed her to get, in some sense, more out of the rattle than *members* who attend to the rattle singularly and employ it in satisfaction of a set of rational guides for use. The "kicker" here is that, seemingly, the very thing that allows her to get more mileage out of the rattle (her visually and auditorally deficient body and her development of perceptual practices appropriate to such a body) is the same thing that delimits her experience of the world as it is composed for us and by us, the world of intentional meanings. For Chris, *objects can only be sources of perceptual stimulation of the sorts outlined above*. When I watched her "do her thing," it was with both joy and sorrow that I appreciated what I was seeing. *Her blindness and her deafness constituted her strongest asset as well as her greatest deficiency.* They sometimes provided her with incredibly intense enjoyment of the simplest things. At other times they were a source of "troubles" equally intense.

My abilities to see and hear allowed me to engage in the practices by which the culturally defined objects and activities of my world were realized. These abilities and actions structured my own experience, pleasures and pains, but did so in a way sensible to other members of society. Obviously, Chris did not comply with culturally prescribed courses of rational activity. Yet in a more generic human sense, she seemed to conduct herself quite rationally. Perhaps she could not give her hedonistic pursuits names like "self-realization," "the pursuit of personal power," or "transcendence," but that she was a pleasure-seeking, world-mastering person made her quite understandable to me. In this enterprise, we were in basic agreement. We just used different technologies to accomplish our goal. This is precisely the idea about persons with mental retardation that is powerfully projected in the epigram to this chapter by Gyorgy Konrad. His paragraph captures so perfectly the paradox of Christina's deaf-blindness and worldessness; she was indeed a "hero of the here and now."

CONCLUSION

IMPLICATIONS OF THIS STUDY FOR ACHIEVING HUMAN INSTERSUBJECTIVITY

All subjectivities seek, in their terms, to fulfill needs and to gratify themselves, and not in any haphazard fashion.[13] Certain needs must be met before others (this is Maslow's insight), and in Chris's case, her survival-related needs were almost exclusively taken care by others. Given this institutional context of her life, next in her "motivational" hierarchy were emotional and perceptual/sensual gratification, and in this regard she was not dissimilar to other humans. She differed primarily in the forms in which these needs were met and in her inability to express these symbolically with acceptable language or postural formats. Many of the rational activities of our culture are built upon these very motivated projects. But I would advance the notion, on the basis of my work with Christina, that the concretization of these enterprises into culturally acceptable forms is *not* what defines our humanity to ourselves or to others. If we can accept and understand the malleability and heterogeneity involved in the expression of these basic projects in the life world, then we can stop one of our central self-deceptions and move away from a view of humankind that raises us above other creatures or that affirms one "kind" of human as better than another. Chris and I may have had our "differences," but these were differences of degree, not of quality. This is probably the most important ethical lesson I learned from Christina.

One of the main differences between us obviously had to do with language. While not having formal language as a shared resource persented all sorts of practical, methodological, and epistemological issues for my work with Christina, it did not make the basic enterprise of understanding one another *essentially* different from that we might observe between two seeing, hearing, speaking adults. As the French phenomenologist Maurice Merleau-Ponty emphasized in his writings, the role and importance of language in achieving mutual understanding of the world may be overemphasized and given too much importance in our scientific studies of human behavior. My work with Christina would tend to corroborate his observation (see Chapter 5 for a fuller discussion of Merleau-Ponty's relevance to this research).

But given this view, what is to be made of my personal attempt to share a world with a very different human being? What can we learn from this attempt? In this regard there are several positions to take. One can "believe in" the phenomenon of intersubjectivity; one can take it as possible that human beings "really" or "in fact" can, and do, share their worlds. Starting from there, my experiences can be seen as providing technical resources and interactional methods for accomplishing this goal—for "starting with two worlds and (to a greater or lesser extent) making them into one." Insofar as the methods and their results are taken to be valid, the further questions can be asked, How is it possible for two worlds to become one in the course of intimate human interaction? That is, are there species-specific characteristics, activities, or aspects of our common "habitats" that make this accomplishment possible? If so, what are they?

Another lesson that might be drawn from my experiences with Chris proceeds from a perspective from which either one does not accept the "real" possibility of intersubjectivity, or one is not interested in discovering whether what we take to be a common world *is* a common world in actual fact. Instead, the question is, How do people start out with the feeling of being cut off from each other and together achieve the mutual feeling of being in touch with each other in the same world? This is precisely what Alfred Schutz, among others, has described as the "working assumptions that constitute people's sense of being in touch with each other." The descriptions of interaction with Chris can be read as our attempts to find ways of being, such that our interaction could be characterized in part by the kinds of working assumptions about which Schutz has written. Thus, we progressively developed "common schemes of communication," "congruent practical relevancies," "mutually defined things to do in the world," common "in order to" motives, and so forth. But even if it is *the sense* of a shared world we achieved, the question can still be asked, Is this not remarkable, and how is it possible for human beings to accomplish this?

These perspectives are not necessarily mutually exclusive, but from either of them the achievement of human intersubjectivity becomes a *practical and empirical issue*—an issue for which, it is hoped, this writing has provided some initial technical resources. By using procedures appropriate to the particular setting in which ethnography is conducted, field researchers can collect data from which the procedures for constituting human intersubjectivity can be made objects for analysis.

THE PRACTICAL IMPLICATIONS OF THIS STUDY FOR CHILDREN
ON THE WARD

From the outset I formulated this research not only as an academic research project but also as action research. The intent was to produce something "practical" for ward staff based upon what I learned. By the end of the project this concern had focused upon the issue of making staff aware that children like Christina made valid choices for themselves and that these had to be taken into consideration when we tried to help them.[14]

In retrospect it is possible to see that a central problem with these "applied" efforts may have been that they were ahead of their time. I wrote for a major "applied" journal in the field an article that provided a technology for direct-care staff to recognize "choice" in children without language. My concern with and technology for recognizing choices made by people with profound mental retardation and no language predates our current preoccupation with this issue. Though my concern was consistent with the philosophy of normalization, normalization was practiced at that time primarily with "higher-functioning" people and was not as much employed with more-involved children. Thus, there was no organizational or programmatic foundations on which professionals could implement recommendations made in the article. Even if they read the article and agreed with it, there were at that time few programs that could, or would, accommodate such an orientation. This still remains true today, even though there are now many curricula developed for "decision making."

This is partially why, I think, there was little reaction to this article in the literature at the time and why the staff at the state hospital did not radically alter their procedures with these children after my training sessions. These ideas were just "too far out," as one very competent administrator remarked to me at the time.[15] It was with sadness that I left the ward after almost three years (the last as a volunteer), the practices and conditions of life almost identical to those when I first arrived.

There was only one practical, action-oriented result of this work that was appreciable, and that was the habilitative progress made by Christina herself. The idea of using procedures such as those described above in order to empathize with and understand her perspective proved highly effective in allowing me to promote meaningful learning experiences for her,[16] and during the period of my involvement with her she progressed considerably in areas that staff did not believe possible. In my notes are many records of the staff gathering around me and Christina and noting how "incredible" it was that Christina could sign for "more music" or stop at the road and proceed slowly across the intersection with her arms outstretched to show she was blind. There was no question from my own point of view, or that of the staff on the ward, that the subjective understanding of Christina's experience of the world provided an effective basis upon which to "construct" (perhaps "facilitate" is better) a meaningful habilitation program for her. Further, all who worked on the deaf-blind ward agreed that the choices made by these children should be taken into consideration when designing these programs. Some of the staff began to base their work with the children much more self-consciously on the preferences expressed by each particular child. For a short period of time there was some progress made, at least from my point of view.

It is unfortunate, but tremendously predictable, that soon after my leaving the ward there was a large staff turnover. The head of the deaf-blind program, Michael Gaddy, who was an excellent administrator and instrumental in the support of my work with Chris, followed the route of all competent human services professionals; he was promoted and sent to Sacramento. Most of the direct-care staff either burned out or similarly got promotions within the hospital, and soon there was no one on the staff who could continue to reinforce and build upon the work I had done with Christina. I left a large paper record of this work in her file in hopes that staff would read it, and even suggested they do so on the occasions I visited the ward (recalling our discussion of client files, I knew I had little hope of this actually happening). Thus, several years later when I visited her, I was not surprised to see that she had lost many (although not all) of the competencies that she had developed while I worked with her. Today she remains in many important ways the same person I met some twenty years ago.[17]

On
Understanding
Without
Words

3

■ AFTER COMPLETING the study of Christina at the state hospital described in the previous chapter, I undertook a comparative observational project involving a child with rubella syndrome living with her natural family (Goode 1980a, 1985). I hoped that this research would both remedy the almost total lack of natural observational data about families with such children and allow me to compare the role of family and state hospital in the development of a child with rubella syndrome—that is, compare observations of Christina to those of a similarly affected child who had never lived in a state institution.

In Chapter 5 I examine in some detail the relation between quantitative and qualitative methods in research on families with retarded members. In this chapter I only raise some of these themes briefly in order properly to frame the family case study. First, there was (and still is) an absolute lack of natural observational data on families with retarded members. Most research employed traditional methods of clinical observation, questionnaires, tests, and interviews. At the time of the study (1978–79) there were *no* articles in the literature, save for parental self-reports describing the everyday lives of such families. A plethora of published quantitative studies reported aggregated data and their averages and trends and typical patterns of data. But in pursuit of such general knowledge we had completely abandoned or had lost the "family" as something that we know as part of our everyday life. If one means the social group that many of us are familiar with as part of our own daily life, I literally could not detect a single "family" in the professional research literature. Unfortunately, this, aside from a handful of exceptions, is still true today.[1] Why this is so needs to be understood in a broader context.

This situation was not at all unique to research about families with retarded members. In fact, it was generally true of many areas of research and was the subject of much ethnomethodological writing in the 1960s and 1970s. Critiquing the epistemological foundations of social science research, early ethnomethodologists (for example, see Cicourel 1964; Garfinkel 1967; Sacks 1963) asserted that no matter how intellectually satisfying and precise, quantified descriptions of social reality often failed validly to portray or represent how everyday events occurred, who they were produced and experienced by those who actually lived them, in short, what they actually consisted of. An important thread of their observations was that while social sciences often produced elegant, complex, and technically impressive analyses of events in the everyday world, these analyses had far more to do with theories and textbooks per se than with the actual experiential features of everyday social life. Most research was, and still is, performed in satisfaction of a narrow, principled version of scientific method, creating forms of knowledge extrinsic to and divorced from the "real course time of the phenomenon's making" (Garfinkel, personal communication, 1978). From the perspective of societal members living everyday life, the most commonly accepted procedures of the "hypethetico-deductive method"—generation of hypotheses, testing of hypotheses, the operationalization of variables, their measurement, and the analysis with reference to theory, and so on—are basically esoteric and strange (if not unreasonable) forms of inquiry grounded exclusively in professional-scientific interests and theories about social events. Such forms of knowledge can actually contradict the lived realities of everyday life.

The way people construct the social activities of their everyday lives is not in satisfaction of scientific versions or theories of phenomena (of which Garfinkel's 1967 book is replete with illustrations). Everyday phenomena are constructed in an orderly way by those who live them, with or without the existence or conduct of professional research. Ethnomethodologists propose that everyday human existence is the raw stuff upon which social scientists depend for dissection and measurement. But ethnomethodologists also assert that such operations *constitute* the reality they claim to uncover, and they perform these operations while unknowingly depending on the orderlinesses of the everyday world. People would continue the production of these orderly everyday realities with or without the conduct of measurement-oriented research, which in any case fails to comprehend their logic and practices and prefers, instead, to examine them according to some extrinsic method or theory.

Given such observations, one should not be surprised at the irrelevance of most practical applications of quantified social science knowledge.[2] Nor do ethnomethodologists look toward refinement of existing quantitative techniques as a way to solve this problem of relevance and utility. Instead, they identify two different, if not incompatible, visions of everyday life—one where persons unknowingly live in a world inhabited by variables, indexes, frequencies, and correlations that await the work of research scientists to be revealed; and one in which the practices of inquiry do not dissect the world in accordance with some previously (or endogenously) defined theory or scientific protocol and which is in some way more faithful to the experience of everyday life. Based on the case data presented below, I argue that in clinical disability research only knowledge that is resonant with the practices of everyday life will likely be useful for purposes of application or intervention.

Ethnomethodology in clinical research sometimes reveals the failure of academic sciences to produce knowledge that is useful in case-by-case social engineering. Good clinical method should begin with punctilious observations of behaviors and situations as the "patient," or "client," sees them (see Laing and Esterson 1964; Sartre 1956). The irrelevance of objective and quantified descriptions of everyday life to such a clinical enterprise is a reflection of the inability of objective methods to retrieve and incorporate detailed descriptive data generally. It is also one implication of methods that reflect the priorities and doings of researchers, rather than those they study. As is illustrated below, both the theory that one applies to, or draws from, the phenomenon under analysis and the concrete features of the phenomenon are dependent upon methodology (in the ethnomethodological sense). If a methodology fails to retrieve the orderly and observable features of everyday life in some fashion, then it will be possible to have elegant, refined, and technically impressive knowledge that has little, or even a contradictory, relation to the realities of persons' lives (for a more detailed discussion of these issues, see Chapter 5).

With regard to the most common methods of studying social groups, families, or whomever, ethnomethodology basically argues that these methods do not capture a hidden reality that can only be known if studied "scientifically." In ethnomethodology's view these methods constitute a scientized version of the world replete with phenomena of interest to those who employ them. Moreover, ethnomethodology has observed that these methods appear to be founded upon essentially folk, or nonscientific, conceptions and understandings of everyday life, sometimes masquerading as very abstract theoretical ideas about phenomena (in this case, families with retarded members). They are usually uniformed by any direct, unprejudiced inspection of everyday phenomena, and thereby produce data that bear an essentially ambiguous and indeterminable relation to the phenomena they purport to represent. To the degree that clinical scales, observation, and testing substitute for direct observation of families with retarded members, such procedures may actually obfuscate our understanding of these groups rather than enhance them.

It is in these senses that I approached this study not as just another case study. It was from the outset a research project that was recognized as unique in the literature, and thereby of some importance. It was a first step into a world that had been unknown to researchers and that had escaped any serious scientific documentation: the world of a family with a severely and multiply disabled child. It was also an opportunity to demonstrate the power of ethnomethodology to display this world.

This chapter focuses upon the communication practices family members engaged in with a deaf-blind child. The collection of field data lasted for almost one year, and during that time I amassed over one thousand pages of handwritten notes, though several thousand pages of observations and analysis could have been generated from the available data. Thus, the topic of communication was only one part, albeit an important one, of the findings about the family.

■ THE SMITHS

I located the Smiths with the aid of Christina's mother, having requested that she help me find a family with a child with rubella syndrome that had not been raised in an institution. She recommended the Smiths to me as a family that had made an exemplary adaptation to their adolescent daughter, who, like Christina, was deaf, blind, and without language. In many ways I found her assessment of this family correct.

The Smiths were a middle-income family of four residing in a blue-collar suburban California community. The father, Joe, worked six days a week as a machinist to support the family's modest but ample lifestyle. The Smiths owned their own home, two cars, and a motorcycle and took occasional vacations to the desert. The home was furnished with antiques and new appliances, some of these paid for by Barbara, Joe's wife, who worked in her home as a provider of day care to local children. Barbara, who had been a secretary before marrying Joe, had primary responsibility for the care of the children and the home, an arrangement that had begun with the birth of their first daughter, Bianca. Bianca had been born with rubella syndrome and was, at the time of this study, thirteen years old, deaf, blind, profoundly retarded, and without language; and because of her cerebral palsy, she could not walk or grab objects normally. In terms of disease sequelae, she was in many ways comparable to Christina, with the important exception of her cerebral palsy, which significantly decreased Bianca's ability to explore her environment. She wore leg braces, had to use a walkette to ambulate, and did so in parachute position (that is, with knees together to help support her weight). She wore thick glasses and bilateral hearing aids. Bianca displayed no oral or sign language. She had few self-help skills and had to be fed, dressed, and taken to the toilet. She appeared to a naive observer to lack the most rudimentary of social skills, preferring to self-stimulate and rock off in her own world. Six years younger than she, Tanya was introduced to me as Bianca's "older younger sister," and she did seem to exhibit a maturity beyond her seven years. She was a very beautiful child who was quite cooperative and helpful to me during my research.[3]

My first impression of Bianca was that she was not, by conventional standards at least, a very pretty child. She had, in addition to the apparatus she wore, a somewhat misshapen body, scoliosis, and irregular teeth and hair. Along with these attributes she had a rather nasty habit of manually transferring large amounts of saliva to objects or persons before touching them. She was a wet affair, and this may have been responsible for Bianca's awful (and underground) nickname at school—"the slug"—a name given to her by her teacher, who actually cared quite a lot for her. From the human services point of view, Bianca was a very low functioning, multihandicapped, alingual, and nonambulatory child with poor cognitive, social, and medical prospects. To the average person on the street, she might have appeared a pitiable, hopeless, monstrous child, to be feared or resented. She was not seen this way by her family.[4]

■ METHODOLOGY

After I contacted the Smiths by phone and visited them at home to explain the purposes of my study, they expressed interest in participating. I began to visit their home twice a week and built a good rapport with the family within a couple of months. For a variety of reasons this was not difficult to do. The family had an interactional style that was resonant with my own, and I was soon invited to come and visit "anytime." I also obtained permission to visit and observe Bianca freely at her special education program at school and began to visit her in that setting.[5] I was thus generally a welcome visitor at both sites and was able to make observations without constraint. Over the course of the next nine months I was to observe Bianca at home, in school, and occasionally in the community (for example, at MacDonald's or shopping). In the home, I was able to observe throughout the day and evening, purposefully sampling the daily life cycle of the family. I spent at least two hundred hours at the home and the school.

As is my customary field technique, I adopted the posture of participant-observer and did *not* take notes during my observations. Instead, I carried a cassette tape recorder and recorded experiences in the field. The recorder was always on except for accident or error. I used these tapes as audio field data from which I later wrote field notes in my office. While the recorder clearly had an effect on the observation sites, it had less of a reactive effect than constant note taking would have. It also allowed me to attend to the observations per se rather than the recording of them. In my experience with the tape recorder, the family normalized somewhat to its presence, so that this field technique was successful in producing detailed and meaningful data about the everyday life of this family.

Thus, the field notes presented below were produced by listening to these tapes and writing at leisure in my office. This accounts for the relatively high degree of detail, including quotes, that would be unavailable through direct observation, note taking, and recall. I wrote a short set of field notes in the traditional manner (that is, from memory) on the day of the observation in order to highlight important events on the tape while they were fresh in my mind. I organized field notes in historical sequence in notebooks. At the end of the data-collection period, I subjected these notes to a content analysis, in the traditional ethnographic manner. Notes judged to represent data on specific topics—for example, in the current case, communication—were collected and subjected to more scrutiny. Selections from these notes appear in this chapter.

■ COMMUNICATING WITH BIANCA

Although I have excerpted from the field notes the materials dealing with the issue of communication as I found it in my observations, this was not an issue of my own making. There was a conflict between professional-scientific versions of family communication and those more naturally available to family members in the home before my entry into the situation. A short while after entering the field, I realized that I had been cast in the role of liaison between school and home and had become an arbiter in a dispute between these two settings. Through choosing to observe both settings, I had inadvertently delivered myself to the battlefront. Consider these field notes.

Before my entry into the situation, Barbara and Steve, Bianca's teacher, exchanged information by writing notes in a small notebook that Bianca took to school and back. As of late, "hassles" had developed, and these notes had become fewer. My entrance provided the perfect knowledgeable, reasonable, sympathetic, and neutral observer to whom each side could appeal the reasonableness of its position and indirectly lodge its complaints against the other. It was perhaps two weeks into the study when I began to feel much like the unsuspecting walker who had inadequately circumvented the neighborhoods dogs' obstacle course.

What I had discovered was a history of fairly serious conflicts between assessments of Bianca made at home by her parents and those made at school by professionals. Similar to what was observed on the ward with Christina, Bianca was socially constructed, and antithetical claims were made by school staff and family members. They disagreed *in detail* about Bianca's capabilities and appropriate treatment for her. So diametrically opposed were these constructions of Bianca that it was initially shocking, even given my previous observations of similar phenomena on Chris's ward.[6] At the time, I was a bit naive about the situation; now I understand that this was (and is) a very commonplace occurrence with such children.

Parents who have lived with children with severe disabilities often disagree about professional assessments of their children. Many of these parents have discovered what I have referred to elsewhere as the "systematic clinical underestimation of competencies in the family context" (Goode 1984). Often, when they point out their conflicting observations to clinicians—for example, that Johnny can communicate well at home despite his having "no" language skills—the parents are regarded as uncooperative or unrealistic. If they persist and their claims appear, from the clinical perspective, to be patently false or absurd, these parents may be regarded as "delusional" or "disturbed." Verbal and written remarks to this effect in school files substantiated this view of Barbara, who was seen by staff as at least unrealistic and possibly delusional. As is described below, in the face of a bleak communication assessment she was insistent that she and Bianca communicated quite well and that Bianca could "tell her everything."

Many years in the field and observing many families with children with severe disabilities have me led to the conclusion that part of professionals' unwillingness to accept conflicting parental testimony regarding a child's in-home competencies is due, not to inaccurate parental perception and reporting, but rather to the failure of professionals adequately to understand the empirical details of everyday family life with a child like Bianca.[7] At the time, the school made some "token" attempts to visit Bianca at home, to check out the claims made by Barbara. This consisted of two or three one-hour visits per school year and in no way allowed those visiting to learn family life to the degree and the detail required seriously to consider Barbara's claims. That was a task possible for me, given the time available to me for observation. But the problem was not just that the school staff did not have time to do the observations necessary, it was also in the way they approached these observations and indeed the family itself. At least at the time of this study, the clinical and special education staff at Bianca's school used their "objective" knowledge of the child as the standard against which parental testimony would be judged. They had the authority and objectivity of science behind them. Assuming competent administration of assessment instruments, they could be seen as having both a fair and objective view of the child, a norm-referenced definition of her (ab)normality, and no motive to distort the child's situation.

It was against this ground of scientific and professional work that the figure of a "delusional parent" emerged. Because the legal and educational institutions of our society empowered clinical and educational professionals (the agents of science in this scenario) to have the final say about Bianca, it was taken as given who was right and who was wrong in such conflicts. Parental intimacy with the child, viewed not as a particularly trustworthy basis for testimony, was instead dismissed as subjective and was sacrificed to scientific objectivity. Intimacy was taken as a barrier to dispassionate scientific knowledge.

As David Helm (personal communication, 1987) pointed out, there are often legitimate professional concerns about children like Bianca, even if we grant that they may function very well in the home environment. The child's ability to function with *unknown* others is part of such concerns. Thus, while professional language assessment may completely ignore actual *in situ* communication practices of families and even transform their narration into symptomatic expression of emotional illness on the part of the parent, this is not to say that tests determining the degree and ways in which persons can communicate with unknown others in their society are irrelevant or unimportant. The criticism is that such approaches are used to override truthful parental testimony about their own communication with their children. The ethnomethodological observations about the shoddy epistemological underpinnings of many "scientific" studies of human behavior also are relevant here. To maintain that there are methodological and theoretical problems in the scientific models that form the basis for the research that grounds clinical instrumentation is not to maintain that clinicians are doing a bad job or that they are dishonest and uncaring people. But they were, in Bianca's school and unfortunately in many others, trusting of science to a fault. In my own view, they failed to realize how little we really understand about human communication and how little trust we should have in textbooks on such topics. This is not meant to reflect on their moral character so much as on the strength of their professional training and of science in human services.

In Bianca's case, the situation between school and home embodied the ethnomethodological observations about mainstream scientific data and methods. The paradigmatic and objective knowledge of the professional was taken as "the truth," against which parental descriptions were judged—this in the face of the obvious fact that parents had a detailed and intimate knowledge of everyday affairs with the child. This situation was also somewhat parallel to that of Christina, where the direct-care staff's knowledge of the child was not recognized as important for her habilitation, and where professional-scientific definitions of Christina ultimately prevailed. Just as the ethnomethodological project of identifying and describing the orderly features of Chris's world was in a sense a corrective to her "scientization" and related "faulting" and negation as a person, so this ethnomethodological project about the orderliness of familial communication with Bianca can be read as a corrective to the family's situation.[8] It is hoped that the reader will appreciate the capabilities of ethnomethodological description to provide information pertinent to such a corrective. Through an examination of the details of the family's conflict with professionals about Bianca's communication, I attempt to show how parental descriptions that contradict even our most basic and reasonable assumptions about reality may be important markers of phenomena that are as real as they are inconsistent with currently prevailing scientific models.

■ BIANCA TELLS ME EVERYTHING

To most outsiders and professional staff at school, Bianca appeared to lack any kind of communicative competence. In formal testing situations (at least those that were available at the time of the study) she would engage in autistic-like behaviors, including autophotic play, rocking, tactile self-stimulation, and the like. While in class, she appeared to be generally unaware of her surroundings or the actions of teachers and therapists. She was not "with it," as Steve would say. She was described at school as having no language and little communicative behavior except for her ability to display emotional likes and dislikes. She was considered to be one of the most "low functioning" children in the school.

After observing Bianca several times at school and listening to the staff's descriptions of her, their basis for their low estimation of her competencies became clear. Given their relationship with Bianca and the history and organization of the classroom, they assumed that they knew Bianca fairly well and without prejudice. The course of my observations at school over the year led me to believe that within the organizational life of that institution, they did know and understand Bianca. But what they failed to realize was that this all to familiar "person" was someone they (as participants of the special education school) helped make; Bianca was given life, an identity, and particular attributes through their relations with her. They knew "Bianca-as-she-existed-in-the-organization-of-a-special-education-school." It was the limitations of such a form of knowledge that school personnel failed to appreciate.

This was also true for Bianca's parents. Both parties to this argument failed to appreciate adequately the concrete social-organizational differences that existed between school and home. The professional view, continuous with dominant professional models of communication, construed communicative competencies as attributes of individuals, rather than as properties of social systems. Professionals held constant, or irrelevant, the context within which communicative skills are displayed, interpreted as to meaning, and judged. Professionals wanted to know about "Bianca's" (emphasizing here the possessive) communicative abilities and how they fit into the "everyman," or "anyman," approach to communication;[9] that is, they were interested in formal language assessment. With regard to such a conception of communication, Bianca was correctly found to be highly deficient. Staff at school had accurately revealed what Bianca could not do as a communicator to everyman. And while this may be a meaningful and even important assessment to make within special education, data reported herein seriously questions the utility of such a notion of communication for any understanding of what and how Bianca and her family communicated. The family did not organize communicative practices with regard to any professional idea or theory. Parents, on the other hand, failed to grasp the legitimacy of the professional concern with "everyman" communication (see below).

After a short time in the field I began to see that despite the mistrust school staff had of Barbara, there was definitely something to her claims about being able to communicate with Bianca. While the school looked at communication in a highly general, "everyman" way, the family took an entirely idiosyncratic, tailor-made approach. Because these two theories of communication, the "everyman" and the "idiosyncratic," were employed by two different sets of actors in two separate and mutually exclusive settings, no one perceived the contradiction between them; indeed, since each had a different purpose and organization, this would have been difficult, if not impossible, to do. The family's concern was with establishing a practical, effective communication system with Bianca. It was not with assessing her communication against formal language practices and then providing training in lacking skills. The family had to communicate with Bianca because she was a valued member of their family. The school did not. After a very short while in the field, I began to become more interested in Barbara's ways of communicating with Bianca, seeing in them a rich and more open field of communication that did not involve formal language in any sense.[10] As much as possible I would suspend judgment about what she told me or what I observed in the home. Since both she and her husband appeared to me to be very reasonable and even careful observers of their own lives, this was not difficult to do. From what I could gather, the topic of "communicating with Bianca" had probably always been a naturally occurring issue for Joe and Barbara. Its thematic and problematic character is well illustrated in the following data.

> We are sitting in the living room while Bianca is finishing her dinner at the table. She is clearly visible to all of us. I am facing Joe and speaking with him when he interrupts and says, "Look what she's doing now." Bianca is jerking her head to one side in an odd, vigorous, and repetitive motion. The action is not self-abusive but borders on self-violence. I turn to Joe and ask him if he knows what she is doing. He says no because this behavior started only recently. I conjecture that it could be because she is angry. Then ensues a lengthy conversation between Joe, Barbara, and myself in which we try to figure out the meaning of Bianca's actions from "the look of things." We entertain a number of alternative explanations—she is angry, frustrated, in pain, or bored. In the end we acknowledge that the behavior's recent appearance makes it difficult to interpret. Joe comments, "I don't know now, but we'll figure it out if she keeps it up."

Barbara had previously referred to these difficult times in her communication with Bianca as "guessing games." This gloss, as well as the field note above, points to the parents' clear cognizance of the extraordinary and sometimes problematic character of their communication with Bianca. Although they maintained that communication with Bianca was both possible and effective, this did not appear to me to be a delusional or unrealistic claim. They were not denying that there were problems in trying to understand Bianca and did not appear to be unrealistic in how they appraoched their communication with her.

Nor were they bothered even by their own pejorative characterizations of not being able to understand Bianca. To the parents these reflected the pragmatic stance they had to take with respect to the enterprise of communicating with their daughter. Sometimes, within what was perceived to be a generally effective enterprise, one failed, and that was just part of the territory. This essentially pragmatic orientation probably accounted for the fact that there was rarely mention of "communication" per se and that most of the discussions about communication were in problem-solving contexts; that is, communication was thematized in order to address concrete and immediate difficulties understanding some particular gesture or behavior.[11] The family was thus not at all interested in Bianca's performances as they related to some theory of communication. They were not embarrassed at all by inconsistencies in their claims or work with Bianca, nor were they interested in Bianca's communicative competencies. Instead, in the home Bianca's actions were given meaning with respect to a rich background of family knowledge and practice. Only when this orientation failed did parents openly address the theme of communication, as if the theme of communication required a pejorative ground upon which to emerge as a figure. By and large, however, communication with Bianca proceeded unremarkably and without commentary. It appeared basically to "work."

At times practical tests were designed to reveal the correctness or incorrectness of specific interpretations of Bianca's messages. These tests were clearly makeshift. They were natural experiments in sense making with Bianca, but without regard for any scientific criterion of adequacy of proof or procedure. For example, if, when Bianca stamped her feet at the dinner table, she quieted down after a parent gave her a piece of fruit, then the pounding was interpreted to have meant "I want fruit." If she refused fruit but did not mind being picked up and taken to the couch, then the pounding was taken to have meant "Take me to the couch." Whatever quieted her down at these times was what she had wanted all along. In this teleological form of inquiry, done without exception in a straightforward and unembarrassed way, the proof of the pudding was always in the eating. This is not intended as an ironic description of the parents' practices with Bianca. These events might be flawed from a scientific perspective, but optimal from a familial one.

The reader may have detected a contradiction between the claim of "complete" communication and the open acknowledgment by these parents of communicational disjunctures and problems with their daughter. The contradiction here rests upon the difference between doing something and talking about doing something.[12] Usually communication with Bianca was not problematic and remained unthematized. Family life with Bianca proceeded without incident, day in and day out. Occasionally this mundane existence would be interrupted, normal family interpretive devices did not work, and the "family conversation" became seriously disrupted. Yet this fact did not damage the overall state of communicational affairs. As some of my notes indicate, when one watched Bianca and Barbara communicating, it was artful, balletlike in precision, and uncannily accurate. For the present it is important to note that the apparent contradiction between doing communication with Bianca and talking about it was not seen as such by the parents. On the one hand, the parents were "realistic" about the limitations of their communicational relationship with their daughter; on the other hand, family members generally communicated with Bianca with great effectiveness. It is within this context of mundane and non-noteworthy communication that the proposal "Bianca tells me everything" is considered.

■ FAMILY RESOURCES TO ACHIEVE
UNDERSTANDING WITH BIANCA

The minutiae of familial interaction reveal the "lived order" of communication between Bianca and her parents. The term "lived order," adopted from Garfinkel's 1978 seminar (Department of Sociology, UCLA), is employed to alert the reder to the simultaneity of idiosyncratic and socially ordered aspects of all mundane social reality—in this case, the communication between Bianca and her parents.

Essential to the ethnomethodological view of social reality is the notion that social facticities and social orders of everyday life do not exist as general, free-floating norms and social structures. Instead, experienced "realities" are seen as a collection of individual and highly concrete scenes of social action that have a certain particularity (just here, just now, with just these features) and a social structure, or generality (the orderliness of, for example, a conversation that can be made concrete at any particular time with any particular social members). All everyday social realities are seen as working in this way. With respect to {communication between congenitally deaf-blind children with rubella syndrome and their parents} (the brackets indicating, or bounding, the lived order in which we have interest), there are a certain actual number of such communication networks, all of which would be found to have both idiosyncratic and common features. The word "lived" is meant to sensitize the analyst to the idiosyncratic features of the interaction; the words "order" and "orderliness," to the common or regular features.[13] Indeed, when listening to parents of children with rubella syndrome converse about communication, this is precisely what one hears, parents comparing notes, that is, comparing common and particular features of the communicational arrangements they have worked out with their children.

The following notes are intended to display this lived order of family communication with Bianca. They will be a unique blend of the particular and the general as embodied in this family. An appreciation of the data in these terms is essential to a coherent reading of them.

Finally, for purposes of explication I have analytically separated the discussion of family communication into topics: routine, layout, likes and dislikes, and the body. An all too obvious caveat about such a list of topics is that they are analytic distinctions and in some sense arbitrary. Their separation in an important way violates the essential wholeness of all everyday events. This family's world, as all worlds, was a unity and had a wholeness that, similar to the way a photo cannot capture the grandeur of a mountain expanse, cannot be recovered by writing or analysis.

ROUTINE

It has been said that we are creatures of routine. Observations of the deaf-blind children on the hospital ward had corroborated this proposition to a large degree. Christina and the other residents appeared to enjoy the predictability of the ward routines and would become upset with their interruption. They were "institutionalized" and had incorporated institutional routine as part of their knowledge of the world.

When I first arrived at the Smith home, I was told that Bianca was no exception in this regard and that she and Barbara had worked out many routines together. To understand Bianca, Barbara informed me, I would have to know these routines. This recommendation I took quite seriously, and by observing and participating in family life I became knowledgeable of these routines. That is, I began to appreciate the utility for the family of mutually understanding the concrete detail of a prospective series of "tasks at hand" (Schtuz 1970) or, by way of definition, of sharing routines.

In its most commonsensical usage, shared routine was not

difficult to appreciate in the Smith household. For example, after only the first few observations, I could easily see that Barbara and Bianca shared knowledge such as "you go to the toilet before dinner" or "you sit on the porch after your music activity." The shared ordering of these relatively large blocks of time and activity were the cornerstone of communicational practice with Bianca. The more I observed in the home, the more convinced I was of this fact of family life. There was a definite and describable recurring orderliness to mealtimes, bathroom visits, recreation, and so on. A repeated detail of temporally ordered tasks was a ubiquitous and observable part of family life from the outset.

The most convincing evidence of the *shared* reality of routine with Bianca was actual interaction with her. Being a participant in these routines and within the communicational structure inherent in them allowed me direct access to routine as an interpretational resource. As with Christina, being interior to the family world, as best as I could achieve this through participation, was the best way to understand "understanding Bianca." The following incident exhibits this well.

After observing Barbara feeding Bianca several times, I volunteered to feed her myself on the next visit. Barbara was pleased at my offer to help, accepted, and on the next visit planned to occupy herself with various household matters while I did so. The next trip to the house, I fed Bianca. For a while things went well enough. Previous observations had acquainted me with some of the details of mealtime practices with Bianca. But at the point I was supposed to help her drink some milk (Bianca had a tongue thrust when she swallowed and could only grasp the glass using two hands in a "pincer" fashion, which made drinking quite messy), I failed miserably. Part of the assistance in drinking milk called for me to hold a saucer under her chin and catch the milk that spilled out of her mouth. Unfortunately I had only observed this and had never done it, so my technique was somewhat lacking. Milk spilled all over Bianca and me. When I saw the milk all over her lap, I tried to stop her from drinking, but she became very impatient with me and grabbed my hand and saucer, putting it in exactly the right place that it needed to be so that no milk would run down her neck. Bianca was teaching me the details of her mealtime routine known to her and her parents. She was making up for my deficiency as a new member of that network. She was demonstrating the praktognosic knowledge that was necessary for that routine's production. After living through such events one could not help but believe in the intersubjective reality of routine for family members.

Shortly after this event occurred, the following took place. Barbara came in and told me that Bianca needed to have a saucer placed under her chin when she drank, because she had a tongue thrust and would get wet otherwise. I told her that Bianca had just shown me how to place the saucer. Both parents enjoyed hearing about this and proceeded to tell me that Bianca would show me her routine, what she expected me to do, if I let her. Joe said, "She's the one who most wants to have her routine followed exactly." She made sure that Barbara did not forget to give her medicine after dinner; and when you put her to bed, she monitored everything you did. Did you put the right number of blankets on? Was the bed rail up? Were her leg braces standing in the corner? I asked Barbara what would happen if you tried to change something in her routine—if you did not give her medication for one evening? Barbara answered that at first Bianca would not like it at all, but that she could be made to accept it. Joe added that for a while they would probably have to give her apple juice in place of medication.

Not only did the parents feel that Bianca understood routines but also that she could teach routines "if you let her." I found this claim to be accurate and increasingly came to appreciate the degree and quality of Bianca's skills and knowledge in the home.

Routine constituted so great a communicational resource for the family that in order to understand many of Bianca's gestures and actions, one already had to be familiar with routine. This put me in the odd but tolerable observational position of having to know the routine to be able to see the ways Bianca was showing it to me. Imagine, for example, that I had no idea of the use of the saucer at mealtime. How would I have interpreted her requests to hold the saucer under her chin (obvious communications to her parents)? Or consider Bianca "counting blankets" I had to ask the parents what she was doing, in order to make meaning out of what I was seeing. I observed that she was looking down at the bed, apparently doing something, but I could not figure out what that was. After the parents told me that it was her monitoring to see if the correct number of blankets were put on, I could then clearly see her doing just that at every subsequent bedtime, and I could also competently and routinely put Bianca to sleep. I also had to remember various other elements of this bedtime routine. But there would have been no way for me correctly to interpret Bianca's gestures at bedtime if the parents had not explained to me their relevance to the details of the bedtime routine.

Thus, it was Barbara and Joe who, as competent, knowledgeable teachers of communicating with Bianca, enabled me to tolerate the ambiguous observational position of needing to understand routine before I could understand Bianca. Their constant willingness to fill in the details that I needed in order competently to interpret Bianca's limited expressive repertoire was what made my epistemological position more bearable. But while I did learn in some very great detail what these routines consisted of, they remained less available to me than to Joe or

Barbara. They were very deep and detailed phenomena for them—replete with contradiction and ambiguous history. They were also for them automatic and natural. For me, these same routines were objects of research construction, had to be worked at to be known, and were never of the same detail and accuracy as the parents' version. In certain ways research knowledge of these matters was inferior to that of parental knowledge.

Through participation in family routines, I collected observations that showed how routines were treated as things, factual matters, by family members. Consider as just one example Joe's remarks about using apple juice as a substitute for medication. Part of the significance of this proposal, and of many others made by the family about routines with Bianca, is the way it treats Bianca's expectations about receiving medication after dinner as a factual mundane matter. Her expectations as part of this routine event are treated as "things" that if not acknowledged and dealt with will have certain repercussions—repercussions that could be avoided if certain strategies were employed. This was undoubtedly a lesson they learned from history. These kinds of remarks to me were the strongest indicator that routine was an intersubjectively shared resource in negotiating daily life with Bianca. What was implied by Joe's remarks, what was not said in so many words, defined family life even more strongly than what was said.[14]

As employed within family life, routine did not only refer to gross divisions of time and practice such as "mealtime" or "bedtime" (that is, a notion of routine that corresponds to our commonsense usage of the term), it also clearly involved finely detailed fragments of these larger activities. Consider the saucer and milk at mealtime. When one speaks of "a" mealtime routine, one glosses the punctilious detail of tasks that are serially performed and constitute the actuality of the meal as a lived order. These tasks and their meaning were asymmetrical but mutually understood matters for parents and Bianca. That is, at mealtime

Barbara and Bianca each had responsibilities that were recipro-
cally designed for the other and recognized as such. These tasks,
or subroutines, had their own detailed sequential order and organization. In their performance Barbara and Bianca were often
united in coaction that defied description in anything other than
dyadic terms. These subroutines were indefinitely deep practices, with always more aspects to appreciate. A good example
might be those practices within lunch associated with the provision of milk to Bianca. The use of the saucer was only one part
of a very complex routine around milk. It had to be poured in
such a way that Bianca could see the glass and the milk container. It had to be poured immediately before it was offered to
Bianca to drink. On subsequent presentations the milk was "fake
poured" (meaning that the closed milk container was lifted to
the glass as if it were open and milk was coming out of it) because
the milk in the glass might have been sitting there "too long" and
Bianca wanted her milk fresh. The glass had to be filled to such
a height, presented at certain times and not others. In the last
presentation no "fake pouring" was necessary, since Bianca understood and accepted that she had to finish up whatever was
in the glass. And this is just with regard to the provision of milk
at lunch! It was Bianca that held one to this level of routine as
keenly as she did to the more gross divisions of time and practice
associated with the word. Her expectations in this regard were
quite influential in the organizing of communication with her.[15]

Because of the intimacy and duration of their relationship,
Barbara and Bianca had built up a huge body of routines with
each other. They used these routines in interaction with each
other in order to read the other's behavior, to allow them to treat
behavior as "signs" within a routine. Compared to a normal child
of her age, Bianca had a relatively small repertoire of expressive
behaviors. She could express emotional opposites such as
happy/sad, angry/content, confident/unsure, and had a somewhat limited capacity to use a language of action (for example,

show that she wanted the sandwich by grabbing it). She had, relative to a nondisabled adolescent, an extremely limited range of postures, paralinguistics, and physiognomic expressions and had to rely upon others to interpret these expressions. In the home, where persons shared projects and relevant understandings as well as a long history of life together, such interpretations for the most part were done unremarkably, unequivocally, and mundanely. When parents verbally supplied the social organizational context of Bianca's gestures, they transformed her limited expressions into something with specific, context-relevant meaning. This is illustrated in the following note.

> A very interesting interpretive procedure is used by Barbara, one that reminded me of those I employed with Christina. At one point during the evening meal Bianca became very upset and began making sounds of displeasure and fidgeting. Barbara turned to me and offered an explanation, "She wants her milk." I asked her how she knew this, and she said that Bianca usually would have gotten her milk by now, but she (Barbara) had forgotten tonight.

In this note an affective display was perceived by Barbara as a sign related to something within their shared routine. These forms of communication, massively available to observation, I began to call "routine signs." Their display was known as it was embedded into specifically comprehended contextual conditions (for example, that forgetting the milk was a complainable matter). The symbolic character of Bianca's communicative act resided in the way parents would understand the display as referring, strictly speaking, to something other than itself—for example, that a complaint was a request for milk. By the use of the shared resource of "what goes when" (and "what goes where"), a very limited set of expressions were allowed to take on an incredible variety of meanings. Bianca's actions became "indexical expressions" (Bar-Hillel 1954) whose sense relied upon "background expectancies" (Garfinkel 1967), and in that regard did not essentially differ from normal linguistic forms of communication. This process of reading Bianca's actions as indexical expressions was the foundation stone of communication with her.

Routine signs were thus essentially circumstantial forms of communication. Despite this and the potentially high rate of interpretive error one might think was built into this kind of understanding of one another, communication with Bianca was sufficient for all practical purposes. This was remarkable to me. So sufficient were these forms of communication that there was a complete absence of signing (teaching signs of the deaf) or any other formal language training at home. While Barbara was clearly devoted to her daughter, this lack of language training did not strike the school (or myself) as in Bianca's best interests. In one instance, when Bianca was "asking" for her milk, I suggested to Barbara that we give her a sign for "more," since this would facilitate her communication with a wider audience. Barbara's response was very revealing about the functional necessity of formal language for family life. She agreed that she should be teaching her signs because one day she might have to leave their home (although they intended to let her live with them as long as possible). But she justified her having not done so by saying, "It's because we just know her so well, what she wants. . . . [Joe] doesn't sign at all, but I should make her do that."

I do not want to debate the ethics and implications of this choice (something we might indeed want to do, even after understanding it "emically"), but the mother's remarks direct our attention to the superfluity of formal language to family life with Bianca. Inclusion of symbolic signing activity in family life would have created an unnecessary redundancy to action, at the not insubstantial cost of having to teach Bianca and interrupt family routines. The symbol would only summarize what was already known, was obvious and understood by the participants. Symbols were clearly functionally dispensable, if not dysfunctional, to family life. Again, this is not to debate their utility to Bianca in communicating with persons outside the family. Because symbols were extremely difficult to teach and redundant, they were seen as impediments to the relatively brisk-paced household routine.[16]

Routine was thus a powerful and ubiquitous presence in almost all family interaction with Bianca. Because it was shared by family members, it constituted a massive and detailed body of practical knowledge upon which interpretation of one another's actions or omissions was possible. Routine entailed asymmetrical knowledge for parents and Bianca. It denoted both detailed microlevel practices and the organization of these into large temporal units. Although unique to the communication practices of the Smith household, their system of routine signs more often than not proved sufficient for all practical purposes when interacting with Bianca.

LAYOUT

To understand Bianca I found that shared knowledge of spatial arrangements within the home was as important as shared ideas about temporal ordering of activities. If we consider the strictly analytic basis for distinguishing between space and time in any observed instance of social action, we can begin to appreciate the critical role of shared layout in almost any instance of family life with Bianca, such diverse scenarios as Barbara and Bianca going to the bathroom after dinner, Bianca crawling into her bed to wait for me to play guitar for her, Bianca crawling into the den on Friday night to wait for her father to come and build a fire in the fireplace, Bianca crawling up to her room to play her light game by opening and shutting the door. These and many other interactions with Bianca evidenced and relied upon Bianca's knowledge of household spaces and locations of objects.

As with routine, the meanings of space were experientially mutually constituted. Over time certain places had become asso-

ciated with certain activities and events. As is typical of families
that live in their own homes for many years, the rooms of this
house had very rich associations for the Smiths. Even in the relatively short period that I worked in the home, Bianca and I managed to build up such a store of shared spatial knowledge (as my
remark about her waiting for me to play guitar on her bed shows).
And as with routine, the parents displayed an indefinitely deep
knowledge of places and their events. I would always be finding
out further details about this room, that box of toys (that once
was another box that Barbara's brother had built), the window
shade in Bianca's room, the rocking chair, or what have you. This
drawer or closet was forbidden to children; this was the closet
where Bianca would go and hide when she was upset; and so
on. In describing life with Bianca, I found a kind of intersubjective, shared "spatialization" of family life (bear in mind of course
that this academic-sounding term stands for something that was,
for the family, completely ordinary and unremarkable).

The degree to which a shared layout was a fact of family life
with Bianca is seen in the following field note, produced after my
first visit to the household.

> Barbara gave me a tour of the house, showing me all the
> different rooms and pieces of furniture. I asked her whether
> Bianca stayed only in her room, and she shook her head.
> She told me that Bianca knew every room in the house,
> whose it was, and what was in it. On weekends she enjoyed
> playing in the whole house and had toys in all the rooms.
> Barbara narrated how Bianca used to crawl up into Tanya's
> room and get into bed with Tanya. I asked if she used all
> the rooms equally, and Barbara said no, but that she did go
> into each of them, depending on what she wanted to do.
> She said that Bianca knew the whole layout of the house.

Participant observation corroborated Bianca's knowledge and
use of household spaces. She could regularly be seen moving

purposively through the home, crawling up stairs, opening doors, or searching through closets or boxes for toys. Although there is no way to "prove purposiveness or that Bianca had the detailed knowledge of the home the mother claimed she had, observation suggested that she was aware of the various rooms and their associated activities. She also appeared to know the arrangements of the furniture, objects, and other belongings in the rooms.

Layout, like routine, drew my attention to shared spatial knowledge at various levels of generality. That is, it denoted spatial knowledge that involved both a general knowledge of the home—for example, the rooms and their relation to one another—and spatial knowledge related to very small areas, such as the space behind the bed or between the magazine rack and toliet.[17] These different levels of spatial knowledge were evidence by Bianca and used by her parents in their interpretation of her actions. Such knowledge also constituted a set of background expectancies against which behavior was both perceived and explained.

As with routine, knowledge of layout was asymmetrically shared. Knowledge of layout, while sufficiently similar to allow family life to proceed, was specific to the individual member's perspective. While Bianca may have seen her room as "the place where I can go to be alone and play such and such games," it was perceived by the parents as "the place where Bianca goes to play and can be left unsupervised for a reasonable period of time while we are running errands or entertaining visitors." The asymmetry of the knowledge reflected the different practical uses to which spaces were put by Bianca and by other family members. While these practical uses may have themselves been functionally related (the place where the child likes to play alone is the place where the other can leave the child to play alone), there was a difference in the association with specific places by particular family members according to their particular practical interest in that space. On the other hand, the general limitation to this perspectival knowledge of space was what Sartre called a "shared facticity" (no family member ever violated the basic laws of everyday reality, tried to walk through a wall, fly, or the like). Thus, while places did have very different meanings for family members, they were in some existential/ontological sense the same physical places for them.

Documentation of the shared spatiality of family life raised some inescapable methodological issues. The shared body of spatial knowledge evident in Bianca's interactions was complex and cannot be adequately explored within the context of this (and perhaps any) writing. While a full discussion of the documentability and describability of family life cannot be provided here, two brief issues can at least be pointed to—the massive amount of data that could be required and the detail, or punctiliousness, of that data. As is described in Chapter 5, the amount of descriptive data required to show what one knows about any particular family can be incredible (a selected outline of topics from my field notes could have involved me in several thousand pages of writing). So one may well ask, when do I stop describing something and know that I have described it adequately?

A related issue is the degree of detail that may be required in documenting family activity. How much does one need to describe, and when is enough enough? These are complicated matters that get raised for observational researchers as part of the course of their work. Consider the phrase taken from field notes on the bathing procedure used for Bianca. "Barbara lifts and rotates Bianca from the bath and puts her stomach down across her lap." When I used that description to familiarize a nonfamily caregiver with Bianca's bathroom routine, her comment was that there was "no way" that she could get her out of the water and onto her lap. This signaled to me that the description lacked sufficient or relevant detail to allow her to reproduce the bathing routine as described. These words gloss what was in the original scene of observation a swarm of perceptual details, the hand being placed under the neck just so, the other hand on the right buttock, the left leg of Barbara extended against the outside edge of the tub, even the flexing of muscles that were not directly observable in the cooperative bathing effort; all these were part of the *in situ* action glossed by my field note but not recorded in it in so many words (see Chapter 5 for a more detailed discussion of the issue of descriptive adequacy). It is worth considering, then, what criterion of detail would ensure that one had really described something adequately.

As with routine, layout was an aspect of family life with Bianca that resisted formulation into a clear calculus or finite set of propositions. Layout was shared knowledge that grew out of their shared lives, and it was heavily relied upon by Barbara in interpreting the meaning of Bianca's actions, and apparently vice versa. During my relatively short nine-month data collection in the home, many of these phenomena were just beginning to emerge for me. I have in these remarks only named these phenomena, described them, and begun to explore some of their features, which themselves were probably undergoing continuous change undetected by my method. This should not be mistaken for a systematic explication.

LIKES, DISLIKES, AND THE BODY

I have explored here two aspects of parent-child communication primarily to provide the reader with the kinds of observations that would be necessary to begin to explicate how these persons could have achieved mutual understanding without shared formal language. Likewise, in explaining emotional disposition and bodily resources for communication with Bianca, I am concerned not so much with a systematic explication of these topics as with a brief description of them and their relevance to the communicative enterprise.

I became aware of knowledge of emotional dispositions and

preferences through Barbara's and Joe's remarks that Bianca could "be a brat" and "sabotage" things. These remarks signaled the existence of specific knowledge of one another's emotions and of the relation between these emotions and specific objects, places, or activities. Such knowledge played a central role in organizing life with Bianca and was also an important tool used by Bianca to exert influence on family members. Consider, for example, how Bianca would summon her mother after being left on the porch too long.

> Bianca has been outside for a while now, and Barbara and I have been walking around the home on various tasks. When we come downstairs Barbara remarks that she can hear that Bianca has pulled her hearing aid molds out of her ears and that they are feeding back. I stop to listen for a high pitched whistle. Barbara is out onto the porch quickly, scolding Bianca for taking out her aids. (Note: subsequent observations corroborate the fact that this mechanism was used regularly by Bianca to summon her mother; because of the potential damage to the sensitive aid, the white sound whistle invariably brought her quickly to Bianca's side.)

This use of objects or practices to anger her parents was a very common way for Bianca to initiate interaction. A tremendous number of examples of such incidents are available in field notes. Sometimes, during these, Barbara would refer to her as a "brat," and sometimes Joe would say Bianca really knew how to "get you." Through such phrases it was clear that the parents had accepted as a matter of family life Bianca's knowledge of their emotional reactions to things, especially what bothered them. Consider Bianca's use of knowledge of emotional dispositions to "get you." This meant in family vernacular that Bianca would do something purposefully just to get you angry or to get back at you. On two occasions I witnessed Bianca go to her father's end table in the parents' bedroom and take out one of the bullets that he kept there in case he ever had to load his gun. Bianca knew that this object was strictly forbidden to her, and she would get it specifically to anger her dad. Once he watched her scurry out of the living room, knowing she was angry at him, and said, "She's going to get the bullet."

But shared knowledge about positive emotional reactions was also part of achieving intersubjectivity with Bianca. Her parents would place Bianca in certain chairs or present her with favorite objects. Although I did not directly witness this, parents told me that Bianca would present them with things that they had lost of that belonged to them. They felt that Bianca understood that they were attached to these objects. Thus, the family shared a mutual knowledge of emotionality, of likes and dislikes, that also formed part of their communication.

Finally, shared understanding of the human body was also a conspicuous and basic part of the understanding displayed by both mother and daughter. Each understood in a tacit way the resources and limitations of the human body as a medium or locus for experience and practice (see Polhemus 1974). Both mother and daughter depended upon attributes of that body as assumed resources in their projects with each other. These attributes and bodily functions included visual and auditory perception (although Bianca's were degraded), emotions and their facial display,[18] paralinguistic properties of voice (relied upon heavily by parents in speaking to, praising, or castigating Bianca), touch (used as both reward or punishment), and gesturing (pointing, reaching, grabbing, deflecting). These were parts of what the human body allowed parent and child to share about each other's actions. In short, Bianca and her mother shared enough of the same world as conspecific that they could understand that world commonly. They participated together in a species-specific "effector and receptor world," or, by way of short hand, the human *Umwelt* (von Uexkull 1934). This very deep way of sharing was evident in any and every interaction with Bianca. It is what made their exchanges, communication, and understanding specifically human (see especially Chapter 4 for a fuller discussion of these topics).

■ "EVERYTHING" FOR ALL PRACTICAL PURPOSES

Consider the above, the reader may appreciate how communication was for the family's practical purposes with Bianca not only possible but effective. Participating and observing family life revealed an unusual degree of shared knowledge among them. Barbara particularly could predict Bianca's behaviors with uncanny accuracy. Together they had built this relatively refined, intimate, and unique communication system. Although this assessment is antithetical to the clinical picture of their relationship, the reader may now see why clinical objectivity could never detect such a state of affairs as I had observed through long-term in-home observation. Acknowledging the ultimate political character to any claim of correctness, I believe that I was descriptively more accurate regarding the family's *in situ*, actual communication with Bianca. The school was more knowledgeable of how Bianca failed to participate in formal language.

By looking at Barbara's claims of complete communication with Bianca, I want to pursue the conflict between the two ways of looking at communication evidenced by the school and the family. As a representative of the scientific community, I too experienced some problems regarding Barbara's claims of "complete" communication with Bianca. At times I felt that my empathy with her and my neutrality as a scientific observer were very much in conflict.

The claim of complete communication was made on the first visit to the home, as evident in the following notes.

> We are in Bianca's playroom, and she and I are on the bed. She begins gesturing at me, waving her arms across

her body and moaning. Barbara interprets her behavior for me. "She is telling you to move because you're blocking the light from the window." Bianca is holding a small piece of plastic to her eye while she is lying on the bed. Barbara says, "She knows what she wants," and almost simultaneously Bianca reaches over and tries to push me off the bed. I move to the end of the bed and Barbara remarks that she probably won't like that either. Sure enough, in a few seconds Bianca again reaches out toward me, indicating her displeasure with my sitting on her bed. Barbara says, "She's telling you to get off." I get up and go over and sit down near Barbara, who has naturally taken a seat away from the bed in a position that does not block the light from the window. She says in an excited way, "The longer you spend with her, the more you realize that there isn't one thing, honest to God, that Bianca does not tell you."

There are a number of communicational features that emerged in this incident. First, we see how Barbara narrated the meaning of Bianca's actions for me in order to make up for my own ignorance of the various bodies of knowledge I would need in order really to interpret Bianca. Barbara offered the explanation that I had to spend a lot more time with Bianca to understand what she was telling me.

Barbara's remarks were consistent with my own observations of normally perceiving and communicating persons who are in relationships with alingual or partially lingual deaf-blind children. Intimacy provides the normal person with an avenue of access to the intentional communication of these children. This is a "social fact" of these relationships (see endnote 13). This is not generally known in the professional literature because most professionals do not study the "lived orders" of these families. This is complicated by the fact that there may be only one or two people who actually know the child well enough to understand what he or she means, and sometimes these people may be unwilling to share (for reasons of self-protection) their experiences. Years of experience have taught me that the person with the most intimate relationship with the alingual child invariably has the authority to interpret action with validity and that such a person may have some relatively strange things to report.[19]

Barbara's proposition was that such interpretive entitlement would come for me by spending time with Bianca. The consciousness of Bianca that she possessed came out of their material practices with one another over a long course of time. She basically said that one had to do it, to practice it, to become good at it. At the same time, she was no empiricist. She subscribed to no "theory" of communication but instead reported on what was the case between her and Bianca. Sometimes she would make extraordinary claims about communication with Bianca. I began to characterize these extraordinary claims as "esoteric" communication practices. While I was able to observe instances of these practices, I could not engage in them with Bianca directly.

My relationship with Christina prepared me to accept that a well-articulated nonsymbolic communication system could exist with an alingual child. And that same relationship made the possibility of esoteric communication acceptable, if not easy to document or justify. It was interesting that Barbara employed the phrase "honest to God" in advancing her claim of the completeness of Bianca's communication. These words anticipated the professional (and for that matter commonsense) skepticism that she knew would be a result of her statement. I found a curious parallel between her position and my own in presenting a similar claim about Christina to my colleagues in sociology, who I also knew would not believe me (Goode 1975b, 48). Despite the fact that we shared no symbolic communication system, I often knew what Chris was thinking (and part of what I knew was that she often could do the same with me). Both Barbara and I had been interior to such experiences and recognized that their disclosure would call forth professional and commonsensical objections. These experiences did not fit well with the dominant models of how human beings understand one another.

Esoteric communication is well illustrated in the following note about a relatively mundane event. I had been talking to Barbara while she was preparing dinner in the kitchen. We were comparing notes about Christina and Bianca. During the course of the conversation the follwing was said.

> "You know, Dave, the other night the most amazing thing happened. Bianca knew that she was going to have tortillas before she ate 'em, even before I started cooking them." I ask Barbara whether they were on the table and whether Bianca could have smelled them. She says no."She just knew—we don't know how—she just knew we were having tortillas."

Initially I had some trouble with Barbara's statement. Granted even that Bianca could have known about the tortillas (and this was Barbara's preoccupation with this incident)—given her communicative repertoire, what could Bianca have done to inform her mother that she had this knowledge? There was no imaginable action on her part that I could come up with, and thus the situation as Barbara described it to me somehow did not seem possible. The communication she was describing did not seem procedurally sensible; it was unaccountable in some scientific sense. While I could understand, based on my relationship with Christina, that esoteric communication of this type could occur, there were no rational or academically relevant resources that I could bring to bear in understanding the event.

Revealingly, my problem was not even an issue to Barbara. My problematic perception of this affair was completely in contradiction to how she offered it—that is, as an assumable matter, requiring no comment or justification, as an ordinary matter of fact. This matter-of-factness is evident in her preoccupation with how Bianca could have known about the tortillas. At no time did she, or her husband, find it remarkable that they could have known that Bianca knew. What was highly problematic for me was a presumed element of their account of the incident, a provoking confrontation between the all too obvious and the unthinkable.

I later questioned Joe and Barbara about the claims they made concerning "esoteric" communication with Bianca. Both parents gave their own versions of "you just know" in some cases. They also had no way to specify how, procedurally speaking, you did this; but that you knew was unquestionable—you just did. One way to understand the parents is to see them in the position of having had an experience that they cannot document or rationally account for and about which they suspect others will have suspicion. I understood the parents' testimony in this light, that their difficulty at documenting and accounting for the "facts" of the achievement of intersubjectivity with Bianca did not reflect the fictitiousness of those "facts" so much as their resistance to formulation into acceptable, commonsensical language.[20]

If we consider more precisely what could have made these phenomena difficult to formulate into language, there are three distinct possibilities. First they may have consisted of observable practices for which we have no current name or language and, following the cultural relativity of language argument (Whorf 1956), were thereby problematically available to consciousness. Second, they may have consisted of practices for which we have names but which remained hidden to Barbara and the observer. Third, these practices may not have been directly observable; for example, they may have been mentalistic phenomena that did not observably appear in the commonsense world. It may also be that each of these possibilities contains an element of the truth regarding this "you just know" aspect of communication with Bianca. On the basis of data collected in the two case studies presented in Chapters 2 and 3, esoteric communication should not be ruled out of serious intellectual consideration on the basis of its looseness of fit with prevailing materialistic conceptions of human communication. It is important to acknowledge that the human sciences are still in their infancy in their study of communication and that we know less about all matters related to human behavior than some experts would have us believe. Discovering how exceptional human relationships provided for exceptional communication—this is part of what Bianca and her family's story has for us. Perhaps their hyperintimate existence together reminds one of the isolated twins who developed their own personal language. Perhaps some of these less-understood mechanisms of communication are brought into play because of the exceptional condition of the communicative relationship, as, for example, in the case of the Smiths. Or perhaps these mechanisms are part of any long-term and intimate contact. Husbands and wives report after years of cohabitation that they have become able to predict behavior and know the thoughts of the other. As a matter of observation, when I watched Bianca and Barbara communicating, I often felt that I was privy to activities in which persons were not necessarily "to be considered closed and self-contained . . . forever cut off from one another because of their bodies" (Edmund Husserl).

Regardless of these analytic/explanatory possibilities, the important point to understand is that as a scientist I had to confront my own skepticism about Barbara's propositions and accept that indeed she might "just know" without being able to explain how. As my tenure in the home came to a close, I reached an orientation to the field such that I would take up recommendations made by family members as factual until proven otherwise, no matter how absurd they might seem at first. That is, if a claim was made as a matter of fact, it was so treated unless counterfactual evidence made it impossible to do so. As mentioned above, not all parental claims had this character. But of those that did, I began to consider these in the light they were

offered, rather than judge their rationality. I was led to this position because doing otherwise would have meant rendering such
claims false or ironic through importing into the scene some extrinsic professional or lay theory. This was what I and other ethnomethodologists objected to in the first instance, and such a
procedure employed knowingly would have made my study of
the family as epistemologically flawed as the more mainstream
family research. Such a method would have been antithetical to
the purpose of the project and would have contradicted the details of what I saw, that Barbara was incredibly knowledgeable of
these affairs and was not unreasonable or delusional during the
home visits I conducted.

What is critical for the reader to take away from this discussion is the realization that as researchers or clinicians it be-
hooves us to refrain from judging claims made by parents that
not only fail to resonate with our professional models but also
may not sound sensible or even rational to us. The affair with the
tortillas summarized this important lesson about the importing
of extrinsic rationalities into observational research; perhaps in
quite a reverse fashion, through a phenomenological style of observation, we are being called upon to examine our own rationality in a critical way. Perhaps we are being called upon to listen
and observe with even greater vigilance rather than medicalize,
rationalize, and delegitimize that which does not fit.

Unfortunately this is a different temptation to resist, even for
ethnomethodologists. Pollner and Goode (1990) discuss in a critical way the ethnomethodological study, published by Wikler and
Pollner in 1985, of a family that was diagnosed as having a rare
psychiatric syndrome of *folie à famille*. A child in this family was
diagnosed as profoundly mentally retarded and without language, and all the family members claimed that she could speak
and was not retarded! The study employs as its point of depar-
ture the diagnosis made in the clinic that the child was mentally
retarded and that the family was delusional, in this sense really

paralleling the situation in the Smith family with regard to Bianca's communication assessment at school. The Smiths' claims, and the Wikler and Pollner family's claims, were derogated and ridiculed, unlike the objective knowledge of the clinic, which was assumed to be the standard of truth and correctness. Through the authority of the clinic, the family's delusion was "established" institutionally. Much to the dismay of ethnomethodology, the same occurs in the research; Wikler and Pollner uncritically employ the clincal frame to analyze data, thereby mistakenly importing the extrinsic clinical logic into the research process. No prolonged in-home ethnography was performed, and no serious attempt actually to consider family claims was made. Instead, familial behaviors were constructed as elements that contributed to a delusional system.

In direct contrast to this kind of symptomatic interpretation of families, I propose that when one enters a home and observes a communicational network, such as that in the Smiths' home, it is highly likely that processes of communication are really occurring, even when difficult to observe, document, or even discuss. Specific properties of these networks, these lived orders of communication, reflect the specific communicative competencies and styles of those involved and their shared lives. Communicational competencies and forms of such networks may not travel well outside the home. They may not exist or may be undetectable in other contexts, such as in clinics and schools. But this being said, these communication practices may nonetheless be extremely real and effective forms of achieving understanding. For children like Bianca and her parents, they may indeed allow for them to make known to each other "everything for all practical purposes."

■ DISCUSSION AND IMPLICATIONS

In the next chapter I provide a detailed discussion of many of the implications of this examination of the Smiths' communication for our understanding of human intersubjectivity and language. In this section a brief examination of some critical implications is offered. First, to what degree, or in what sense, was the communicational relationship between Bianca and her parents abnormal or extraordinary? To what degree and in what senses were they in a position with regard to one another that was different from that of normal communicators?

As Schutz (1970) noted, the knowledge we share with one another in the everyday world is partial, incomplete, and incoherent. Understandings in the everyday world are good enough for practical purposes and would not stand up to the rigors of scientific rationality (see Garfinkel 1967). Yet we do not think that our communication is incompete, incoherent, and partial, or that we fail to communicate. We are generally satisfied with how the conversational machine works (Sacks 1963) and have developed specific conversational strategies for when it becomes problematic. Thus, it could be argued that the essential nature of communication with Bianca was much the same as communicating with anybody else. In any communicational enterprise two subjectivities are in a position of using whatever resources may be at hand to achieve their mutual purposes. At times we all lack significant information about the other subjectivity. With persons who cannot communicate with formal language, we may even lack a sense of what significant information might look like or how it is obtained through the course of interaction. Communicative networks involving persons without formal language demonstrate that verbal communication is part of a "total communicational act" (Watzlawick 1973). To treat verbal communication as the basic vehicle for human understanding is to fall victim to what Merleau-Ponty (1962) called "the ruse of language." The lack of a shared normative symbol system between Bianca and Barbara, and between Christina and me, did not transform our communication work together into an entirely different enterprise. We were two (sets of) people trying to understand one another with the resources we had available. Many of these resources are undoubtedly used in "normal" communication, but because of the "ruse of language," they go unnoticed and unappreciated; at least this is my view. It is only in certain kinds of relationships that some of these nonlanguage resources become highlighted for us: communicating with a baby, a deaf person (if you do not sign), a person with a stroke, an Alzheimer's patient, a person from another culture without any shared language, and so on.[21]

What was peculiar to the Smiths (and other families who had raised children with rubella syndrome) was that a prenatal disease process had put them in a notably unique and ambiguous communicational relationship with their daughter. Without any shared formal language, the family had to rely *exclusively* upon nonformal-language communication resources, and this gave their communicative praxis with Bianca a certain audiovisual, somatic detail. It sharpened for them the uses of these nonformal-language-related resources. Communication proceeded with Bianca without comment and was adequate to everyday life with her, except when it failed and was then rendered a problematic and thematized aspect of family life (for example, see the field note about "guessing games"). Thus, a contradiction existed for this family: they were interior to an incredibly efficacious nonformal-language-based system that achieved intersubjectivity with Bianca, but the deaf-blind alinguality of their daughter created all sorts of difficulties for the Smiths. "Guessing games" and "communicational tests" are not common to most family's communication networks. It is important that we acknowledge the differences in communicating with Bianca, while still appreciating that the observations above probably reflect tacit features of normal communication about which we are unaware.[22] Certainly one would not be surprised to see similar findings in studies of interaction with very young children, mentally retarded children, or, so long as we are careful about the juxtaposition of people with mental retardation and animals, in communicative interactions with other species.

There were several purposes in presenting the details of this communication system between Barbara and Bianca. First was convincingly to exemplify an instance of ethnomethodological observation—that is, observation and explication of the phenomenon of communication as displayed in school and home. Part of this observation was a critique of the way the clinical, objectivist, quantified language approach to communication could not begin to comprehend the reality of communication for this family and could admit to these types of data (see Chapter 5 for a more detailed illustration and discussion of this observation). The objectivist approach defines, manipulates, and measures variables and attributes that are theoretically reasoned as being constitutive of communication.

In a literal sense, it is quite accurate to say that despite the millions of dollars and man-hours spent researching communication, human science today does not have an adequate grasp or understanding of a single instance of ordinary or extraordinary family communication. In fact, we are only beginning to study and understand what a conversation of any type consists of, and how it is achieved by co-conversationalists (see Sacks 1963; Sacks, Schegloff, and Jefferson 1974). The problem from the research perspective has been the failure to engage in a critical process of exploratory description, coupled with an insensitive application of theory and statistically oriented, natural science method to all social research issues, including studying families with severely retarded children. In the clinical world, clinicians formulate a professional model of communication (based upon research and commonsense notions about communication) and then make problematic the actions of their "clients" by virtue of the clients' lack of fit to this professional model.[23] In both clinical and research approaches to communication there is a reliance on "description-deficient" scientific data that bear an unknown relation to the actualities of everyday communication practices. These data can constitute an impediment to generating pragmatically relevant knowledge.

Another motivation in presenting these observations was to explore the possibility of, and perhaps illustrate, an essential incompatibility between an objective, scientistic version of human existence and one that is directed more at the retrieval of what is experienced and actually produced by people in their everyday lives with one another, day in, day out. Ethnomethodologists remind us that it is this everyday reality, this ultimate stuff of human existence, toward which science ought to direct its inquiry. The studies of central tendency and typicality eviscerate the wholeness and richness of this everyday existence and transform it into something unrecognizable to the persons who are actually participating in and producing the realities under study. To a large degree knowledge so produced may be irrelevant to the actual phenomenon it seeks to represent or encode. It may even be contradictory to the actual experiential details of the case, as with the Smiths.

The Smiths did, and will, conduct their communication with Bianca as they did, without cognizance of any sort of scientific understanding of their activities. They were in fact doing so despite having been labeled delusional by professionals who relied on such understandings. The lack of relevance of the kind of logic that underlay professional wisdom in this area cannot be any better illustrated than by how it missed the Smiths' communication with Bianca entirely. Its problems cannot be solved through the refinement of statistical or clinical method. It may be that the whole worldview that comes along with such methods is extrinsic to and inconsistent with the experience and production of everyday social existence. If this is true, then it is no surprise that such methods produce knowledge that is not useful in organizing and changing everyday events.

As part of achieving some modesty about their own work, scientists should acknowledge that (literally) any number of theories could have been used to study the Smiths' communication with their daughter. An anthropologist might have explained what they did in terms of their participation in culture; a primatologist might have emphasized their species-specific behaviors; a psychiatrist could have talked in a language of denial, projection, and guilt; and so on. As was noted by sociologists of knowledge earlier in this century, analytic possibilities are limited only by human imagination. But what must impress one is the way all these scientists would unknowingly depend upon the communicational practices of the Smiths, what they did together ascientifically, this ultimate stuff of human life done without respect to extrinsic logics and theories. One might say that there are *n* ways to describe Barbara and Bianca interacting but that all these would depend upon what Barbara and Bianca did together as a matter of their everyday lives together. Without implying that it would not be interesting or useful to take any of the above disciplinary stances, I would suggest that the problem with scientific models or theories and their associated methods and data is that they are models, theories, or amalgamations, and not representations of the phenomena themselves.

The final motive for engaging in this writing was to demonstrate the utility of this form of inquiry in retrieving family life as lived. I would submit that these data, filled as they are with my own personal interpretations, contradictions, and ambiguities, present a more accurate portrayal of the relationship between Bianca and Barbara than is available in clinical files. Whatever interventions one might choose to pursue with the Smiths, an understanding of their lives as understood and lived by them would benefit us enormously. It enhances our understanding of the meaning and impact of interventions on family life. Case studies such as this reveal far more than anecdotal information and should be an ongoing part of scientific studies underlying clinical practice with such families.

The value of ethnomethodological research for clinical intervention cannot be overestimated. Of course, this research is time-consuming and costly in terms of effort and emotion, but I am convinced that such studies are important nonetheless. As a methodology for exploratory research, the ethnomethodological case study can serve as an excellent vehicle to sensitize practitioners to critical dimensions of a phenomenon. For example, the current study has served that purpose for language researchers/clinicians. The involvement of the researcher directly with the phenomenon allows him or her to understand what are the important questions, to whom, and why. Exploratory research will reveal new phenomena. In this mode, the very existence of phenomena hinges upon the possibility of genuine discovery, facing the object in itself rather than with professional blinders. The existence of naturally organized familial communication systems of the type described above is important news not only to students of psychology, sociology, or communication, but to clinicians who work with people with disabilities and their families. If clinical work is about effecting the everyday behaviors of people, then an understanding of what "everyday" consists of is an imperative part of the clinical corpus of knowledge.

Because of the ability of observational methods to retrieve everyday life, a limited number of case studies should serve to validate or discredit, as in the current study, results that have been obtained using more-traditional research approaches. This is a way to use observational studies to "triangulate" data and results. This would potentially enhance the validity of large-scale studies using more quantitative approaches.

A sufficient emphasis upon investigating {naturally organized communication systems in families with alingual children} (where brackets again mean "lived order") would promote a better understanding of human communication generally, as well as have specific application for populations with communicational dysfunctions or idiosyncracies. As stated above, it may well be that Barbara and Bianca's communication reveals powerful and tacit features of human communication, generally speaking. These skills are more than likely embedded deeply in everyday family communication, although less easily recognized.

The clinical applications of such knowledge can be very powerful. Exploratory research such as in this chapter cautions the clinical world to remain open to new ideas about communication. The documentation of the Smiths' communication system entails a recognition in principle of the existence of probably hundreds of thousands of other such systems. An understanding of the lived order of such networks, their commonalities and differences, may prove useful in designing (re)habilitation curricula and even specific techniques of communication that could be taught to persons about to enter into relationships with others who lack formal language. Such an understanding of these naturally organized, lived orders of communication will also allow us to help parents in their role as teachers. As was said in the introduction to this study, we know very little about the everyday lives of families like the Smiths, and this hurts clinicians who seek an understanding of the lives of those they work with that is fuller than is traditionally available in the clinic. Such an understanding would deepen the logic of intervention. It might lead to more-effective intervention and, failing that, at least to an appreciation of the communicational competencies that do exist, even if they cannot be further developed.

There is yet a whole other area of implications of this work regarding our understanding of child-adult interaction more generally. Along with others (Mackay 1974; Sacks 1974) I argue (see Chapter 6) that critiques similar to the one offered above concerning the traditional approaches to research in families can be made with respect to studies involving children generally. That is, numerous studies of child-child or child-adult interaction have dissected these natural events without regard to their everyday orderliness. As noted by Sacks (1974) and his students, children have not fared well in the scientific writings of adults. These writings are flawed from a technical perspective; they are adult centered and do not represent children as children see themselves, or childrens' activities as they are achieved "in their real time making" (Garfinkel, lecture, Department of Sociology, UCLA, 1973).

It has become my firm belief after participating in case-study research for more than twenty years that what is lacking in our current knowledge of human behavior is the most basic descriptive understandings. Our current emphasis on extremely refined techniques scientifically to dissect human existence is either premature or entirely misdirected. If we accept that we know as little about the construction of many everyday phenomena as we do about communication, then the choice for contemporary human science seems clear. It can continue to refine itself into pragmatic superfluity, or it can begin at the beginning and conduct the range of descriptive studies that are required. The current measurement-and-modeling orientation in research is an elegant preoccupation that human science can ill afford. It is a kind of measurement madness.

The details of the study of the Smiths point the way to a more systematic examination of these lived orders of communication without formal language. These details point to the existence of a domain of phenomena, although the study is not an explication of this domain. But even this single case displays the potential of ethnomethodology to reinvest the fullness and realness of everyday life back into the social and clinical sciences. It is this fullness that informs and grounds the program of ethnomethodological research and provides it with potential relevance to human services practitioners who require practical answers to everyday human problems, and to scientists who seek knowledge of everyday reality and its social construction.

Reflections
on the Possibility
of Understanding
Without
Formal Language

4

■ ONE VARIANT of thought about human language proposes that shared formal symbolic language is the distinguishing feature of human beings and of being human. In fact, although the idea is of ancient origin, today the notion that without language human beings are less than human is a common theme in the writings of many academic disciplines and professions. Sociology is no more or less guilty of this mistaken idea than such disciplines as psychology, linguistics, or neurology. In sociology, so entrenched is this notion that it is found in introductory textbooks as an obvious—and, I would add, completely unexamined—axiom about human society.

The concept has appeared sporadically throughout history but appears to "well up" with some regularity. Recently we find it in Oliver Sacks's *Seeing Voices*. He writes, "Language, as Church reminds us, is not just another faculty or skill, it is what makes thought possible, what separates thought from nonthought, human from nonhuman" (68).[1]

Those who have been fortunate to experience relationships with children like Christina or Bianca, or with others who fail to develop or who lose formal language skills, know what this proposition about human communication and human beings is inadequate in the following senses: (1) that rich, complex, multi-faceted, and maturing social relations with such children are achievable without shared symbolic language; (2) that language is not a necessary precondition for thought and reflection (although the quality or character of that reflection may not be available to us); and (3) *that the faculty of language, albeit with a power qualitatively to transform one world or reality into another, is just one of many human faculties that allow us to experience and participate in what Merleau-Ponty (1962) called the human* Umwelt *and* Welt (see immediately below for a discussion of these terms).

Another variant of the idea that people without language are not people is that society without language is impossible or not really society. Again, from within the Smiths' microsociety or mine with Christina, such a proposition is suspect. This formulation of the essentiality of formal symbolic language for the possibility of society is found in textbooks in sociology as well as texts from clinical disciplines. Yet Jan van Dijk, a pioneer in the clinical assessment of children with rubella syndrome and a clinician by training, stated, "Society without language is not society" (1968, 6).[2]

My analysis seriously questions these prevailing biases about formal symbolic language and its role in human life and society generally, taking a somewhat opposing viewpoint that formal symbolic language is rooted in practices of bodily intersubjectivity that provide the unexamined grounds for human intersubjectivities of all kinds, including those based upon formal symbolic language, nonformal symbolic communication, and nonsymbolic communication.

Reflecting upon these issues, I employ the analytic distinction of *Umwelt* and *Welt* suggested by Merleau-Ponty (1962, 327).[3] The term *Welt,* or "world," is intended as a gloss for the socially produced world in which language is used to organize and assign

meaning, make institutions, produce objects, create environments, and so forth—a world, as Schutz would say, that is given
to us largely by our predecessors, that we one day produce and
recognize ourselves, and that we transmit to our progeny. This
term is suggested in conjunction with that of the *Umwelt*,[4] or the
biological aspects of humans. The endowment of the *Umwelt* is
a species-specific receptor-and-effector world that is available
through our experience of being a human body. The word *Welt*
refers to the reflexive, self-constituting, essentially social character of humans, rather than this vulgar, unearned biological potential and worldly situatedness that all humans receive, in one
degree or another, by virtue of having been born. In this chapter
this distinction is treated as a critical though entirely analytic
one in that the experienced world, the reality of everyday life in
which we find ourselves, is apprehended by us as a whole, as a
unity without analytic distinction, that is, as "the world." Merleau-Ponty's work provides iterative insistence on this "monistic"
understanding of the human world, given in its wholeness and
then dissected and refracted by humans for their various purposes.

Do humans have a "biological lexicon" that forms the grounds
for their participation in the world, including expressivity and
understanding? The answer to this is in some ontological sense
yes. Our comprehension of what this biological lexicon is and
what it consists of is clearly a result of practical reasoning and
documentary procedures of the human sciences. Can observed
instances of the bodily endowments of perception, expressivity,
and intersubjectivity simply be explained as biological potentialities of an *Umwelt*? It would appear that the answer to this is no.
The *Umwelt* is not a state or even a stable set of processes. It is
permeable to the reflexive construction by people in society.
Thus, perception, expressivity, understanding, and the rest are
demonstrably influenced by culture, place, historical time, and
so forth. Human biological potentialities are reflexively consti-

tuted through participation with consociates, learning of the practices of society through which everyday reality, the world, is socially constructed.[5] And of course, this world is experienced in this way as a relatively natural, nonconstructed world.

Thus, the analytic distinction between *Umwelt* and *Welt* is not intended as a characterization of how events are constructed in everyday reality. It is merely a useful heuristic to facilitate organization of an answer to the question.

To preview the argument, these case studies indicate that human understanding or intersubjectivity occurs within the everyday life world, of which *Umwelt* and *Welt* are two different aspects. Within the life world, understanding or intersubjectivity is inclusive of communication; that is, communication is one kind of intersubjectivity between people. Communication is inclusive of langage, language being one form of communication. Understanding the world and others begins without the resources of language and is strongly influenced by uniquely bodily forms of expressivity and communication. These forms of understanding and expression are anterior to, and the grounds from which, language emerges for most of us. *It is the lexicon for the conversation with our bodies* (see below). There are certain things that human beings share understanding about that have little to do with formal communication.[6] I argue that what was known in common by the children and adults described in the studies was more than what can be communicated and certainly far greater than what can be spoken, written, or signed. The understanding that existed between children and adults in these studies reflected these nonlanguage, perhaps noncommunicable, primordial understandings of the human world.[7]

The dual sensory impairment and perhaps other forms of cognitive impairment prevented children from perceiving and recognizing certain forms of bodily expressivity (for example, facial expressions of emotion) and inhibited the development of formal language. But this fact did not prevent them from sharing other forms of bodily expressivity. Communication was available to them through their sense of touch and proprioception, through residual sight and hearing, and, most important, through the engagement with their society that their senses and the structures of their societies permitted. The communication that children and adults achieved in these two studies occurred (with the exception of esoteric communication) through the mutual production and interpretation of "indexical expressions," which in this case, because of the alinguality and deaf-blindness of these children, consisted almost exclusively of bodily and gestural nonlanguage indexical expressions. The interpretation of these bodily indexical expressions was highly asymmetrical (those produced by the children were interpreted by us through language, and those produced by us were interpreted by children without language), but they were very clearly sufficient to permit communication, for all practical purposes, between us. By treating understanding in this practical way, we suspend the notion that there is a way to decide whether understanding "really" occurs, and instead pay attention to the interactions described in these studies and their practical outcomes.

When looked at this way, the evidence in these studies that human beings with and without language can practically understand and communicate with one another in many ways is so clear and so massive that one has to ask why the framework for thinking about this question was, and today still largely is, about the very *possibility* of communication and understanding existing. When speaking about this work, I am forever being asked questions like How can you communicate with them (children with rubella syndrome) if they have no language? or How is it possible to communicate with them? I think it could be entirely appropriate, in light of what I have come to understand in these case studies, to rephrase the question thus: *How is it possible for children with deaf-blindness and no language and adults who see, hear, and speak to fail to understand one another?*

■ INDEXICAL EXPRESSION

As noted by Garfinkel and Sacks (1970), the recognition of indexical expression is as old as writing. The phenomenon can be generally as the *essentially situated, or occasional, character and interpretation of expression.* While such expressions have primarily been written about by linguists and usually refer specifically to language behavior, indexical expressions have also been conceived of more broadly than just as words and sentences. As explicated by Garfinkel and Sacks (1970, 14), Edmund Husserl wrote about "expressions . . . whose sense cannot be decided by an auditor without his necessarily knowing something about the biography and purposes of the use of the expression, the circumstances of the utterance, the previous course of discourse or the particular relationship that exists between the user and auditor." This approach to the understanding of verbal expression has been extended by the ethnomethodologists more generally to refer to other forms of human expression. A. V. Cicourel (1974, 88) writes:

> The general significance of indexical expressions . . . is to be found in their use by members for locating speech *and non-oral communication* within a larger context of meaning by instructing the speaker-hearer to link an expression to the clock-time; the type of occasion on which it occurred; the speaker and relevant biographical information about him; the place; the intentions of the speaker; and the kinds of presumed common or special knowledge required for endowing the expression with obvious and subtle meanings. (Emphasis added)

Although still referring primarily to the production of language expressions here within a commonly assumed world of members (masters of a natural language), Cicourel reminds us that earlier formulations of indexical expression included non-oral forms of language communication. I contend that many (but not all) of the features of indexicality characteristic of formal language expressions also apply to indexical nonformal language or even nonsymbolic expressions. Nonlanguage indexical expressions, signs, or indexes are mutually produced and recognized by children with deaf-blindness and no language (nonmembers) and adults who see, hear, and speak (members). Although there are many differences between language-based indexical expressions and nonlanguage expressions, they are both essentially geographically and temporally situated, and socially and biographically circumscribed, forms of expression. "Membership" as traditionally employed by ethnomethodologists, however, does not account for the shared forms of expression that are not natural-language based but have been observed in relations with children like Chris or Bianca. In reading the ethnomethodologists, one might think that intersubjectivity and understanding one another is only an affair of language (a writing, speaking, signing game). While it is this, it is not only this. It is, in my observations, unfortunate that the ethnomethodological usage of this term "member" may hinder us from realizing that we understand one another not only because of the sharing of a natural language but because of a broader sharing that is involved in our mutual membership in the human *Umwelt* and *Welt*, because of being in and sharing a world together. There are clearly kinds of knowledge that go along with this membership in a world.

■ EXPRESSIVITY AND KNOWLEDGE OF THE BODY

Since the publication of Darwin's *Expression of Emotion in Man and Animals*, the topic of the body's expressivity has been part of the modern study of humanity. Although some of the earlier studies of bodily expressivity tended to be more biological or psychological in approach, the modern understanding of bodily expression emphasizes its socially constructed and indexical character. For example, Poole (1975, 101), in a review of the philosophical literature on bodily expression, reaches the following three general conclusions: (1) there is no expressive body activity that is not expressed by a body in particular; (2) no expressive body activity can be significant without a specific historical and ethical context; and (3) meaning is only diacritically significant—that is, in different historical and ethical contexts, specific content (meaning) will be different. Thus, the modern conception of bodily expressivity emphasizes its embeddedness in the world, and its meaning as emerging from specific involvement in that world, that is, as indexical expressions.

Perhaps the single intellectual figure most associated with the analysis of bodily expression is Maurice Merleau-Ponty, whose *Phenomenology of Perception* provides a tour de force reembodiment of the basic problems of philosophy and is particularly instructive in interpreting my two case studies. Merleau-Ponty specifically rejects mechanistic interpretations of the body for phenomenological ones. In one of the most powerful statements ever written about the body, he states:

> In so far as I have a body through which I act in the world, space and time are not for me, a collection of adjacent points nor are they a limitless number of relations synthesized by my consciousness, and into which it draws my body. I am not in space and time, nor do I conceive space and time; I belong to them, my body combines with them and includes them. The scope of this inclusion is the measure of that of my existence; but in any case it can never be all-embracing. . . . The synthesis of both time and space is a task that always has to be performed afresh. Our bodily experience of movement is not a particular case of knowledge; it provides us with a way of access to the world and the object, with a "praktognosia," which has to be recognized as original and perhaps primary. My body has its world, or understandable world, without having to make use of my "symbolic" or "objectifying function". (140–41)

Such a description includes a rejection of mechanistic characterizations of either persons or actions. The phenomenological approach precludes us from treating the body as a mechanism or collection of mechanisms. Merleau-Ponty describes the body as a unity that is "always implicit and vague" (198). He repeatedly warns us of transforming a person into a being-in-itself, a non-self-conscious being, rather than a being-for-itself, a unity with a true self, or consciousness. In dealing with our understanding of "damaged" people, he is quite specific: "If the patient no longer exists as a consciousness, he must then exist as a thing" (122). He is equally explicit in instructing us that understanding the spatiality and motility of damaged persons can only be understood by a method that *"involves treating the human subjectivity as an irresolvable consciousness which is wholly present in every one of its manifestations"* (120; emphasis added). This seems consistent with how I and the Smiths experienced the alingual deaf-blind other, as a consciousness wholly present in an admittedly different human manifestation. Such a conviction was behind the project of trying to identify with Christina's experience of her world. This experience of these children is also common to families and friends. This explicitly phenomenal and consciousness-granting interpretation of bodily action is well suited to describing the kind of membership that characterized the bodily understandings (intersubjectivities or knowledge) that existed between the children and adults in the studies.

If we approach the body, or bodily expressivity, from within such a framework, then we become interested in the ways bodily expression is situated within a world, provides human consciousness with access to experiences in a world, a knowledge of practice or doing (praktognosia), and does so without reference to symbolic or objective function. The importance of this practical world and of its attendant understandings, as original and primary, is critical for our understanding of deaf-and-blind children without language. This phenomenological approach to bodily knowledge and expressivity best explains the data contained in these case studies and also explains how bodily knowledge and expressivity served as a resource to children and adults in achieving understanding.[8]

The motility of the body was one of the most important ways children and adults communicated with one another. It was always possible to recognize indexical expressions as bodily motility of children. Borrowing from Husserl, Merleau-Ponty writes that we can understand "motility as basic intentionality. Consciousness is in the first place a not of matter of 'I think that' but of 'I can'" (137). This understanding of human motility as conveying basic intentionality was a cornerstone in the communications between the adults and children in the studies. Indeed, the movements of the children became, after a time for me and for the parents naturally, an indexical expression of their intentionality. The indexical part of this statement is critically important. It reminds us that communication through the motility of the body is a form of indexical expression as defined above: the movements of these children's bodies were not formally labeled by participants as "indexical" but were seen to have meaning through their emergence within a particular situation, at such and such a time, in this particular place, with these particular children and adults, with such and such a shared biography and understanding of others' motives, and so on. (In other words, indexical expressions are given meaning within a certain "lived order.") This can be seen in both studies repeatedly. Adults interpreted the movements of the children as indicating a basic intentionality of action that referred to the concrete everyday situation in which it was manifest. In this way it was a vulgar competence of staff on the ward to recognize Christina's "escape" from her part of the ward as an "attempt" to get to the piano. Or Bianca's climbing the stairs after lunch was seen as her "going to play in her room."

It should be understood that this interpretation of bodily expression of intentionality was also available to the children. Christina and Bianca, as well as other alingual children observed, could apparently understand the motility of staff as indexical expression. Thus, when a staff member would pick up a child lying on the floor and push him or her in a direction, this movement of the other was perceived by the child as a specific request, from a specific person, under specific conditions. Almost invariably such expressions of the adult bodies were taken as requests on the part of the staff to "go that way." Often these requests took on a very concrete character—"Go that way to the door to the dining area (which is the next part of the day's routine)." To the children, the movement of adult bodies could take on indexical significance in many situations, and a variety of significances depending upon the intention of the adult. In fact, the mere initiation of a bodily interaction with the child was always an expression of specific intention, whether it was to tell the child to go a certain way, to let him or her know the adult was displeased or pleased, or to let the child know that an action should be done this way or that and to ensure that the child saw it the same way. All these forms of bodily expressivity through the movement of the adult body were accessible to children as indexical communication.

Another critical form of bodily expressivity that was understood by adults in the studies as indexical body expression was facial, vocal, and bodily displays of emotion. These displays of emotion were understood without their explicit analysis being called forth in so many words. The expression and recognition of emotional disposition was a ubiquitous and ever present resource in the understanding of the children. Movements of the child's body, and facial and vocal displays of emotion, were interpreted by adults indexically. Likewise the children were able to recognize and interpret the adults' displays if emotion through the motility of the adult body (for example, hitting or harshly shaking a child), voice (yelling, insofar as the child had residual hearing), physiognomic expression (insofar as the child had residual sight), and perhaps esoteric aspects of communication (for example, a person's "vibes") was also involved. (For a discussion of how these lexical items [motility, expression of emotion, the mute bodily knowledge of place] get built into communication and are given specific meaning, see below on the conversation with our bodies.)[9]

Bodily expressivity of intention through motility and of emotional disposition through bodily movement could on any particular occasion fail or succeed. This was understood by the children and adults in these studies, who, like other people, were not always successful in conveying their intentions to one another. This is to say that bodily indexical expressions are similar to other forms of indexical expression in that they are recognizably successful and unsuccessful instances of communication. The operating assumption is always that they work, unless shown otherwise.

■ THE SOCIAL CONTEXT OF BODILY EXPRESSION

If we accept that (1) it is possible to understand the body's activities as expressions of human consciousness and intentionality (that is, as communication) *and* (2) that the body itself carries with it certain forms of mute common understandings of or relations with the human world, then it is important to acknowledge how these expressions and relations are socially constructed and given meaning by men in the everyday world. In the text above describing these forms of bodily expressivity, it is already evident that they must be discussed as indexical expressions, that is, as social productions and recognitions taking on concrete meaning through their essentially situated emergence. Even the silent forms of understanding and the membership in the human *Umwelt* that the body grants us are of the world (*Welt*) of people; they are part of the lexicon of bodily expression.

How can we think of the social situation within which bodily expression and understanding occurs? I am thinking now about the social situation within which the adults and children in the studies understood and communicated with one another. One answer is available in the writings of Alfred Schutz (1973), whose description of the phenomenology of everyday life characterizes much of human interactivity as "working" in the world of daily life.[10]

> World of daily life shall mean the intersubjective world which existed long before our birth, experienced and interpreted by Others, our predecessors, as an organized world. Now it is given to our experience and interpretation. All interpretation of this world is based upon a stock of previous experiences of it, our own experiences and those handed down to us by our parents and teachers, which in the form of "knowledge at hand" function as a scheme of reference. (Schutz 1973, 208)

The "wide-awake and grown-up person" acts within this world of daily life, with other people and within a natural attitude that he or she experiences as "reality." Acting within this natural attitude, a person perceives and experiences the world as intersubjective from the outset, a world in which human beings have an "eminently practical interest" (208). This world of everyday life is the "scene and also the object of our actions and interactions," which are of pragmatic interest to us (209). The meaning of bodily and interactional phenomena is a result of our reflections upon these spontaneous activities within the natural attitude.

Schutz devises a vocabulary to understand the events in the world of daily life. He speaks of "conduct" as subjectively meaningful experiences emanating from our spontaneous life. Conduct does not refer to conscious intent but rather to the relatively unconscious activities of inner and outer life—habit, tradition, and affect, for example. When conduct is devised in advance (that is, conscious), based upon a preconceived project, it is called "action" whether it is overt or covert (here deviating from Weber). To distinguish covert action (for example, thinking about what to do in the next half hour) from overt action (carrying through with a plan to bring about some end), Schutz uses the term "working." "Working . . . is the action in the outer world, based upon a project and characterized by the intention to bring about the projected state of affairs by bodily movements. Among all the described forms of spontanaeity that of working is the most important for the constitution of the reality of the world of daily life" (212). It is through working acts that the self creates its sense of now, realizes itself as a totality, communicates with others, and organizes spatial perspectives. Schutz writes about communication within the world of daily life:

Social actions involve communication, and any communication is necessarily founded upon acts of working. In order to communicate with Others I have to perform overt acts in the outer world that are supposed to be interpreted by Others as signs of what I mean to convey. Gestures, speech, writing, etc., are based upon bodily movements. . . . My participating in the on-going process of the Other's communicating, establishes . . . a common vivid present, *our* vivid present, which enables him and me to say: "We experienced this occurrence together." (218–20)

Finally, Schutz characterizes the world of working as the

paramount over against the many other sub-universes of reality. It is the world of physical things, including my body; it is the realm of my locomotions and bodily operations; it offers resistances which require my effort to overcome; it places tasks before me, permits me to carry through my plans, and enables me to succeed or to fail. . . . By my working acts I gear into the outer world, I change it; and these changes . . . can be experienced and tested both by myself and Others. . . . I share this world and its objects with Others; with Others, I have ends and means in common; I work with them in manifold social acts and relationships, checking the Others and checked by them. And the world of working is the reality within which communication and interplay or mutual motivation becomes effective. (226–27)

Although Schutz's remarks are clearly not directed to an analysis of a languageless world of daily life, or working or communicating together that does not include the resource of language, when I first read this text, as a graduate student working with Christina, I was taken, as I am now, with the many ways that Schutz's characterization of the world of daily life captures the lived experience of the organization of life with these children, including communicating with and understanding them.

Indeed, the children and the adults in these studies were constantly involved in "action in the outer world, based upon a project and characterized by the intention to bring about the projected state of affairs by bodily movements." They did this "work" in an eminently practical fashion. This work consisted in whatever practical activity they did together: eating, walking, dressing, playing, learning, and so on. While they did not have language as a mutual resource in these practical activities, or a stock of practical knowledge, as Schutz describes ours (members'), adults and children both lived and experienced in direct and indirect ways an intersubjective world of daily life, the interpretation of which rested upon previous shared experience. They observably and reportably shared a stock of knowledge at hand, not given to them by their forefathers, as Schutz describes members' stock of knowledge, but manufactured together on the ward and on the basis of these shared experiences. They had ends and means in common, shared motives, and were involved in projects together, checking one another in the course of these projects. The "projects" formed the basis of hospital and family routine. They involved acts done in the outer world, performed by both children and adults, that were communicative—that is, used signs to others that needed to be interpreted in order to convey their meaning. It was from within these projects that indexical bodily expression was interpreted by both children and adults.

■ A CONVERSATION WITH OUR BODIES

When I think of the bodily communication between myself and Christina, or between Barbara and Bianca, the word "working" brings to mind the bodily, effortful, and physical character of that communication. The characterization offered by Schutz of communication with language is also very reminiscent of the bodily communications noted in these studies. There occurred a kind of conversation with bodily gesture. For example,

> I would greet Christina by placing her hand on my face. She would then gesture for me to pick her up. I would pick her up, and Chris would lock her legs around my waist and vigorously bounce up and down, indicating to me that she wanted me forcefully to throw or lift her up and down with my arms. I would do that often until my arms tired, which Chris could sense. She often would put her right (good) ear to my mouth, telling me she wanted me to talk or sing into her ear while I bounced her up and down, and so forth. In this somewhat routinized but lively greeting, a kind of *conversation with our bodies* occurred, a communication with bodily signs that resembled in some ways a conversation with language.[11]

Of course, verbal conversation as normally produced is also a conversation of our bodies. But I use the latter term in contradistinction to the notion of conversation that employs formal language (signed, spoken, written, or computer or otherwise mechanically assisted). In the kind of simple description I offer in this paragraph I think we can witness a conversation of the body that does not use formal language, although it can be symbolic. The items of the conversation with our bodies were indexical (drawn from the lexicon of expressive bodily possibilities granted to us through the *Umwelt*), just as many of our conversational utterances are indexical expressions drawn from the lexicon of the spoken word. Indeed, the idea of a biological lexicon of bodily expressive possibilities fits well with this notion of the production of indexical body expressions as part of a conversation with our bodies.

This same characterization of indexical bodily expressions embedded in mutual projects and understood from within the stock of practical knowledge at hand also applies to the communications between Barbara and Bianca. This indexical conversation of the body may be a generic communicative form with such children and, like conversation for us, constitute the most dominant and present form of communication with them.

I am not arguing that the Schutzian description applies exactly to that of the daily world of the children and adults in the above studies. Not having the shared resource of language structured, in so many ways, the concrete particulars of how the world of daily life could be produced together and experienced. It made quite problematic any simple description (such as those given to us by Schutz) of what the "stock of practical knowledge at hand" was for the children and adults. It created an asymmetry of a radical kind in the distribution of social knowledge and in the modes of interpretation of the other's actions. But in addition to these deviations, one is impressed with the parallels between Schutz's description of working in the world of daily life and the actions observed with the children and adults.

The role of language in working together and communicating with the children was complicated. On the one hand, language could not be a shared resource for working together with them, since they did not possess language. Whatever communications adults and children did together could not use words or formal sign language. This is why the indexical properties of bodily expression were so important to the adults and children in these studies. This form of expression and communication was the only avenue through which they could work together in the world of daily life. On the other hand, the adults in these studies were late twentieth-century users of American English and as such perceived, acted upon, and created their world in ways peculiar to their mother tongue. It would be a serious mistake to think that the adult, language-based view of the world did not profoundly structure the interactions with these children. As was discussed under the notions of the natural attitude and the social construction of Christina, language clearly played a critical role. These children, unlike Victoire of Aveyron, were clearly products of human society and institutions. Not only were they socially constructed through different forms of language, they also felt the structuring of their world by the American-language-using adults in very direct ways, even though they may not have understood what was being demanded. Indeed, the twentieth-century American-language version of the world (and specifically its West Coast variant) was the dominant culture of the ward, its ideological supremacy enforced by its agents, the adult caretakers, an ideology having specific properties and requiring specific actions. When I characterized the childrens' life on the ward as an endless series of corrections, this correction was to the normal form—to the actions and specific properties required by idealized language descriptions (as "production accounts"). This is to say that the idealized stock of knowledge for the adults formed the "ground" against which "kids goofing up" emerged. So, while the children possessed no language, and while formal language did not constitute a mutual resource in communicating with them, it was a powerful and ubiquitous force in shaping their physical and social lives.

■ THE ESSENTIAL RATIONALITY OF INSTITUTIONALIZED ACTION

One interesting feature of both these studies was that when one understood the concrete projects, the membership of those performing them, their place and their purpose, and so forth, the actions of these children lost their pathological quality. Christina rocked as a part of the rhythm of her everyday life in the state hospital. Bianca did not use symbols, because her participation in other forms of communicative activity within her family obviated the pragmatic need for language. In a sense, both these children were institutionalized[12]—one in an actual physical institution and the other in the institution of family (though this phrase partakes of two different uses of the term "institution" in sociology, it is not misleading). The bodily expressivity of both children was understood from within these social-organizational structures. Bodily signs made sense with respect to these situations; they were "geared into" them as part of the work of these children. It also bears mentioning that the strategies of mimicry and long-term observation I employed to understand Christina's world made explicit the "work" she was doing.

■ SOME METHODOLOGICAL REFLECTIONS

Jürgen Habermas has characterized the bulk of Western science as having "epistemology . . . flattened out to methodology" (1971, 68). He accuses contemporary sciences of ignoring the problem of world constitution. This kind of critique is not applicable to ethnomethodological or phenomenological studies, which hold as problematic the epistemological status of their own text. While the method of these studies has its own weaknesses, ignoring the problem of world constitution is not one of them.

One way to read this book would be as a reflection on the method ("logic of inquiry") required by the question, How is it possible for deaf-and-blind children without language and normally seeing-and-hearing adults with language to understand one another? The book proposes ways of understanding children with rubella syndrome, and our social relations with them, that are phenomenological, involving suspension of the assumptions of the everyday, or natural, attitude. As such, the studies and this writing are instances of what Schutz describes as the "paradox of the phenomenological proposition." The phrase refers "to the mundane world-concepts and language which are alone at the disposal of the communicating phenomenologist. That is the reason why all phenomenological reports are inadequate because of the attempt to give a mundane expression to a non-worldly meaning, and the difficulty cannot be met by the invention of an artificial language" (1973, 257). The reader can see in this statement the essential and unresolvable issue posed in my initial work with Christina.

This kind of inadequacy is a characteristic of this inquiry. Despite what may appear as my radical reconstitution of these children and our relations with them, the tools of this reconstitution are essentially mundane and, by practical necessity, of the natural attitude. There is no real answer to this epistemological aspect of the method, but there is a sense in which the reflexive awareness of the problem changes the quality of the problem, once posed, and changes the relation of the observer to the written observations. One thus needs the awareness that in understanding these children, the answers to the most important questions are found in the conversation with our bodies, and not in any text.

■ DISCUSSION

The two studies point to communicative resources available to human beings without formal language. The adults and children in these studies were able to achieve complex, communicative practices through which, with the exception of "esoteric" communication, practical intersubjectivity was a product. I used a heuristic distinction between *Umwelt* (the biological, the being-in-itself) and *Welt* (the essentially social, self-constituting, being-for-itself) to characterize these communicative resources. While the children and adults did not share the resource of language (part of the *Welt*), they did share many other resources of the *Umwelt* and *Welt*. The biological potentialities endowed us by the *Umwelt* were described as a kind of lexicon of the body. This lexicon consisted of bodily motility and posturing as ways to display intentionality and emotions and of silent forms of understanding, such as "knowledge of place" or "praktognosia," that were part of the "body's understandable world." It was from this lexicon that socially organized communicative practices based upon "work" together were constructed.

This lexicon was given life through specific instances, or "lived orders," of socially structured communication practices. These practices consisted in the mutual production and recognition of indexical expressions of the body, expressions essentially situated in this production and interpretation and taking on their meaning in a fashion similar to that of conversational utterances. A kind of "conversation with our bodies" occurred, although one in which the perception and comprehension of indexical bodily expressions was highly asymmetrical. This asymmetry was primarily a product of differences in sight, hearing, and cognition between the children and adults of the study. These differences, as significant as they were, did not prevent the mutual achievement of intersubjectivity through communicative practices using the indexical properties of bodily expression. Conversations with our bodies occurred within a social context—our joint "projects" in the world of daily life—without our "working together" with what was known in common, within the flow of shared events that allowed participants to say that they had "experienced these occurrences together." It was from within this totality of what was shared, though it was asymmetrically shared, that the conversations with our bodies were given meaning by the adults and children described in the studies.

Through this characterization of the studies, it is possible to interpret the particulars of each case.

The phenomenon of "multiple identity" (each child being

granted different and conflicting "identities," or "selves") observed in each study served as a way to make overt the tacit, unreflexive, natural attitude toward these children employed by the various adults who surrounded them. Recognition of these organizational expressions of the unreflexive social construction of these children served as an invitation in both studies differentially to construct interaction with the children. By attempting to suspend, to deconstruct and examine, this natural attitude, I was propelled into "work" aimed at reorganizing my peceptions of and relationship with the children and the family. In the first study, the "in order to" motive was to describe the everyday life of Chris as it was experienced by her. In the second study, making explicit the naturally occurring communication practices between the family members and Bianca was of analytic concern. Thus, the recognition of the natural attitude in the social construction of the children served to point out the possibility of reconstructing them, and our relations with them, in these ways.

The various strategies employed with Christina were designed to allow the researcher access to aspects of her world of daily life (*Umwelt* and *Welt*). The deaf-blind simulations sensitized me to aspects of the *Umwelt* as experienced by her and, when failing to do so, also instructed me about her way of being in this *Umwelt*. The analysis of field-note descriptions of Christina sensitized me to the ways I participated unknowingly in the same processes of social construction that I observed others engaging in within the natural attitude. Mimicry allowed me more directly to experience and understand the essential rationality of bodily expression and action. Spending the long periods with Christina allowed me to identify with the organizational aspects of everyday life as lived, with the projects that characterized her existence and within which her body, and other bodies, served as the primary vehicle of expression. Understanding these routines of daily life allowed me to comprehend the social situation of mutual communication with Christina and other children. Obedient passivity was an interactional strategy that allowed Christina to initiate and organize bodily interaction according to her own motives and priorities, thereby giving me a clearer comprehension of the system of relevancies and motives contained within her expressions. The use of videotapes of music making and other activities was another way to suspend the normal perception of events and to review them with an eye toward Christina's participation in the taped events. The discussion of Christina's use of the rattle attempted to locate Christina's version of object over against that of the adult speaker-hearer-seers. These are the ways that the materials can be brought directly under the auspices of the vocabulary of Schutz, Merleau-Ponty, or Garfinkel and Sacks.

In the study of the Smiths, the intersubjectivities of the family—the partially shared human *Umwelt*, the jointly produced routines of everyday life, the commonly understood spaces of daily life, the shared likes and dislikes, and their common biography—can similarly be understood as aspects of bodily indexical expression or as shared knowledge of the *Welt*, as described in this chapter. It was within the "work" of the *Welt* that bodily expression was indexically interpreted and took on specific meaning.

The discussion of esoteric communication in these relationships cannot be subjected to the same method. Because this kind of communication by definition resists description as a set of communicative practices, it can be documented only through verbal description of unaccountable experiences of intersubjectivity. It can be substantiated, in any practical sense of the term, only through experience, and then becomes a kind of knowledge revealed only to those who are practitioners. Be this as it may, the existence of these forms of intersubjectivity would appear to be part of our relationships with children like Christina and Bianca. We should not discredit these claims on the basis of their looseness of fit with prevailing models of communication.

In essence, the central observations of these studies are that in Christina's society of the deaf-blind ward and in Bianca's family, building an everyday world together consisted exclusively of conversations with our bodies, and that such conversations are constructed of nonformal-language-related bodily expressions or gesticulations, produced by particular bodies, with specific biographies, at some specific time, in particular relationships, as part of a historically specific scene, and interpreted as such— that is, indexically, by interactional participants. One formulation of these studies' essential recommendation about the constitution of the everyday world is, Society exists through a conversation with our bodies.

■ ARE THESE PHENOMENA ETHNOMETHODOLOGICAL PHENOMENA?

A final question about the communicational practices reported in these studies: does their discovery constitute the existence of "radical phenomena" as defined by Garfinkel (1991, 16–17).[13] Posing this question is also a way of asking, in what sense are the phenomena articulated in these studies ethnomethodological phenomena?

There are several aspects of Garfinkel's definition of "radical phenomena" that I would argue are well satisfied by phenomena observed in these studies. First, the communicational phenomena were reportable, and were so only with firsthand observation. Second, they were discovered and could not be imagined. Third, the phenomena could not be recovered with a priori representational methods, nor were they demonstrable in terms of classic sociological studies. Fourth, the investigation of these phenomena through traditional sociological methods would have lost the phenomena (indeed would never, and did not, discover the phenomena in the first instance). Fifth, the phenomena were locally and endogenously produced, naturally organized, and reflexively accountable in and as of details. If space allowed, a discussion of how these phenomena fit these requirements of the definition would be in order. That not being the case, the reader will be forced to rely on his or her intuitive grasp of how this might be so.

A sixth requirement of Garfinkel's definition is that the existence of the phenomena—in this case the conversation with our bodies that is not formal-language based—be a "foundational issue" in a discipline concerned with the production of local order in and as practical action. I interpret these studies as pointing to precisely such phenomenona: (1) a nonformal but symbolic and indexical expression of bodily gestures that are largely unrecognized but are nontheless part and parcel of the construction of the everyday life of deaf-blind children without language, and (2) nonsymbolic and perhaps nonexpressable forms of praktognosic knowledge that also constitute the basis of shared experience and mutual understanding. I must admit, however, that the "extraordinary" source of the materials—participant observation in the reality building between alingual deaf-blind children and speaking, hearing, seeing adults—provides few clues to how these kinds of nonformal-language-related bodily indexical expressions are constitutive of our own daily lives. When language is added to the interactional equation, when the interactants are members, the communication of pre-, extra-, and nonlanguage bodily expression becomes, in my experience, difficult to see.[14]

While there has been much work on "nonverbal" or "gestural" communication in the past twenty years (see Birdwhistell 1960 or Kendon 1967, and very recently deFornel's 1991 discussion of iconic symbols), most of the discussion is of how gesticulation works within the context of formal language exchanges. The two studies of the deaf-blind describe "another level," if you will, of how bodily expression may "work" in everyday settings. Insofar as this is true, these studies suggest that previous discussions of the role of bodily gesture in communication are incomplete and that the role of the bodily gesture in everyday life, as primarily an addendum to or mediator for verbal communication, needs to be reconceptualized.

On the other hand, the sense of how this other level may work, indeed, how it is to be thought about and reported upon, reflects the irremediable "language-ification" (that is, formulation into natural symbolic language) of these bodily practices. I tried to indicate the depth of this issue in reflections on my own construction of "Christina's world." There is a certain inescapable contradiction in *writing* that the body has ways of expression and participation in the local production of social orderliness that are not formal-language based. It is indeed a kind of absurdity to attempt to describe these ways and their practices by engaging in the acts of writing and production of words. Thus, while I would maintain that the existence of these phenomena point to a foundational issue in the construction of the local orders of everyday society, I have to admit that I have less of an idea how we might talk about these phenomena. I frankly mistrust many of my own formulations of these phenomena precisely because of this language-ification process. In terms of the mainstream interests of sociology, including ethnomethodology, I can claim only to have provided names to phenomena that need to be appreciated and observed in more detail, by many more scholars, and in a variety of human situations.

The seventh requirement of Garfinkel's definition is that the phenomena be available to the policies of ethnomethodology— for example, to the policy of ethnomethodological indifference. In my own interpretation of these studies, the phenomena they point to would appear to satisfy this requirement. That this is true may again not be as obvious as in some of the earlier parts of this definition. There are certain aspects of this work that would appear to contradict this principle. For example, the institutional context and history (that of the mentally retarded person living in a state institution) was, as Pierre Bordieu might put it, an "objectivity of the first order" (Bordieu and Wacquant 1992, 7)[15] and contained within it a certain discoverable/observable moral or valuative order that was constitutive of the lives of these children. These children were observably socially devalued, stigmatized, and punished people. This devaluation and degradation as human beings involved members who occupied specific roles in this process, and their construction of these children as medical or custodial objects was discussed in the research. Although these observations have a clear moral basis and are not indifferent in the sense that they are uncaring or neutral, I do not understand them as contradicting the policy of ethnomethodological indifference.

Nor, as I described in Chapter 3, do I regard as contradictory to this policy the studies' point that professional research about children with deaf-blindness essentially and irremediably "missess" the world of such children. Such phenomena are "discovered ironies" and, I would argue, are immediately observable, reportable features. Such observations do not violate the essence of the principle of indifference, since the principle does not mean that one cannot find ironies or make statements about the relative efficacy of different sense-making procedures in comprehending specific problems. To say that all reasoning is mundane, practical, and essentially situated is not to say that all reasoning works equally well in the world. The device of indifference is not intended to shackle the eyes of an observer and make him or her unable truthfully to report when members are ineffective, evasive, confused, self-defeating, self-deluding, or what have you. The essence of the policy of indifference is that one should see all discussions of fact and methods, including one's own, of what is or is not the case, as local phenomena and contingent accomplishments of persons with particular motivations and practical interests in making claims about outcomes and the efficacy of procedures and methods. There *are* reportable differences in how persons act. The differences are discoverable, however, and *only discoverable.* Having discovered them and understood them does not mean that one can necessarily do better or that one even wants to do better. Matters of method and findings are simply not up for principled discussion, which, as Lynch (1991) points out, is what makes ethnomethodology somewhat incorrigible and even incomprehensible to other sociologists.[16]

The last requirement of Garfinkel's definition asserts that radical phenomena describe orders of detail that are immortal and part of the work of the streets. He describes this work as ordinary, commonplace, vulgar, familiar, unavoidable, irremediable, and uninteresting. In some ways these characterizations fit the phenomena described in these studies. Once described, the observations seem vulgarly available and something that somehow should have been obvious all along.[17] The phenomena indicate an orderliness of detail in the societies studied. Within these societies they were ordinary, uncommented upon, unavoidable, uninteresting, and so on.

Summarily, these phenomena located by studies are radical phenomena, even if they are difficult to label and even to see in more ordinary, everyday interaction.

A last comment about the phenomena reported in these studies as ethnomethodological phenomena: the ambiguities and misgivings I have acknowledged about my own work have also characterized ethnomethodology's reaction to these studies. These studies remain basically uncited in the ethnomethodological literature, partially because ethnomethodology does not know what to do with them. This is not a complaint, because to some degree I am in the same relation to them. But to the degree ethnomethodology and other social sciences continue to ignore these studies and their implications, they needlessly give away one of the only examples of research that has focused on the question how the body structures and participates in the construction of the orderliness of everyday social life.

Wittgenstein wrote, "To imagine a form of language is to imagine a form of life." Can these studies be said to have discovered a form of language, an indexical bodily language, that is a deep but tacit aspect of our form of life and provides us with understandings as sure as that of formal languages? Is not this language the form of human life in which we and children with deaf-blindness and no formal language (and who knows how many people in relations with non-language-using persons) participate? These are questions that need to be examined by future researchers.

Construction
and Use of Data
in Social Science
Research

5

Once epistemology has been flattened out to methodology, it loses sight of the constitution of objects of possible experience. . . . The positivistic attitude conceals the problems of world constitution. The meaning of knowledge itself becomes irrational—in the name of rigorous knowledge. In this way, the naive idea that knowledge describes reality becomes prevalent.

—*Jürgen Habermas,* Knowledge and Human Interests

■ THE ANALYTIC DEVICE: THE PHONE EXERCISE

On the first day of an undergraduate course on sociological theory, the ethnomethodologist Harold Garfinkel handed to students an assignment titled "The Phone Exercise: A Demonstration of How Sociology Operates on Everyday Life."[1] Students were asked to obtain a cassette tape recorder and record the following examples of ringing phones: three cases of a phone ringing summoning you; three cases of a phone ringing summoning someone else; and three cases of a phone ringing for you, but as a simulation.[2] As with many initial assignments in ethnomethodology, and bearing out Garfinkel's many remarks about the utter sensibility of everyday action, when students were asked to collect data on these mundane telephone occurrences and to consider them as worldly phenomena, they were in disbelief and displayed a lack of comprehension ("Did he say phones?" "Does he really want me to make recordings of phones?" and so on). Garfinkel reassured them, and questions related to procedure were answered.

Students were asked to bring in their recordings to class in one week and to be prepared to play examples. What happened was that each example played was indistinguishable from the next, in the sense that the example consisted of a silence, ring, silence, ring, sequence. The only problem in playing the examples were technical; for example, some people had to "find" the phone ringing on the tape, which in some cases was preceded by extensive silences. But by and large the experience of hearing the examples was a tedious and monotonous affair of rings and silences. Students quickly reached a kind of intolerance with the procedure and began to wonder what this was all about.

At this point in the exercise students became so doubtful of its sense that they had to be reassured. Garfinkel asked them to tell how they got these examples on tape. They reported their stories, some of which were innovative and humorous.[3] The stories were unique, although a kind of pattern also seemed to emerge. *Nobody* had had trouble getting the examples of the simulated phone call. Whatever the particular circumstances, obtaining these examples was a relatively straightforward and efficient affair. However, with the nonsimulated phone calls, students reported various degrees of difficulty in obtaining the recorded examples. All agreed that compared to the simulated examples the nonsimulated examples were time-consuming and sometimes technically difficult to obtain. Students agreed that each type of phone call was experienced by them as a very different kind of event, even though they had a ringing phone as a commonality.

In the next part of the exercise the following analytic was written by Garfinkel across the top of the blackboard: "An Analytic

Device to Identify the Problem of Social Order" (later he called it "An Analytic Device to Understand Sociological Theorizing"). It consisted of four columns labeled in the following order: {lived order}, methodic procedure, data/rendering/description, and techniques of analysis. Garfinkel then used the students' experience of the phone exercise to explain what these concepts meant.

LIVED ORDER

The reader will recall that the concept of "lived order" and its centrality in ethnomethodology was briefly described in Chapter 3. By "lived order" Garfinkel meant to refer to an orderliness of everyday life, examples of which were the three types of phone calls the students were asked to collect. The words "lived" and "order" refer to aspects of what actually occurs and is experienced in everyday social action. The word "lived" alerts the observer to the essentially situated and historical character of everyday action (to paraphrase Garfinkel: that it is composed of just these people, at just this time, at just this place, doing just this—the "justs" of everyday structures of everyday actions that are social in origin (such as taking turns in conversation, queuing up, getting directions, driving on the freeway, offering a description of what you are doing, and so on). The term "lived order," then, calls our attention to both the contingent and socially structured ways societal members construct/enact/do/inhabit their everyday world.

Ethnomethodologists generally have noted that the lived orders of the everyday world are both relied upon and ignored by societal members. Every American English–speaking adult, for example, knows in incredible detail and as a matter of practical production and recognition the structures involved in taking turns in conversation, or in supplying the necessary "continuers" to allow conversation to go on. In this sense this everyday orderliness is known.[4] But it is not known in a way that is conscious and reportable. Indeed, when persons are first made aware of the complexities of the system of taking turns in conversation, they are often dumbfounded and flabbergasted by its existence, even though they can produce it in detail. Thus, the lived order is often something that is known but unremarkable. It often escapes the reflection of scientists but constitutes the basic practice, framework, and resource within which they make their own work sensible.

One way to look at ethnomethodology's outlook on the social construction of "reality" is to understand that ethnomethodology sees a world that is composed exclusively of ongoing, situated, lived orders. "Lived order" is not a term from a school of relativistic philosophy, which might maintain that reality is essentially subjective. Lived orders are the ongoing daily work of societal members, work that is their powerful creation and interpretation of the social structures of everyday action (see especially Garfinkel and Sacks 1970). Their "work" (Schutz 1962) expresses both their social and cultural machinery, as well as their personal commitment to employ this machinery at "just" that time, and so forth. It is from within such lived orders that matters of fact, relevancy, method, adequacy, techniques, and the like, are decided as practical mundane matters, be this done in science labs or on freeways.

With regard to the phone exercise, the lived orders Garfinkel was asking students to examine were the lived orders of trying to get the different kinds of phone ringing on the tape. As indicated in Table 1, he wrote down the examples under the "lived order" column heading: {phone ringing for you}, {phone ringing for someone else}, and {phone ringing for you, simulated}. (As described in Chapter 3, the brackets are used to make clear that the text is offered as an index of some actual, observable instance of a lived order.)

TABLE 1

GARFINKEL'S PHONE EXERCISE AND ITS APPLICATION TO SOCIAL SCIENCE
RESEARCH

(Lived Order)	Methodic Procedure	Rendering/Data Description	Analysis Technique
THE PHONE EXERCISE			
(phone for you)	microphone, oscilloscope, paper drive (where ⌇⌇ = ring and ----- = silence)	---⌇⌇--⌇⌇---	frequency, digitalization statistical analysis
(phone for someone else)	same as above	---⌇⌇--⌇⌇---	as above
(phone for you, simulated)	same as above	---⌇⌇--⌇⌇---	as above
———	———	———	———
(parent sexual satisfaction)	clinical scales	scale scores	statistical analysis

APPLICATION TO WAISBREN 1980, GOODE 1990, AND GOODE 1983

Waisbren 1980

(parents react coping, impact of dd child)	questionnaires, interviews	scale scores interview answer numerically coded	statistical analysis ANOVA content analysis

Goode 1990

(family coping with dd child)	participant-observer audio-taping	audio tape, field notes from the tape	content analysis, reflection

Goode 1983

(adaptation of deinstitutionalized adults in community)	videotaping, audiotaping	videotape, audiotape, field notes from tapes	transcription, repeated viewings and hearings of tapes discussion of tapes

METHODIC PROCEDURE

"Methodic procedure" refers to any systematic, rationally conceived set of data gathering activities that are reasoned to encode, record, capture, or reflect features of phenomena that are under investigation. When such procedures are objectified and sanctioned by scientific associations and professional groups, they become the grounds for defensible and sanctionable knowledge or truth. Through such "gentlemen's agreements," researchers judged by peers as having performed these procedures to some consensually agreed standard of adequacy are thereby entitled to report upon "what is real" and "what is actually going on."

Garfinkel then proposed to the students that we administer a highly objective and defensible method to analyze our data about the ringing phones. He proposed that we take the tapes of the phone calls and hook the recorder up to an oscilloscope and paper drive that could produce a visual record of the screen of the oscilloscope. Assuming that such procedures were done up to the standard of scientific adequacy, the procedure would produce data on a paper drive in which a line would represent a silence and a squiggly line would represent a ring of certain amplitude, frequency, and temporality. Persons with the disciplinary perspectives of physics or engineering might well claim that the objective properties of the phones would thereby be encoded, captured, or reflected.

Interestingly, as Garfinkel pointed out, the data would produce in each instance a record that would at least appear to the eye as so similar as to be identical, that is, a pattern of straight lines and squiggles that would look like this:

The irony of this procedure is of course that the objective data so produced fails to identify or distinguish between the lived orders of those phone calls for those students. While the data can be methodologically defensible from a scientific viewpoint, they nonetheless fail to record what it was that made those ringing phones the phenomena they were for the students, that is, what made the phone sensible to them from within the sociohistorical stiuation in which they found themselves. The recordings capture only the physical properties of rings and silences without recovering the lived orderliness in which telephone rings and silences are inexorably embedded. The example is intended to show how objective scientific method can utterly fail to retrieve critical aspects of a phenomenon while remaining faithful to a principled version of itself as good scientific methodology.[5] This observation is graphically illustrated in Table 1, in which the data produced by the oscilloscope/paper drive appears identical for each type of lived order.

METHODIC PROCEDURES IN STUDIES THAT QUANTIFY
HUMAN ACTION

In most research related to disabilities, a form of methodic procedure is adopted that administrates to lived orders some extrinsic theory about them through some quantifiable behavioral scale or questionnaire. This allows lived orders to be dissected into variables and quantified, or asks those living lived orders to reflect upon theoretically defined aspects of that lived orderliness as numerical matters according to some questionnaire or clinical scale. This lets researchers treat these lived orders as collections of numerical variables. Two of the examplary research articles I deal with below are about families of children with severe disabilities. The paragraph above has particular importance when I come to consider the article that is representative of the "normal science" in that field of study.[6]

By way of simple illustration, if a researcher was interested in understanding the sexual behavior of parents soon after the birth of a severely disabled child, the researcher might ask parents to fill out an Index of Sexual Satisfaction Scale. (Although I will not cite a reference to a particular published scale, such a scale does exist and this example is, and features of this scale are, not ficti-tious). The scale consists of a list of strongly worded items about sexual relationships and is accompanied by a set of instructions that tell the respondent to employ a Likert-type scale (a five-point scale ranging from "strongly agree' to "strongly disagree," with a neutral middle) in rating the items. There is a space for the respondent's name at the top. The instructions begin with the statement "This is not a test." The items apparently are common-sense phrases about various aspects of sexual relationships that have been reasoned by the scale constructor to relate to sexual satisfaction. There is, before any "data" is collected from any set of parents, serious reason to doubt the descriptive validity of such a scale.

There is ample room for self-distortion in reflecting about so personal a matter as sexuality, which may or may not be "thought about" analytically by the respondent in any circum-stance other than this. There is also the obvious fact that the scale will be read by an other, whomever, which is why the in-structions begin as they do.[7] Thus, self-distortion and lack of ano-nymity present serious influences upon the sort of answers persons might give. Then there is the matter of the items them-selves, simplistic and commonsense formulations about what is reasoned to be "satisfying," or "good," sex, and dissatisfying, or "bad," sex. Is it "good" or "bad" to argue after sex? (It is bad in the scale I refer to.) Is it satisfying or unsatisfying to feel that you do not want to talk to your partner after sex? (It is unsatisfying according to the scale.) When someone responds to such items, do we learn about their perceptions of their own sexuality, or their reactions to a social scientists commonsense reflections about what sexual satisfaction ought to consist of?[8]

The answer appears to be the latter, because when we look at how such scales are developed, or how they are validated, there is almost no naturalistic observation of families or, in the case of sexual satisfaction, this being admittedly infeasible in our culture, even self-reports of how people perceive their own sexual satisfaction. Typically, as with the scale under consideration, validation means (1) statistical correlation with other clinical instruments purported to measure the same variable or construct, (2) correlation of test scores with a statistically produced sexual satisfaction factor, and (3) correlation of the test with clinical interview information. When observation is done to validate the scales, it is clinical observation, usually highly structured and in a very unnatural setting for the person being observed—for example, in a professional clinic. The judgments in these settings also evidence a professional perspective that is used as the ultimate interpretation of behavior (Pollner and Goode 1990). And it is not at all clear that these professional judgments travel well to the settings in which actual behavior occurs.[9]

The way such scales are used in collection of data is well known. If we used our Index of Sexual Satisfaction with six couples and averaged the scores of each couple, we would then have a number that is presented by researchers as reflecting the degree of sexual satisfaction of that couple. Although somewhat of a simplification, let us suppose 1 meant low satisfaction and 5 high satisfaction. The scale is administered to six couple: couple A gets a 1.5; couple B a 4.8; couple C a 3.1; couple D a 4.1; couple E a 2.0; couple F a 4.6. Within social research generally such numbers can be found in the literature and offered as valid indicators of relative degrees of satisfaction. The descriptive fact about scientists who investigate phenomena through such procedures is that in any particular case they are in no position to judge the relation of the number on the sexual satisfaction index to that of the lived order of sexual satisfaction of that couple. Indeed, there may or may not be anything at all common to the couples whom we have data about in terms of the degree or quality of their sexual satisfaction level. There may or may not be, as evidenced in

the actual lives of these couples, comparable phenomena related
to what one might call sexual satisfaction. Whether there are or
are not such commonalities is not revealed by the administration
of clinical scales. Quite the reverse: through their administration,
such scales create comparability between units of measurement
(see Cicourel 1964), whether they exist as part of the local orderliness of events or not, precisely because each respondent in the
end fills out a questionnaire and is assigned a number. Actual
similarities and differences between couples, whatever these
may be and however they may be knowable, are not matters for
consideration.

Following Garfinkel and Sacks's (1970) formulation of "ethnomethodological indifference," Michael Lynch (1991) warns
against the use of paradigmatic ethnomethodological accounts
of scientific procedure that make them appear ironic or imply
some moral judgment about their goodness or badness, effi-
ciency or inefficiency, validity or invalidity. My own interpretation of these authors' posture is that it is not intended to mean
that one cannot say anything specific about such matters in particular instances of professional or lay production of knowledge.
Their position does not ignore the worldliness of such concerns
or their observability, but rather maintains that whatever one is
going to say about such matters is only discoverable, observable,
and interpretable with respect to *particular instances* (lived orders). As Lynch points out, this outlook on the practice of science
turns against the prevailing dominant ideology regarding such
matters, particularly for those who employ quantificationist
methodologies as described briefly above. By placing matters of
methodology back into the everyday settings they emerge from,
"ethnomethodological indifference turns away from the *founda-
tionalist* approach to methodology and that gives rise to principled discussions of validity, reliability, rules of evidence, and
decision criteria. The implications of this can be threatening and
even incomprehensible for sociologists" (88).

How do ethnomethodologists "see" methodic procedure as part of the researchers' lived order of doing normal research? Probably the best single statement of this perspective may be in the work of Lynch, writing in summary of ethnomethodological studies of [scientific discovery work in laboratories and related scientific settings].

> These studies emphasise the singularity, quiddity, or as Garfinkel puts it . . . , the haecceity ("just thisness") of discovering practices. This emphasis differs remarkably from the prevailing aim in the social sciences to explain general patterns of events rather than single episodes, but to put it this way is to misunderstand the issue. The point of studying haecceities is to disclose an order of local contingencies of the day's work: unique assemblages of equipment for recording and enframing data, improvised methods for getting experiments to work, uncanny procedures for selecting "good" data and cleaning data of artifacts, expedient ways of getting results and getting them again. . . . Assemblages of haecceities gloss the embodied and interactional work of doing experiments and demonstrating results. They identify *Lebenswelt* practices, although they do not index a foundational centre—a transcendental consciousness—intentionally related to a coherent phenomenal field. (Lynch 1991, 98)

Thus, what is found by looking at the assemblages of haecceities that are characteristic of the work of quantitative researchers interested in families with severely disabled children is indeed a certain *discovered irony*. That irony is the same one that Garfinkel illustrates through his telephone exercise for the students and that turns out to be true for many other branches of social science research that follow similar methodic procedures: the adherence to principled forms of method that unreflectively rely upon the existence of lived orders creates forms of data whose relation to the lived order as produced and recognized by those involved is entirely problematic and even irrelevant.

This discovered regularity in how family research gets done,

part of a larger assemblage of social scientific practices, has particular implication for disabilities research. As soon as one takes
on an action framework or clinical framework in research, one in
which application of knowledge is a clear intention and focus,
the degree of fit between lived order, methodic procedure, and
data becomes much more critical. Without this requirement of
research, the fit between what researchers claim actually to be
the case and lived orders that are being studied (for example, the
daily lives of families with severely disabled children) is simply
not an accountable issue for researchers. When clinical procedure or change agentry is to be based upon research, it is often
then, when things do not work according to the researchers' predictions, that the irony is exposed.[10]

Through an explication of methodology in this fashion, perhaps ethnomethodology, referring to Habermas's epigram for
this chapter, is trying to "unflatten out" methodology through a
reintroduction of epistemology.

DATA/DESCRIPTION/RENDERING

Garfinkel defined this column of his chart with other synonyms
such as accounts, representations, analyses, explanations. By
these terms he meant the physical results of the administration
of the methodic procedure. In the case of the phones, these were
the cassette tape of the phones and the resulting electronic record (oscilloscope) and physical record (paper drive). The most
common forms of data in studies of families with severely retarded children are clinical scales and questionnaires that have
been numerically coded and electronically saved in, for example,
a computer data base. Having collected such data, most researchers allow the record (renderings, representations, and so
forth) to stand for or on behalf of the observable features of the
object. At some point in the research process, it is the data that
are reflected upon, analyzed, explored, and discovered—no
longer the lived orderliness that is under investigation. The data

are the "corpus" to which the researcher is held strictly account-able. What he has measured, on what level, and with what com-pleteness becomes the preoccupation, and quality of analysis is a reflection of his and his colleagues' technical sophistication in manipulating statistical data. People actually engaging in sexual intercourse are far from the researcher's mind, but not so the numbers on the sexual satisfaction index and his strategies to analyze these.

Data, descriptions, or representations, are (to borrow from a Garfinkel lecture) "a more or less relevant ensemble of pertinent matters." Such data sets are representations, or signs, or indexes, of some actual state of affairs with which they may or may not be (in some practical sense of the term) "congruent." As with the ringing-phone exercise, data produced through such clinical-ob-servational scales and similar techniques fail to render what it was that made the lived order recognizable to participants in the first instance. The data sets miss in some integral and particular way the identifying features of the local orders that they seek to represent. Thus, the paper-drive data of the phone calls fail to retrieve any of these identifying features. The numbers from the Index of Sexual Satisfaction fail to reflect defining features of ac-tual instances of this phenomenon for those under study.

TECHNIQUES OF ANALYSIS

The last column of Garfinkel's analytic device, techniques of anal-ysis (also called "scheme of detail" during the semester), refers to the specific operations that are performed upon the researcher's data. These commonly include "cleaning the data," statistical inspection and graphical representation of data, statistical ma-nipulation and analysis of data, diagramming, sequencing, mod-eling, content analysis, outlining, and so on. Such operations can be done upon a corpus of data to any degree of detail, depending upon the researcher's time and interests. Data is available for multiple uses and can be, and usually is, used many times before any analysis is completed. Data may be recalcitrant to research-ers' efforts because of matters related to technical expertise, but they do not resist or prescribe the detail or intensity of method-ologically rigorous analysis that can be brought upon them.

Almost all effort in educating researchers on the graduate level is devoted to developing expertise in carrying out techniques of analysis for statistical data. This technical ability distinguishes a researcher from an everyday layperson. It is this that occupies much of the professional discussion in our journals and meet-ings. Despite the fact that such expertise has underwritten im-mensely successful careers, social researchers have preoccupied themselves and their students with a relatively narrow set of methodological concerns, represented by Garfinkel's fourth col-umn.[11] One of the lessons of the phone exercise is that one could analyze with immense detail those phone recordings and would never come up with the identifying features of their lived orderli-ness. No matter how detailed or rigorous the analysis, if the data already miss the identifying feature of the lived order under in-vestigation, then none of the findings will reflect these features. As described under this column in Table 1, one could subject these recordings to a procedure of digitalization and statistical manipulation, but such analyses would not recover what made the three kinds of phone calls different from one another. Like-wise, one could creatively analyze the data from our study of sexual satisfaction in couples who have given birth to severely disabled children, but if the data already exclude the identifying features of such phenomena, those features will not be found in the analysis.[12]

■ APPLYING GARFINKEL'S ANALYTIC DEVICE TO RESEARCH STUDIES EMPLOYING QUANTIFIED-SCALE SCORES, DESCRIPTIONS, AND VIDEOTAPE AS DATA

Because Garfinkel's device is intended as a way to locate and understand how societal members—in this case, professional social scientists—analyze lived orders, it can be used to explicate virtually any attempt at lay or professional "fact finding." In this section, three articles employing three different kinds of data are analyzed through Garfinkel's device.

Two of the three articles deal with families with children with severe disability, the other with a man with severe disability who lives in a community residence for people with disabilities. The first study, by Susan Waisbren (1980), is a cross-cultural study of families with such children in the United States and Denmark and employs common social science methods of questionnaires and interviews.[13] The next study, by Goode (1990), is the case study using field-note data from one famly with a child with multiple handicaps that was presented earlier in this book. The last study, by Goode (1983), is a video-data-based case study of a man with severe disability who lived in a community facility.

As presented in Table 1, there are no formal differences in the overall logic of inquiry, or method, that these articles employ. All of them can be explicated through the categories of Garfinkel's device, indicating the analytic capability of that devices to subsume forms of social science inquiry. Each article describes the use of methodic procedures that are argued as "adequately" (more will be said on this word below) encoding a phenomenon of interest (a lived order, if you will), whose names appear in the first column of Table 1. Each article employs some version of a professional, not lay, approach to data collection and analysis, produces a massive corpus of data, and has fairly technical ways to analyze and operate upon this data in order to show "what is really going on."

NORMAL SCIENCE STUDIES OF FAMILIES WITH SEVERELY DISABLED CHILDREN

Waisbren's 1980 study represents the "normal science" approach to studying families with severely disabled children. It is a matched-pair study of two samples of families, one from Denmark and one from the United States. Families are compared regarding the "impact of the handicapped child" and "parents' perception of services." The bulk of the article tries to validate results through a lengthy and detailed discussion of the methods (clinical instruments, sampling, techniques of data analysis). Parents in each country were invited into a clinical setting, submitted to structured interviews that were numerically coded, and filled out clinical interview schedules. The results of those interviews and questionnaires were then analyzed statistically (ANOVA) to determine if there were any significant differences between these two cohorts of families in terms of impact of the child on the family and parental perception of services.

Remembering Garfinkel's telephone exercise and the discussion of its application to normal, or common, social science practices of research, a certain irony is observable in Waisbren's relation to the lived orders she is researching.[14] It is important to understand that the "lived order" she is interested in and that is announced in the introduction and conclusion to her article is the behavior and feelings parents exhibit after the birth of a handicapped child. The article's conclusions are replete with references to how parents act and cope with the situation with which they are confronted. The "discovered irony" is the same that was discussed with respect to the Index of Sexual Satisfaction. At no point in Waisbren's study is there any indication that she or any of the research team ever observed parents and children in their homes, shopping, in the doctor's office, or any other setting of everyday life.[15] The researchers involved in this study are entitled to make some claims about the lived order of {parents of newly born handicapped children reflecting upon their experiences through responding to clinical scales and interview questions at the clinic}. The analysis of that lived order would include the particulars of the instruments and questions, the social interactivity of reseachers and parents, and other aspects of the local organizational arrangements evidenced in the situated practices of the data-collection situations. The researchers are *not* epistemologically entitled to talk about {parents' coping strategies}, {impact on the family}, and any other matter having to do with actual, *in situ*, everyday action.[16]

The epistemological structure in such a method unreflexively allows the aggregate of parental reflection and testimony, numerically coded and analyzed, to stand on behalf of the lived orders of interest. That this is done in an unselfconscious way—and, indeed, that it is never a matter of embarrassment or critique from reviewers—says something about the generality of this practice and its acceptability as part of normal science. Using nomenclature familiar to ethnomethodologists, this analytic device can be represented in this instance as follows:

$$\{\text{impact of handicapped child on family}\} = \{\text{parents responses to clinical instruments and questions}\}$$

Here the equals sign means "assumed isomorphism."[17]

The important point is that the aggregated data employed by Waisbren stand, similar to that in our example of sexual satisfaction, in a very problematic relation to the affairs of everyday life that they are intended to capture, encode, or reflect. Of course, some of the data can bear an important relation to the researchers' understanding of these families. These kinds of data can be both instructive and misleading about the everyday lives of such people. Parental "accounts" of family life are serious matters that should be listened to in some serious way. But they are best elicited and appreciated in the local context in which they are produced, and the standardized instrumentation to which subjects are forced to respond in the typical research situation probably obfuscates our understanding of their lives as much as it helps.[18]

REFLEXIVE ETHNOGRAPHY AND DESCRIPTIVE DATA

As noted in Chapter 3, there are very few descriptive studies of family life that have involved intensive and long-term observation in the home, and I am aware of only one involving a family with a severely disabled child. This is the study reported in Chapter 3. The chapter (and original article) contains the results of such an in-home ethnography and introduces the reader to the Smiths and Bianca, their daughter with rubella syndrome. As is described, I spent several hours each week, and sometimes longer, with the Smiths and was well accepted by the family. Although part of a more general ethnography of the family, the lived order of interest in this specific study was the communication that existed betwen the parents and Bianca. To recount briefly, the research procedures used were the real-time audiotaping of all ethnographic encounters in the home and at Bianca's school. Field notes were produced later at my office through a "write while listening to the tape" procedure. This procedure allowed for very detailed field notes, with verbatim entries, and freed me from note taking while at school or the home. While the presence of the tape recorder undoubtedly effected the interaction, it nonetheless provided a relatively good solution to the in-home ethnography situation.[19] These notes were then put into notebooks, content analyzed, and used as the basis for articles about the family. The analytic device could be expressed as follows:

{communication with Bianca} = {field observation and production of field notes about communication}

The field notes stand on behalf of the *in situ*, local orderliness of communicative practices with Bianca.

There are no *formal* differences between Goode and Waisbren according to Garfinkel's device. Both researchers collect data based upon some methodic procedure and analyze it according to "professional" criteria and standards. But there is a different purpose and reflexivity involved in the conduct of the two forms of research. My preoccupation in the research is with the strength of my data in remaining faithful to the family's demonstrated and my perceived local orders of everyday life. I am acutely aware that I can never capture this everyday life in an "objective" fashion, and I therefore pay close attention in my own research to the relation between the first two columns of Garfinkel's analytic {lived order and methodic procedure}. Many of my practical preoccupations involved in the physical conduct of research respond to this concern (for example, spending many hours after a lengthy field visit to write notes while the memories of the events are still strong and fresh). In Waisbren, this kind of preoccupation is entirely absent. Rather, her concern is with the practicalities of the research project, that is, with getting a sample of parents into clinics and giving them the appropriate tests and questions (within the allotted budget).

While it would be tempting simply to assert that my descriptive data stands in an obviously stronger relation to the lived order under question than that of Waisbren, this would be an empty assertion. First, I would not say that there is a transcendent and ultimate determinable reality that this method encoded or captured through my own unbiased presence and objective/disinterested observation of the scene. As the Japanese film director Akira Kurosawa reminded us in his film *Rashomon*, the only thing one can be sure of is that people are trying to make sense of what they see, hear, and experience in situated and practical ways.[20] Second, ethnography, even when there is real-time audio data that field notes are based upon, is ultimately a literary affair, since the reader must trust the competence of the ethnographer to have interpreted "correctly" what he or she heard (that is, to have understood the situation in a way that was resonant with the lived orderliness under investigation). There are no validity or reliability checks to be made, and what ultimately convinces readers regarding such matters is the evidenced competence and professionalism of the ethnographer.[21] Finally, any other ethnographer who studied this same family would likely come up with substantially different results. Michael Clarke (1975) remarked that the method in ethnography is the ethnographer. I think this is exactly the case. The logic of inquiry that each ethnographer brings to the situation is a reflection of that individual's sensitivities and insensitivities, knowledge, even physical makeup. Further, the situations that are socially constructed by individuals in the field are very different from one another. If one of my female students, call her Roxanne, were to conduct a parallel ethnography with this same family, I would expect Roxanne's data to be different and her notes to reflect her own sensitivities.[22] Indeed, the "research object" that she would observe would be a substantially different social unit. This could be represented in this fashion:

{the Smiths with Roxanne present} ≠ {the Smiths with Goode present}

Thus, while it would be possible to assert that field notes ought to reflect the actualities of lived orders in some strong, if not isomorphic, fashion, such an assertion would be naive for the kinds of reasons cited above. The relation between the lived orderliness and the descriptive accounts is not obvious and nonproblematic.

Before turning toward some of the conundrums involved in the use of descriptive data in research, we should recall that the issue of methodology was central to the Smiths' concerns about their daughter. During the period that I knew them, the Smiths were involved in a conflict with the school over several issues, one of which was what Bianca could and could not understand and communicate. Bianca possessed a very limited behavioral repertoire that included no formal language signs or symbols, either expressive or receptive. When Bianca was objectively assessed in the school clinic, professionals reached the conclusion that she could express satisfaction and dissatisfaction paralinguistically, but this was the limit of her ability to communicate. The mother, on the other hand, claimed that "Bianca tells me everything," and repeatedly insisted that the child knew much more than she was given credit for. The clinical and parental interpretations of Bianca's behaviors were diametrically opposed and eventually led to a confrontation between them, the school eventually referring to the parents as "delusional" regarding their daughter's "real" situation.

Although it is obvious that this was a conflict over who Bianca was, her social identity, if you will, why do I call this a confrontation over methodology? It was, in a way, a confrontation between the formal, quantitative assessment procedures employed by professionals at the school and the informal, observational ones used by the parents in the home. The two methodologies led to two conflicting conclusions but were embedded in a clear organizational structure in which the professionals' knowledge was legitimated and the parents' delegitimated. This was achieved by the school asserting that their testing of the child was an objective assessment against which the subjective one of the parents was to be judged. The analytic device employed by professionals could be represented thus:

{formal assessment of Bianca} = {Bianca's communication at home}

This device parallels exactly those normal science practices described above, wherein the results of some formal research procedure are taken to be isomorphic with some lived orderliness.

My in-home ethnography seriously questioned the adequacy of that device. I found that an incredibly complex efficacious communicational system had been built up by this family.[23] The way the Smiths communicated had literally nothing to do with what any of the formal-language-assessment tests measured, and was not contained in the theories about communication in the textbooks with which professionals were trained in graduate school. Since no researcher had actually spent the time and effort necessary to live with such a family and directly observe their lives, how the family communicated was entirely unknown to the research literature. What the conduct of the research allowed me to do was to formalize some of the parents' observational knowledge, to validate it and to report it in an acceptable scientific format.

In this sense the Smiths' battle over their daughter was partly a battle over what method was to be used to assess who she was: the hard science or soft science; dispassionate, objective procedures or impassioned, subjective ones?

ETHNOGRAPHIC DESCRIPTIONS AS DATA ABOUT AND OF THE EVERYDAY WORLD

There are very interesting phenomenon one encounters when considering the relation of descriptive data to the everyday affairs they purport to represent. In the case of the Smiths' ethnography, the relation between ethnographic data and the lived order of the Smiths was foremost on my mind. Because Garfinkel taught a radically situated interpretation of members' accounts and practices, I did not consider an objective view or description of the family possible. While constructing the data, I was, on the one hand, "painfully" aware of this. On the other hand, the data was perceived as anchored in and faithful to the research phenomenon, the lived order, under investigation (that is, {the Smiths interacting with Bianca with Goode present}). My experience of data construction was deeply contradictory and ambivalent; I found an unavoidable and essential subjectivity to the way particular formulations and issues about family life got raised in the notes,[24] but felt that these issues were not simply a matter of the author's making, that they reflected "real," if not consensually defined or agreed upon, features of the phenomenon. One must emphasize that this was a felt ambivalence involved in producing ethnographic data. This means that both parts of the contradiction were reflexively identified as essential aspects of data production.

When involved in the production of ethnographic data as a practical matter, one is often confronted by some variation of the problem of descriptive adequacy. What does having a valid, or true, description mean? How much data is required, and with what detail, in order for an observer to say, "I have described something"? Within the article on Bianca I noted that the mother would always have superior knowledge of Bianca and that I could never replicate such knowledge. What then would be an adequate description of that child or, of that matter, the family or any other social group?

These issues were raised while observing the Smiths. They were well illustrated in two events during that study. One was the content-analysis phase of the research under the direction of Garfinkel and Pollner. At the end of data collection I had over one thousand pages of field notes on this family. It was agreed that a content analysis of this data was appropriate. (Garfinkel said, "Go through the data and tell us what you found out. Tell us what you know.") I completed this content analysis and grouped and conceptually organized the identified topics. The outline projected a dissertation that was estimated to be twenty-five hundred pages or more, and frankly, that was leaving out of the outline many topics that I *judged* (and I may be very wrong in those judgments) to be unimportant or of minor interest. The instruction "Tell us what you know" led to an overwhelmingly massive answer. This tells us something about the lived order {of families with severely disabled children}—its description is indefinitely deep, a never-to-be-completed affair, with incredible richness and detail that await the patient and trained eye.[25] The fact that a study seeking to describe a single family with a severely disabled daughter could produce such an incredible body of knowledge, with potentially so much to be said, bears strongly on what a human science could and should be.

In another part of the research the adequacy of description was also reflexively posed. Bianca lived with her parents and younger sister, who had never taken a vacation or spent time apart from her. After thirteen years of caring for her they desperately needed a break. I convinced them to allow Bianca to be cared for at the state hospital where I worked for one week, while the rest of the family vacationed. There was one catch. As the reader already knows, the Smith household ran on exacting and mutually understood routines whose violation often resulted in violent outbursts from Bianca. The mother was concerned that if these same routines were not maintained at the state hospital, Bianca would become unmanageable. She asked me if I would write up the various household routines—mealtime, getting up in the morning, toileting, bathing, and so forth. Though a considerable task, it fit well with my ethnographic research, and I began several weeks of producing detailed descriptions of these routines. The end product was fifty-odd typed pages of descriptions of family routines. The idea was that I would share these with the ward charge and that she and the staff would reproduce these routines at the hospital.

A few days before Bianca was to arrive, I brought Martha, the ward charge, the notebook of routines. She promised to read them. Several days later I helped drop Bianca off. Two days after that I called the ward to ask how Bianca was doing. "Fine. Having a great old time," I was told. I asked about the notebook and if it had helped. I received silence, followed apologetically by "We really didn't use that." (In retrospect, it seems I should have known, but at the time, I was crushed). Martha explained that she had read the material, which was a task in itself, and that she had tried to use it, but had failed. The example that sticks in my memory is her description of trying to give Bianca a bath according to the way it was done by Bianca's mom at home. Martha described her attempts to pull and push Bianca in the ways that I had indicated and how nothing happened. After several minutes of wrestling with Bianca and getting nowhere, Martha decided to "do it my own way." The notebook was put away. None of the household routines were followed, and Bianca did not appear to mind at all the new routines of daily life at the hospital. Thus I learned that the knowledge that Bianca's mom had of her in the home, as detailed, accurate, and incredibly deep as it might be, was not necessarily transferable to other settings. Bianca did not react to her change in scene by insisting that her home routines be honored; rather, she seemed to enjoy "being on vacation," as Martha described it, and doing things differently. After all, Bianca was fourteen and had never had a vacation from her family either!

This incident also reveals something important about the adequacy of descriptive data. While the bath description I gave Martha was quite detailed, it lacked something or other that would have allowed her to give the bath the way Bianca's mom did it. There were many reasons the description did not "work" as it was intended. It lacked specific details, which made it inadequate to the task of reproducing the bath. For example, when I watched the bath, I did so as an outside observer. When I described the movement of the mother and daughter, my words often glossed over what were complex bodily posturing and positioning that were invisible to me (flexion and relaxation of muscles, movements of limbs and hands and feet that were far too complex to observe and describe, some of which were hidden from me in any case and could not be described). There were certain unthought-of discontinuities in the description. For example, the size of the bathtubs at the hospital were much different from those at the Smith's home. The bath at home begins with mom sitting on the side of the tub, something that is not easily accomplished at the hospital. The aphorism "A picture is worth a thousand words" pertained to this situation. This points to a certain inevitable relation that exists between lived orders and the words that seek to describe them, the inevitably incomplete relation described by Garfinkel in Studies *Studies in Ethnomethodology*.

What can be learned from the above is that the adequacy of a description is practical and historically situated. The relation between any particular description and the lived order it seeks to encode or represent is not determinable in some objective sense, since error or completeness can be assessed only against other situated descriptions.[26] While anthropologists and ethnomethodologists take very seriously the "emic" views of participants who produce and recognize the lived order of everyday life, neither descriptive science treats emic accounts as objective, fundamental, or primary.[27] They do not treat the account as a journalist might, but report the description as an observable part of the daily (in this case family) praxis through and with which the family constitutes its own everyday life.

Thus, when considering the construction of ethnographic description, what "passes" for an adequate description is irremediably the product of affairs that are extrinsic to the descriptive data-building process *per se*. In applied social research, seldom do problems of descriptive adequacy have to do with the first two columns in Garfinkel's device. In this sense ethnographic and descriptive ethnomethodology are essentially literary enterprises, found or constructed to be adequate to practical purposes such as publishing, training students in ethnography, training human services worker, and so forth. This practical conception of adequacy of data is in contradiction to normal science, which maintains that adequacy rests with the objectivity of procedures used to collect and analyze data.

VIDEOTAPE AS SOCIAL SCIENCE DATA

The last research study to be explicated through Garfinkel's device employed videotape as the primary source of data. The study was done within the Department of Occupational Therapy at UCLA Medical Center and was an attempt to document the lives of persons with developmental disabilities who had been deinstitutionalized and were newly living in the community. A group of occupational therapists, called the Upward Mobility Project, were attempting to provide services and supports to help this group adapt to community life. Documenting their efforts was also a purpose of the research. Data was collected about both these lived orders through three procedures: participant observation, audiotaping, and videotaping.[28] These data-collection procedures yielded two types of data that were analyzed: audiotape and the field notes based upon them, and videotape and the video transcriptions that were based upon them. These two bodies of data were analyzed through content analysis (audiotape-based field notes) and viewing/discussion, transcription and cataloguing (videotapes and transcriptions). This information is represented at the bottom of Table 1, characterizing the work presented originally in Goode 1983. Thus, the analytic device I used, revealed by Garfinkel's scheme, is represented thus:

{adaptation of deinstitutiona-   {field observation and pro-
lized adults with develop-   duction of notes, audiotapes,
mental disabilities to the $=$ and videotapes}
community}

Because the study used multiple forms of data, the correspondence is between these multiple forms and the features of the lived orders under investigation. It is significant that these forms of data occur jointly in this study. The historical process through which the videotapes were produced was part of a larger effort of documentation of lived order and must be apreciated in this case as such. In other studies it would be possible to rely exclusively upon videotape as the data source.[29] The current discussion focuses on issues related particularly to the production and use of video data.

We now have a collection of three methodical devices relied upon in the construction of three different kinds of data: Waisbren's (1980) device, Goode's (1990), and Goode's (1983). The comparison of these three devices provides one of the basic arguments of this paper. *While all three studies and forms of data are not isomorphic with the lived orders they seek to describe, there are different relations between the data and the events they purport to encode.* In Waisbren's device, details of the data production make it quite possible that the methods lead to information that bears little resemblance to family life as lived. In Goode 1990 the presence of the researcher in the home, coupled with the use of a real-time, audiotape method to produce data and with reflexive awareness of the descriptive problematic, put those data and their analysis in a *stronger relation*[30] to the lived order under analysis. The use of videotape even further enhanced the strength of this relation (although this is by no means guaranteed by the use of such data), while again not "solving" the problem of assumed isomorphism between the first and third columns of Garfinkel's analytic, {lived order and data/rendering/ description}.

In the current study, video functioned in powerful ways to structure knowledge of the lived orders under investigation. The strategy used to study the community adaptation of people out of institutions was to collect individual case data. In Goode 1983 one such case, a fifty-year-old man named Bobby who had Down syndrome, is described. Several analytically important uses of videotape are evidenced in that work.

Collection of video data in this study glossed a real heterogeneity of events, all of which had in common at least the presence of the recording video camera. Camera work was shared by many involved in the project so that in any particular instance I could be either cameraman/observer or subject. The research subjects also took videotape of themselves. Some video was shot in very familiar and relatively nonthreatening circumstances, such as in their rooms. Other videos were shot in very formal and unusual circumstances, such as in a clinic or even during clinical assessment. Tapes that were shot at the beginning were very different from those shot after strong relationships had developed. There was a definite sense that the later tapes had more of a sense of truthfulness and openness. The actual audiovisual quality to the data varied considerably depending on conditions, the exact equipment involved, and its location relative to the action being recorded. Thus, {production of videotape data in the Upward Mobility Project} glossed a real heterogeneous collection of lived orders.

So much tape was shot, with so many people and locations involved, that the management of the data became a central concern of the project. A reel-to-reel half inch tape is an entirely uninteresting and opaque form of data. One hundred of these on a shelf is an absolutely overwhelming collection of "who knows what?" until someone creates a guide to the content of the videotape data. A log of videotapes that had been numbered and dated to be created. This required that persons watch the tapes and record the action seen on the tape in a notebook. This notebook then served as a guide to the video events recorded on the tape and made the tapes more analytically useful and available.[31]

With regard to the documentation of Bobby's adaptation to community life, the basic property of videotape, the machinery-specific recording of real-time audiovisual events, creating an audiovisual rendering that could be replayed indefinitely, was useful in developing an understanding of the lived order of Bobby's daily life. Videotape allowed me to capture "critical incidents" (Flanagan) related to the research object. These selections of "perspicuous happenings" became the basis for a display of what were judged to be important or illustrative features of Bobby's everyday life. These incidents appear in the 1983 article in the form of narrative and videotape transcription.

In one example, entitled "Privacy Lost,"[32] a videotape transcription appears that demonstrates several things about Bobby's life. It was an early tape, shot when we did not know Bobby that well. We had asked him to leave the room while we videotaped an interview with two of his friends. All of us from the project could sense that Bobby did not want to leave, but we could not understand what he was saying to us. The tape documents his attempts to persuade strangers that he should be allowed to stay in the room while his friends are interviewed. One sees repeated attempts by projet members to get him to leave, while Bobby refuses to budge and becomes somewhat emotional. Finally one of the staff suggests that we ask the two friends if they mind if he stays. "No problem. Don't care, honey," they reply.

There were several lessons to be learned from this tape. One was a reflexive lesson about values and providing supports and services. Bobby was put through a lot of stress because of the project staff's insistence that we protect the "privacy" of the two sisters being interviewed. What we failed to see, but what was obvious to the sisters and to Bobby, was that this concern of ours was an imported one. Because these people had come from state hospital communal life, they did not have a sense of privacy in the same way that we did. They had no secrets from one another (or so very few that it made no practical difference).[33]

Another interesting lesson we learned from this tape was how badly we understood Bobby and how much he really understood about what was going on around him. Since this was a tape made early in our relationship with Bobby, we did not understand much of what he said. This experience of Bobby's speech was consistent with his clinical profile, which stated that he was difficult to communicate with and probably understood very little (he was moderately to severely retarded). But while trying to transcribe this portion of the videotape, the very process of constructing the transcript, the repeated viewings and attempts to record exactly what was said and done, allowed me to hear that many of Bobby's misunderstood utterances actually were topically and structurally "good," but ill-pronounced, sentences. By being able to replay Bobby's utterances over and over again, I was able to shortcut a normal process of becoming familiar with

Bobby's speech pattern. It was an interesting irony that those who knew Bobby well did not have any problem understanding what he said (a status many of the project members were eventually to enjoy). All strangers, unfamiliar with his speech patterns, had a lot of trouble talking with him. Language assessors, who knew Bobby for a very short period, never realized that a lot of his "gibberish" made perfect sense.[34]

After I had transcribed the section of the tape in which we had asked Bobby to leave and during which he had appeared to make little sense, I was amazed to see that he had answered perfectly each question we had asked him and had even showed his adequate understanding of the issue of privacy with which we were preoccupied. The problem was that because of his apraxia, we were unable to recognize at the time what he was saying.[35] Thus, in the course of several days of working on the transcription of this videotape, I went from thinking about Bobby as a severely retarded person who made little sense, to thinking about him as a person with unusual countenance and expression, but who otherwise understood himself and his world as well as I did myself and mine. The reality of this transformation was demonstrable on the tape, once I had achieved a transcription of it. In this sense, working with videotape as data can be a powerful device for deconstructing and reconstructing the second-by-second production of everyday reality.

Thus, it would appear that the ability of videotape to allow audiovisual features of a lived orderliness to be played repeatedly, and to be deconstructed and reconstructed through the transcription of video, places the researcher in an unnatural, though powerful, position to speak with some authority about audiovisual aspects of the lived order under investigation. Person A interrupted Person B, or did not. Person C put the glass down and then said, "Who?"—or said, "Who?" and then put the glass down. While Bobby was heard to say, "Runnnnnruh," he in fact said, "Anothu wun." At the same time, this unnaturalness—this vantage point created through a recorded event that allows the researcher repeatedly to view and hear recorded aspects of a lived order—lets the researcher discover features of the everyday orderliness that may not be conscious to those involved in its production, or even consciously recognized by those observing in real time. Sacks used this unnatural relation created by the procedure of multiple viewings of videotape to utmost intellectual advantage (Sutherland, personal communication). He would take a simple piece of tape, say of two persons greeting each other and shaking hands, and play it 150 times in a row. During these multiple viewings, the sensibility of the everyday event would vanish, and the viewers would begin to lose the coherence and unremarkable sense of the event. They would become like "martian anthropologists watching some bizarre ritual" (Sutherland, personal communication).

Thus, videotape data would appear to have two related capacities for their users: one is to recover the audiovisual details of an event in a relatively unequivocal way, as the technical merits of the recording equipment in relation to the situation allow; the other is to destroy the unremarkability and mundanity of everyday events and leave in its stead an unfamiliar and new world with previously unnoticed features.

Video recordings of every lived order capture (relative to the particular equipment and placement of equipment)—to borrow from linguistics—*the syntactic of a lived order*, the what came first, second, and third of an event. Video recordings in no way capture *the semantic of the lived order*, the meaning understood by participants who created the event, or by those viewing the video record of that event.[36]

This is well illustrated by another event that is discussed in the 1983 paper. This videotape was titled "The Bobby Baby Boo Boo Porky Pig Oink Oink Tape" and was a lengthy interview between Bobby and his special friend Art, the facility cook. Both individuals wanted the interview and regarded each other as good friends. The tape reveals a highly asymmetrical and ambivalent relationship, in which Art appears to have the upper hand (he is referred to by Bobby as his "daddy," even though Bobby is older than Art), manipulating and even humiliating Bobby. The title of the tape is Art's pet name for Bobby, and the interview culminates in Bobby's being asked to "bark" during the song "How Much Is That Doggie in the Window?" Although what was learned about Bobby's communication with intimate persons through the transcription of this tape is interesting (the syntactics of the utterances), the meaning ascribed to these events by participants and viewers of the tape is even more so.

One obvious way to view the tape is as evidence of a retarded man's being infantilized because he is too stupid to realize or resist. When this tape was played for psychiatrists at the UCLA Neuropsychiatric Institute's research rounds, this was by far the most common interpretation of the event. Related to this frame of interpretation was that of seeing the tape as displaying an almost "pet owner–pet" relationship between Art and Bobby. Both these interpretations index a viewing of the tape in which Bobby appears as a severely retarded man being victimized by his so-called friend.

An alternative interpretation emerges from the ethnographic context of the tape's production. This tape was made relatively late in the project's life, at a time when Bobby and I had become friends. Watching this interview while it was occurring (I was in the room but not operating the camera) was a terrible experience. When Bobby was asked to "bark," I was unable to control my own reaction (anger) and more or less stormed out of the room. Bobby followed me, and when he caught up to me, I asked, "How could you let him do that to you?" (or something like that), to which he replied, "Calm down. It's all right." I told him that it was not all right with me and left immediately. Thus, my experience of the interview *in situ* was slightly different from the psychiatrists'; I initially saw Bobby as culpable in allowing this humiliation and was angry at him for it.

I was very interested in viewing and working on this piece of tape. As I began to watch and transcribe it, many details I had missed entirely while at the interview began to emerge. The interview was an incredibly competent performance for a man with so deep an apraxia as Bobby. The tape contains many gestures indicating that Bobby is uncomfortable with the role into which he is being cast (baby or doggie), but he seems to do his best to salvage some dignity in the situation, mostly through simple humor and gesture. The content of the conversation is very revealing and includes a recitation by Art of all the things that he does for Bobby and how he "takes good care of him." As I watched the tape several times, the meaning that I had ascribed to the events as I had experienced them changed for me. I began to see that Bobby appreciated full well the social cost of this interview but that it was to some degree a necessary cost if he wanted to receive the benefits of his relationship with Art. Indeed, Art took good care of Bobby, and given the incredibly impoverished circumstances of most of the residents at this facility (they literally had no money and no possessions), the clothes, records, car rides, and late-night sandwiches that Art bestowed upon Bobby were no little matter. As I watched the tape again and again, I began to appreciate Bobby's position in all of this. Rather than evidence his powerlessness and stupidity, the tape began to reveal his adaptive ability and competence. Given the resources and people he had to work with in his everyday life, this was the best solution he could come up with to achieve a certain advantage over the others.[37] When I returned next week and visited Bobby, I apologized for my behavior the previous week and discussed the interview with him. When I remarked that it was really not my place to judge his relationship with Art and that I understood that he was going to have to "put up with some shit" if he wanted to get the benefits of that relationship, he smiled and was particularly animated in his concurrence.

Thus, the meanings (the semantic) of lived orders recorded on videotape do not inhere in the tape (as the syntactic to some degree does). The same piece of tape can serve as the evidence for several different meaning structures, even diametrically opposing ones. In the above example, the same piece of tape could serve as data demonstrating Bobby's incompetence and infant-like features or as data showing his social and adaptive competencies. Realizing that these two interpretations could be powerfully supported by the same piece of tape, I devised an experiment. I would show the tape to students and give them instructions how to see the tape. Some were told that this tape was of a severely retarded man who was infantilized by a more competent person. Others were told that the tape showed what a retarded man like Bobby had to endure in order to get preferential treatment at the facility. *Everyone saw what I told them they would.* I referred to this ability of the researcher to conjure up different semantic interpretations of the same videotape data as *"video sorcery."* This term captures the coordinated interaction that exists between the frame with which the audience views a piece of video data (the way audiences make meaning of the tape) and material organization of the video (the electronically reproduced audiovisual data that are a rendering of the occurrences that actually took place). Because this interaction could be relatively easily manipulated (through what I referred to as a tutorial in how to view the tape), it was possible to play with the semantics of the data and to change for the audience something seen and heard into something else seen and heard. Hence the term "sorcery."

This ability for things to be there and not be there on video-tape, seemingly magically, was apparently even true for the "syntactic" features of the tape. While the electronic coding of particles on videotape remain, from the perspective of the viewer, basically invariant from one viewing to the next, perception of these particles can vary significantly from viewing to viewing and from person to person. This was demonstrated to me in an incident involving the use of videotape on the ward for the deaf-blind children. One day while videotaping Christina, I captured the following incident.

I was videotaping Chris playing with a record player, laughing hysterically as she dragged her tongue across the record and made the sound in the speaker "slur" (Chris here predated the similar use of records by rap music DJs). Without any external change in the conditions of her play, she suddenly began to cry hysterically. This abrupt switch in affect was something that I had seen with several children and that I had termed behavioral non sequiturs. After I calmed Chris down, I realized that I had captured the incident on tape and was pleased that I would be able to show this unusual behavior to colleagues. I returned to UCLA and played the tape for some research colleagues, detail-oriented observers by training, and expected a stunned or interested reaction when we got to the part of the tape where Christina started to cry. There was no reaction. No acknowledgment of the unusualness of the behavior. When I asked them what they saw, they said, "Chris playing with the record player and laughing." I played the tape again, even prompting them at the point where Chris switched affect ("See that?"), but still got no reaction. As I watched the tape, *I* saw the whole behavioral non sequitur sequence in detail, but *they* did not! I decided to replay the tape another time and this time tell them what it was that I was seeing and wanted them to see on the tape. I prompted them at the critical point again. This time each person saw exactly what I described. They watched it a second time and were convinced that the tape was "quite remarkable."

They were quick to point out the extreme shifts of affect in Chris's behavior at a viewing session that occurred several weeks later.

In this incident we see that the sorcery of video can extend to the very audiovisual features of the lived order that are supposed to be "encoded" in the data. To me, the tape clearly evidenced the audiovisual details of the lived order in which I participated. To my colleagues, there clearly was not enough detail in the actual images and sounds to allow them to recontruct the details of the lived order. The electronically produced images and sound served as mnemonic reminders to me, but not to my colleagues. However, once a tutorial was provided on how to see the syntactics of the tape, then indeed those features were seeable on the tape. The seeable features of the tape were the products of the interaction between me, the expert on deaf-blindness present at the actual scene, and colleagues who were trying to serve as helpful coresearchers. But however understandable the process through which the "proper" interpretation was established, this was nonetheless an alchemical "now you see it, now it is gone and has become something else" affair.

These two incidents display two kinds of possible nonisomorphism between video data and the lived orders they are usually considered to have "objectively" captured or encoded. They lead us to the conclusion that when researchers construct videotape as data, the fit between the first and third columns of Garfinkel's analytic may not be as clear or as strong as common sense would have us believe. Videotape data does not "capture" a lived order; it creates a rendered version of that lived order, but one that bears no principled, a priori relation to that lived order (which is not to say that the tape does not have describable features related to the lived order—for example, it has good audio quality; it is too close to the interaction; it is not possible to see enough detail in the faces; and so forth). The important point is that "what is on the tape" becomes the accomplishment of particular instances of viewing and analyzing tapes, and reflects the viewers' relation to the video, their perspective, and especially their familiarity with the lived order and the videotaped rendering of it.

■ SUMMARY

This chapter is based upon a demonstration devised by Garfinkel illustrating how normal social scientists operate upon the lived orders they research. The phone exercise is a demonstration of the epistemological relation between worldly events as produced and recognized (lived orders) and their representation, or rendering, as "data" in social scientific research. The analytic device proposed by Garfinkel to view the phone exercise is not ironic in design; that is, it is not intended to show that all social researchers are guilty of misconducting data. The phone exercise is an illustration, intended to organize our thinking about different worldly events, doing and experiencing something and talking about it, devising some way to measure something and observing it according to some preconceived scheme, analyzing data on a computer, doing a content analysis, and so on. The device sensitizes the reader to the underlying epistemological structure of data's construction and analysis. Depending on some semantic interpretations, it is probably not possible to think about how research could be done in a way that would not be subsumable by Garfinkel's categories.

Thus, on one level there is a certain epistemological parity, or sameness, implied in this treatment of social science research data. Because there is on transcendent, ultimate, foundational, independently knowable reality against which any rendering, or representation, can be "objectively" assessed, *no kind of data can be said to be objectively better or worse than any other kind.* All such differentiations are practical and consensual matters, part and parcel of the embodied work of actually doing research, of living the assemblage of haecceities that constitutes the embodied method of one's science. While the phone exercise and its suggested analytic does throw light upon usually unexamined relations and is in that sense unnerving (or, as Lynch [1991] observes, "incomprehensible") to researchers, it does not imply that social research is futile or fruitless or that social researchers are "dummies." On the other hand, when employing this device, one is led to certain *discovered ironies* of methodology, some of these having been discussed above with respect to each type of data. It is a generic aspect of research that all researchers collect data in social research and thereby essentially and unavoidably reconstitute or recreate their phenomena anew as "data"—indeed a corpus of data that will stand on behalf of "actual" features of the phenomenon. But all forms of doing this are not equally valuable, interesting, reliable, useful, and so on. However, and this is at the heart of the ethnomethodological recommendation, *all such discussions/judgments of method are themselves parts of the assemblage of haecceities, parts of the lived order of doing social science research in whatever form, not apart from it.*

It is interesting to imagine what researchers who have never heard of ethnomethodology might think after reading this chapter. Their judgments, I would suspect, would be quite varied, though I also suspect that almost all would have strong reactions. Here is, in any case, what I would have wanted them to come away with.

- There are no "fixes," quick or otherwise, that can produce an objective, nonrendered form of data.
- The relation between one's data and the lived orderliness under investigation is never simple or isomorphic.
- When one adopts an ethnomethodological perspective toward data, they take on a history, have a specifically historical "production account," if you will.

- No data is objective, and all data, any data, need to be used/constructed with great reflexivity of method (one needs to be aware of the underlying epistemological structure proposed in Garfinkel's device).
- We need to be very suspicious about the descriptive categories employed in our natural language, which are often unexamined in research and form the basis for collecting and interpreting all forms of social research data.

While I do not think that such readers would or should want to become ethnomethodologists, I would hope that they would be increasingly sensitized to the "measurement madness" that exists in the social sciences in the United States and elsewhere. I would hope that they would see that the meticulous observation of the affairs of everyday society is a most sensible direction for social science at this time. I would hope they would have an increased awareness of the value of research methodologies and data that are more likely strongly to represent phenomenal features of everyday life. Finally, I would hope that they would turn attention more keenly to matters of epistemology in their research, as well as to those of methodology.

Kids,
Culture,
and
Innocents
6

My heart leaps up when I behold,
 A rainbow in the sky:
So it was when my life began;
So it is now I am a man;
So be it when I shall grow old.
 Or let me die!
The Child is father of the Man;
And I wish my days to be
Bound each to each by natural piety.
　　　—*William Wordsworth*

■ VIEWS OF CHILDREN AND ADULTS

This chapter is a reflection upon a recurrent theme in the social sciences—the relations between children and adults. Adult-child relations are investigated under a tremendous number of names in social science today. Terms like "language acquisition," "moral development," "socialization," "the sociology of the family," and "the sociology of children" are commonly found in social science textbooks and research. These conceptualizations and the work associated with them, I argue below, represent usually very adult concerns about children and to a large degree may lead us away from understanding children qua children, or, better—as I explain below—kids qua kids.

Some social scientists today are attempting to redefine these domains of inquiry. Particularly, ethnomethodologists (Cicourel et al. 1974; Goode 1979; Mackay 1974; Sacks 1974) and ethnographers (Glassner 1976; Mandel 1990) and phenomenological sociologists (Waksler 1991) have attempted to deconstruct some of these traditional ways of conceptualizing and researching child-adult interaction.[1] As they have attempted to look at child-adult, as well as child-child, interaction from the children's viewpoint, to discover how children think about and organize what they are doing in their everyday lives, many of these observers have come up with the idea that children share a separate way of seeing and doing things that could be described by a term such as "kids' culture." This term combines the idea of adult "culture" (a way of understanding and operating upon the world that is transmitted from generation to generation) with that of "kid" (a colloquial term that most young American persons will use to describe themselves and their friends). Thus, the term implies that if we look at children as they see themselves, we will discover that they have a separate culture from that of adults. Not obvious from the term is that kids' culture is a subculture and exists largely within an unfriendly and repressive adult culture.

Associated with this view of kids as possessing a separate culture, of kids transmitting that culture from generation to generation, is that they also possess interpretive competence equal to (or even greater than) that of adults and that they are potentially, when adults avoid managing their behavior too narrowly and conventionally, more creative, more honest, more expressive—in short, in some ways, more "human"—than adults.

Such a view contrasts sharply with mainstream social science understandings of the younger and smaller members of society. By "mainstream" I mean here those dominant, adult-authored models of socialization and child development and education that are found massively in scientific, educational, and habilitative literature about children. This view generally involves commitment to a commonsense version of children (1) as *essentially* requiring the intervention of adult society to acquire basic human competencies; (2) as tabulae rasae—empty educational slates—bundles of unfulfilled potentialities to be nurtured (by adults) until their full and competent expression in adulthood;[2] and (3) as *growing in relatively clear developmental stages* (physical, sensorimotor, moral, linguistic, cognitive, and social) toward adulthood. In most of the writing about children, with notable exceptions, some of which were cited above, there is the explicit or implicit belief that children possess these features and that without adult instruction and supervision they will fail to become fully and appropriately human. By implication, it has been argued that to be fully and appropriately human is to be "adult." Under such a view, explicit cognitive, linguistic, and social standards (idealized standards) of adult behavior are politically enforced, as a practical matter, as are those by which the humanness and goodness of children are judged. Insofar as one attains these socially valued skills, one is "fully" human and "good."[3] It is this kind of thinking that characterizes scientific thinking about children, disabled or not, and abounds in our sociology and psychology textbooks. This adult way of looking at children is also characteristic of many of our everyday interactions with them, forming a rhetorical foundation stone for adult institutions responsible for socializing the young.

The elements of this framework represent adult commonsense convictions that emerge in adult theories and research on kids. Such beliefs are products and parts of the practical relations that, in most Judeo-Christian societies, exist between children and adults, and within this pragmatic frame of understanding way are "valid." They are part of an ongoing organization of life, part of a social facticity of these societies, and are in this sense functional to the maintenance and reproduction of everyday life. But looked at critically, and particularly from the perspective of children themselves, these convictions may be inaccurate and demonstrably divergent from ethnographic and other observational data. When looked at this way, such convictions emerge as adult-biased—or, to coin a term that parallels the notion of ethnocentricism, *adultcentric*—interpretations of children and their actions.[4] As scientific propositions about the world, such views are "an expression of the sociologists' commonsense position in the world, i.e., as adults" (Mackay 1971, 180). The epistemological implication of *adultcentricism* is that researchers have failed to encounter "children *qua* children and . . . reveal[ed] themselves as parents writing slightly abstract versions of their own or other children" (Mackay 1974, 181).

The position taken by Robert Mackay, Harvey Sacks, myself, and others implies that adult theories and studies of children's behavior represent judgments made by those of a dominant culture about those in a subordinate one, made both overtly and tacitly by adults and often without any regard for or accountability to the subordinate (kids') value system. In a sense these authors advance the position that most of our knowledge about children is missionary-like, largely because adults are culturally in the position of domination and conversion. And like missionaries, we have legitimacy up front on our side, and we do not have to acknowledge or concern ourselves with the natives' beliefs in order to get the job of conversion (that is, socialization) done. Karl Marx described how proletarian belief-action systems may be ignored, mystified, or rationalized by the bourgeoisie, who control the physical and ideological means of production in a society. Similarly, regarding our (adult) treatment of children, we can and often do proceed without expressed regard for children's beliefs or practices. (This causes them to seek areas relatively safe from adult interference in order to engage freely in kids' culture—see below). A more jaded view of institutions responsible for children's socialization/education, like that found

in Jules Henry's 1964 observations of public schools in New York
that he titled *Culture Against Man* or in Laing and Esterson's 1964
work on family schizophrenegenia, may support the parallel between parents/adults and missionaries. In these, as well as many
other studies, parents/adults use every ploy used by those in
charge of colonizing and converting others—brutality, sanctioned punishment, threat, mystification, lying, bribery, co-optation, and the rest.[5] But in the same way that the bourgeoisie sets
the dominant ideology of its era, often to its own advantage and
without concern for the interests and viewpoints of the proletariat, so we as adults have formulated the dominant conception
of children. We mystify children and even ourselves concerning
much of the violence we do to children, calling it schooling and
education, for example (see Henry 1965 or Cicourel et al. 1974,
particularly for an alternative view). We adults have socially constructed children, and often to our own advantage. In the same
way that the economically superordinate (bourgeoisie) enjoy
benefits from their colonization of workers (proletariat), we enjoy
benefits from our colonization of children—psychological and
social remuneration can be ours as parents of children, and in
some countries economic remuneration as well. Adults benefit
economically from children, even if the children are not their
own progeny. Huge economies of medicine, habilitation, education, recreation, and rehabilitation surrounded our social construction of children, from which huge numbers of adults gain
economic advantage, some of whom substantially.

In Western societies we have, to use marketplace language,
"packaged" children, for example, in the ways they are portrayed
in mass media, and particularly television; children are big busi-
ness, and their portrayal in television series and commercials,
while aimed at selling products, is also a powerful force in shaping child and adult conceptions of what a good child is.

Adult dismissal, repression, and co-optation of kids' culture is
multifaceted and not simply an economic venture. Involved is a

deep psychology of often contradictory emotions and thoughts, a psychology that often reveals the unresolved conflicts and fears, perhaps envies, that adults had as children and that they recreate in their institutions for children and their writings about them. It is a notable feature of most contemporary studies of and writing about children (at least those done in the United States) that they continue to use explicitly adultcentric terminology such as "child," "childhood," "children," and so forth, even though "kids" (at least American kids) virtually never refer to themselves with these terms. In America today (with some cultural variation) young persons before the age of ten prefer the term "kid." For this reason I use "kid" in preference to "child," particularly when referring to the kids' perspective on matters. I use "child" or "children" to convey a sense of a construction of youth that is adultcentric.[6]

When one tries to observe what occurs between kids and adults in some relatively nonjudgmental way, being nonpragmatic, nonparental, and not institutionally motivated, the dominance of adult-authored versions of kids becomes immediately obvious, as does the existence of kids and kids' culture. There is a literature bearing upon the existence of kids' culture per se. For example, the pioneering work of Iona and Peter Opie in English schools (1959) and Philip Aries' historical account of the invention of children and childhood (1965) contain seminal material. The Opies' work is particularly critical with regard to the conceptualization and empirical description of a separate culture maintained by children (kids) within an adult-dominated institution (the English private school). In ethnomethodology, the writings and lectures of Harvey Sacks, based upon his own and colleagues' observations of children and adults, inspired a contemporary resurgence of interest in kids' culture. Sacks's colleague Cicourel and several others published a discussion of the ideas underlying the notion of kids' culture in a book titled *Language Use and School Performance* (Cicourel et al. 1974). This book contains studies related to child-adult interaction in school, with an emphasis on the interpretive misunderstandings that develop because of cultural differences between adult teachers and kids. As a classroom study, the book also describes and demonstrates how kids beliefs and actions are molded to fit the requirements of adulthood in society or are ignored or punished. The Cicourel book is one of the best studies of child-adult interaction, and its authors are reflexively aware of their adultcentric position. A collection of studies (ethnomethodological, phenomenological, and ethnographic) of kid-adult and kid-kid interaction edited by Francis Waksler (1991) also attempts to remedy the explicitly adult orientation taken by researchers.

Generally, then, excluding some families and exceptional institutions and groups, "kids" in our society, especially in institutions formally charged with their education or socialization, are either socially repressed or socially invisible—consistently culturally dominated or methodically undetected or misinterpreted—in their dealings with adults. At best, kids achieve a kind of ambivalent recognition from adults, an ambivalence described by Mackay as a "paradox" under which kids' competencies are "simultaneously denied and relied upon by adults" (Mackay 1974, 190). This is demonstrated in the Cicourel book time and again: that kids' competencies are relied upon by teachers to achieve practical purposes such as teaching or discipline but are denied in their reflections upon the kids' roles in these affairs. By and large the adult conception of "children" (in the sense described in the chapter's introduction) prevails in schools for normal kids.

◼ FINDING KIDS' CULTURE THROUGH ITS RELATIVE ABSENCE

In human services for kids who are in some way damaged, such as those deaf and blind like Christina or Bianca, adult recognition and appreciation of competencies is even more tenuous and problematic. As is described in Chapter 2, at the hospital these kids were acted upon and written about exclusively in adult terms. No normal children visited the school or the ward, so the deaf-blind residents did not get exposed to kids' culture per se. But the problem on the ward, as I described above, had to do with the fact that these children not only lacked participation in kids' culture but also lacked a voice altogether to which adults would listen; what they were telling us, we adults were often unconcerned with. So complete was the adult domination of life on the hospital ward, the repression of any "extramural" activity of the residents, that when a friend asked me to take him to the deaf-blind ward so he could meet "the kids," I remarked, "First you'll have to find one." The remark came off as cryptic but really was intended literally.

Written studies and my own observations of normal children and those born deaf and blind suggest that seeing and doing things like a kid is *not* equivalent to a set of biological/existential attributes—that is, being chronologically young, small in stature, and lacking experience. Being a kid consists, at those times when kids can organize their own world without the help of adults, in perceiving and acting upon one's world in socially organized ways that are learned through participation with other kids in ordinary and mundane, everyday interaction. For a variety of reasons, and in real heterogeneous ways, participation in kids' culture is *not* guaranteed to all who are young. Neither is it barred from those with many years and much experience.[7] Kids' culture is a way of "doing" the world that can be almost completely repressed in children by adults. Tuli Kupferberg, the radical, beat poet, and social commentator who became well known as a member of the rock group The Fugs in the 1960s, portrayed this insight in his 1983 pictorial essay "Kiddie Porn." This was a magazine "editorial" consisting of a collection of photographs, taken from magazines and newspapers, depicting young children in various military and paramilitary situations: waging guerilla warfare, practicing with rifles and handguns, participating in confrontational politics, and so forth. Certainly, for many eight-year-olds who are involved in guerilla warfare around the world today, participation in kids' culture is an occasional, if not impossible, affair. Even without open warfare, many children live in climates in which adult issues (religious, political, or economic) are so dominant that it is only with difficulty that they find time for kids' things. For the millions and millions of children worldwide who suffer chronic malnutrition, dehydration, and disease, forty thousand of whom die each day (*Newsweek*, December 27, 1982), participation in the dramas of kids' culture may never occur.

Although these are extreme, but far too common, cases of deprivation of kids' culture, in America lesser poverty also prevents the young from being kids, as may the whims and idiosyncracies of emotionally disturbed or confused parents who employ a wide range of unkind and even abusive techniques in dealing with their children. And even less extraordinary examples are also pertinent. In the middle classes, child athletes can be seen who are "burnt out" by their early teens, a result of the emotional pressure to compete and win that existed in their household, a goal not particularly central in kids' culture but obviously central to adults'. Even more routinely children with some intelligence are transformed into "imbeciles with high IQs," to borrow Laing's phrase. In fact, it can generally be said that adult culture is not conducive to kids' culture, represses it upon recognition more often than not, and focuses most of its effort in conversion of children to adults.

In reaction most kids are smart enough to find the social and physical space necessary to conduct their own affairs. The way they do this is really specific to their own situation. But it is sometimes impossible for specific children to plug into kids' culture even if they do not experience extraordinary situations such as those described above (for example, an only child of a single parent, who may spend a tremendous amount of time trapped in the home alone). In more-urban areas with concentrated populations there are relatively known and accessible "liberated" places—playgrounds and parks, alleyways, rooftops, cellars, street corners, video-game arcades—where kids' culture, rather than the dominant adult culture, forms the basis for participation. But even in these places kids are constantly aware that they are within the surrounding adult culture; Big Brother is really, after all, Big Father (or at least Big Adult).

The existence of these arrangements points to a variability in participation in kids' culture, a variability that is no less interesting in its less extreme forms. For each of us there was a certain quality and quantity of our participation with those of our own generation, which may be biographically ordered *and* reflect regularities in "personality" and structural features of one's environment (for example, being a person of color in a racist society). Whatever our access to kids' culture, most of us are hastened along a path toward adulthood and adult reality. We are led this way sometimes gently and sometimes forcefully. We proceed at unique rates, and with unique experiences of the various defeats and victories we encounter along the way. In the end we tell the story to one another that this was "growing up," although other than the physical analogy, it is not at all clear what we commit ourselves to by using this concept. In most cases, it seems to signal the end of our participation in kids' culture.

■ CHILDREN WHO DO NOT BECOME KIDS OR ADULTS

For better or worse, some persons are denied participation in kids' or adult culture or both. The etiologies of this denial vary and may involve accidental circumstance, willful or unplanned neglect, organic deficit, or some combination of these. Many such children are socially devalued and given deviant labels such as retarded, mentally ill, autistic, multihandicapped, and, in very rare cases, "feral"—chronic social isolates. These classes of children share a higher risk of chronic undersocialization and lack of contact with adults or their own peers. Each category collects youngsters who, apart from the organic insult or disorder they might have, also may have experienced pathological forms of interaction with adults or children. Associated with this chronic undersocialization may be a physical failure to thrive, a failure to develop language and other social skills, and the development of "pathological" behaviors such as stereotypes that are usually interpreted as organic in origin (see, for example, the interpretation of stereotypy in Lewis et al. 1984). This occurs almost always in the case of the retarded child living in an institution. Children with these diagnoses, and others who experience pathological or insufficient contact with adults or kids or both, are often considered to have problems that are primarily due to organic deficits. That is, there is a materialistic and atomistic bias evident in the dominant adult scientific interpretations of these children's behaviors. Even children who are social isolates or "feral" are often interpreted as having physical pathologies that account for behavior not resonant with dominant cultural posturing and expressions. I suggest an alternative interpretation that is descriptively more adequate.

Because the attainment of being a kid is dependent upon participation in kids' culture, it is possible to undergo the physical processes of growth and maturation that we associate with childhood and adolescence without ever becoming a kid. This is what happens to those youngsters who are chronically environmentally deprived; in the more severe cases of environmental deprivation the physical processes of growth are often also effected. And when there is a physical or organic component contributing to the child's inability to access kids' culture, there may be two levels to the child's predicament. Many children are in such a predicament. But in my own observations, very severely afflicted children often fail to become kids for reasons of social deprivation (for example, being excluded from kids' culture through school placement) extrinsic to their organic deficits per se. That is, they are socially devalued, ostracized, uneasily integrated into foster families, and even incarcerated. In terms of the dominant materialistic bias in interpreting their behaviors, these children are usually diagnosed with the variety of developmental disabilities.

One important question we can ask ourselves is what we can learn from these in many ways unfortunate children who never become kids? What does their experience tells us about normal children and adults? In the remainder of this chapter two such case analyses will be offered, one of a "feral" child and the other of children who are born deaf-blind and who live in an institution.

■ THE WILD BOY OF AVEYRON

After my own first encounter with survivalist mountaineering, I knew that the many historical accounts of children who had survived in the woods or jungle just could not have been true. I thought of myself as a pretty intelligent, well-conditioned, and strong adult, and there was no way that a three- or four-year-old would have survived some of the things that I went through. Yet beginning with the myth of the founding of Rome, in which Romulus and Remus were purportedly suckled by wolves, there have been regular historical accounts, some by reputable and learned persons, recounting the capture of a "wild," or "feral," or "wolf," child. These accounts describe children who acted in animal-like ways and who were usually found in some distant area in some forest or jungle. They were often in bad physical condition and suffering from wounds of various sorts. They were said to have been raised by various animal groups, based upon their forms of movement and behaviors. Given my experience in mountaineering and a cursory knowledge of the behaviors of animals with nonconspecifics, I found it incomprehensible that children could survive in the wild or be "raised by wolves."

It was thus with some relief that I read Bruno Bettelheim's 1959 article on feral children and autism. Despite his recently discovered shortcomings, Bettelheim's suggestion that we think of these reports of feral children most likely as reports of lost or abandoned autistic, schizophrenic, or multihandicapped children made sense to me. I agreed wtih him that the vast majority of reports of children raised by animals were false. These were probably lost and or purposely deserted handicapped children who had spent some relatively short time in the woods.

This was *not* the case with Victoire, the Wild Boy of Aveyron, and this is what makes the encounter between him and his teacher, Jean-Marc Gaspard Itard, one of the most interesting in history.[8] For here was a case that could be documented, through newspaper articles of the era, to be a genuine case of a child who lived in the woods alone for a considerable part of his childhood. In a well-known and observationally meticulous series of notebooks, Itard ([1801], 1972) an eighteenth-century pedagogist for the deaf, documented his attempts to rehabilitate *l'enfant sauvage*, the Wild Boy—who had been captured several times over the course of the years and had been known to locals to be an inhabitant of the forests near Caune. Given what we know about his medical condition, it is probable that this was a child whose throat was slit by his caretaker/parent(s) and who was left to die. He miraculously survived and elected to stay in the forests rather than rejoin "humanity." At least, this is a feasible explanation today, given what we know (see also Mannoni 1972; Malson 1972).

In addition, the discovery of this wild boy by the French intelligentsia in Paris made him known throughout France. They looked at Victoire as an example of what philosophers like Rousseau called "natural man," or man without society. Would such a man be a superman—a man free from the evils and restraints of society? Would he be naturally kind, or evil? Here, thought many of the French intellectual community, was such a man, or at any rate a twelve- or thirteen-year old boy who had been in the woods at least seven years, without the benefit of human society. There was some real interest in what this "natural man" was going to be like, although this waned considerably when Victoire was found to behave more like a deaf retarded child than a superman.

Itard however saw the child as a professional and intellectual opportunity. His journals are rightly regarded as some of the most punctilious observations in the history of human science. They are also a most disturbing account of pedagogical futility and a classic failure in the history of special education. When confronted with a child who had successfully survived and adapted to a nonhumanly, naturally ordered forest environment, Itard was unable to facilitate his adaptation to a humanly constructed society.

Itard reasoned that Victoire was the ideal student, the tabula rasa, essentially because he had "never learned anything" about language and culture. Victoire was perhaps a failure at being the superman some expected from "natural man," but he would not be a failure at being the perfect student upon which Itard would create perfect knowledge through perfect pedagogy. Itard would write upon the blank slate—at least these were his hopes when he first heard about the child and went to see him, hopes that were to lay the groundwork for both his and Victoire's fate.

In what was at the time a very bold and noble experiment, Itard attempted to formulate a scholastic curriculum and methods that would allow Victoire to learn the cultural knowledge he lacked. These experiments were based upon the teachings of Itard's teacher, the great Condillac, the founder of what we recognize today as classroom teaching. Itard attempted to teach Victoire speech, writing, arithmetic, and other academic skills, as well as social norms and proper behavior. After many years of hard work by student, teacher, and Itard's housekeeper, substantial progress was not noted, especially in academic and language skills. In fact, Victoire never learned language and never achieved anything like a satisfactory adjustment to society. He died in his early twenties with substantially the same developmental disabilities he had when he was first captured, and without ever having achieved, by French eighteenth-century standards, fully human status.

The accounts of Itard's lessons, of his devoted, repetitive, and sometimes violent attempts to provide Victoire with the culturally valued knowledge and practices that he lacked, are quite moving. Aside from a movie, they have inspired much intellectual commentary, not the least of which deal with how so good an educator as Itard could have failed so miserably with the wild child. In a clear and pointed analysis provided by Octavio Mannoni (1972), Itard is described as having created a very narrow cultural image of Victoire and as unreflexively employing totally adultcentric views (Mannoni does not use this exact term) in assessing his charge's competencies and deficits. Itard saw this child as an *ignorant* savage, that is, as tabula rasa, an empty vessel to be filled up with correct knowledge. Of course, nothing could have been further from the truth. This youngster was undoubtedly one of history's penultimate survival artists, probably was of exceptional natural intelligence and strength, and was described in Itard's journals as displaying, when Itard would take him out on walks in the forest, what we might today call survival skills and knowledge (for example, the ability to hear foods fall and to smell foods and know if they are edible, as well as prodigious physical strength). He was definitely not "an empty vessel." But these behaviors and competencies, when judged from the standards of eighteenth-century French society, were not even considered evidence of human intelligence. In fact, Victoire's actions were decidedly maladaptive to human-ordered relations. He was, until Itard took him into his home, treated as a very stupid person. He was considered by medical authorities in Paris to be retarded and had to be rescued by Itard from an institution for "imbeciles."

In the social construction of stupidity, words such as adaptive and maladaptive usually conceal assumptions made about the relation between an individual and his or her social circumstances. If we were to suspend some of the French assumptions made about Victoire, we could only be awed by the incredible tenacity this child displayed in wanting to live and by the intelligence and strength he needed in order to be successful. To have survived at so young an age as a member of the forest community was an incredible achievement; he was a real Edgar Rice Burroughs hero, and no imbecile or blank slate!

Mannoni (1972) points out that with survival exercises being so common today, we can easily imagine a scenario wherein Itard would find himself having to learn from Victoire in order to survive. When judged by the "standards employed in action" used by the forest society, Itard would have had to become Victoire's student. Such a fantasy was literally unthinkable for Itard. And so "Itard learned nothing from the savage . . . he made him into a blank screen upon which he projected his knowledge. If we have something to learn from reading him, it is not really about the savage, nor about Itard, but about what is revealing . . . in their encounter" (Mannoni 1972, 41). The journals demonstrate, in part, the repeated insistence that Victoire conform to Itard's chronically adult ideas about knowledge, education, children, and adults. Itard consistently ignored what the child already knew, misconstruing Victoire's recreational walks as "play" sessions irrelevant to his pedagogy. What perhaps should have been his central task, to learn from Victoire about human competencies in a nonhumanly ordered, natural world, was assigned peripheral meaning through its designation as "play." Victoire's skills and knowledge, his world until capture, was defined out of existence and relevance. No wonder Victoire remained resistant to Itard's experiment. Instead of beginning with what was meaningful to the particular child as starting points for pedagogy, Itard maintained allegiance to the adult precepts of Condillac's teachings and scientific method. Because Itard embraced these adult edifices deeply and unreflexively, what Victoire knew was specifically labeled irrelevant to his teaching. The important question we must ask ourselves today is, irrelevant to whom, why, and under what circumstances?

When judged by the standards of the adult French middle class, Itard's viewpoint seemed sensible—just as current medical views of organically retarded children seem today. In the long run it was precisely this narrow attitude about what was relevant, competent, and human that contributed to Itard's failure and Victoire's unhappiness. In what must be regarded as a classic meeting between a special educator and a developmentally disabled adolescent, we find no less than an exemplary instance of adultcentric thinking dominating, and in this case perhaps destroying, the education of the young. In Itard's construction of Victoire as savage, unknowing, and deficient, we encounter evidence of the adult cultural narcissism so characteristic of adults' accounts of kids. One cannot help but be impressed with the practical cost of the lessons not learned by Itard. In many ways his encounter with Victoire previsioned current human services failures with children who are acultural.

■ CHILDREN WHO ARE BORN DEAF-BLIND AND RETARDED

In looking at children who lived on the deaf-blind ward, I found examples of children who were denied access to kids' culture—first, because of their sensory, cognitive, or motor disabilities; second, because they lived lives that were to various degrees segregated from those of kids. These children were chronically undersocialized and even exhibited behaviors that reminded me of those described by Itard in his journals. In the case of the children who resided in a state institution, they were also the victims of social rejection and psychological devaluation. Their presence in such a place was a testament to severe, total societal rejection. Even upon initial inspection it was evident that these children were physically, psychologically, socially, and spiritually damaged. They were lonely, unhappy, and suffering to a degree that is, I am thankful to say, not common in our society. They had no "normal" kids to interact with and were denied access to kids' culture.

I observed that there were interactions that occurred between the children on the ward, but these were not expressions of kids' culture, since none of the residents had ever been socialized into kids' culture. Generally, the deaf-blind children displayed a marked disinterest in one another and, with notable exceptions (for example, two children who enjoyed sleeping on each other), tended to avoid each other. Sometimes violence and aggression occurred between children, although it was not always possible to tell how personally directed this was. There were other examples of short-term contact, or violence, or even difficult-to-describe interactions, but this was really the extent of the residents' interactions with one another (which is to say, not that these interactions did not have a richness of sorts, but that they were not expressions of kids' culture). When one wanted residents to engage in prolonged contacts with one another, this had to be done with staff facilitating and shaping the children's behaviors (for example, trying to show the children how to dance with each other).

These children on the hospital ward lived in a completely adult-ordered world and were judged by highly abstract, adult-centric standards. Their habilitation and training was based exclusively, and without relief, upon these adult and abstract notions. The children possessed a wide range of human competencies that went unnoticed largely because they were not within these medical and custodial frames for interpreting children's behaviors, frames that yielded largely pejorative and "faulting" assessments in any case. When one examined the way these children were described in adult documents, there was a complete lack of reference to capacity and a total preoccupation with the details of incapacities. Thus, the children on the ward were not only denied participation in kids' culture, they were also subject to a particularly unsympathetic and negative form of adult culture.

As I described in Chapter 2, these children's viewpoints were entirely ignored in their "training." The adults on the ward occupied a position similar to that of Itard, making adult judgments about desirable and undesirable behavior and holding the children to these. They were indeed missionary-like in acting out the habilitation programs for the children. So indifferent were the helping professionals to the children's expression of choices that such choices were either unrecognized or perceived as insensible by the staff, and this made the children's habilitation look more like animal training than education and socialization. To remedy this situation, to speak on behalf of the Victoires of the deaf and blind ward, I wrote the article on recognizing their choices (see the Appendix).

When looking at the work I did with Christina from the perspective of her participation in kids' culture, I cannot say that I was able to help her directly. Many of the research activities and findings documented in Chapter 2 enabled me to recognize the shared human competencies that Christina and I possessed. While the uncovering of the children's competencies, and particularly Christina's, was important for research and for them, the children did not thereby get closer to kids' culture. This might have been because, at the time, I did not appreciate how critical was access to kids' culture for these children, and indeed for all children, handicapped or not; and I did not make it a priority to bring Christina to playgrounds and other places where kids played.

What I did with Christina was discover our avenues of sameness and show that many of her actions were meaningful, even socially meaningful, including such stereotype as rocking and finger flicking. I was able to do this through suspending (to various degrees and in various ways) the adult perspectives through which her actions and self were constructed. I allowed her to show me versions of herself, in her own terms. This may parallel what happens in kids' culture, in its better moments, although I was clearly an adult doing "research." But it is also true that I repetitiously refer to myself in my field notes as Chris's "superplaymate" and that much of what we did together during certain periods of our relationship certainly resembled kids' play in many ways. So while I would not say that our relationship helped Christina gain direct access to kids' culture via interaction with kids in her peer group, I would also not say that what we did together was entirely unrelated to kids' culture. In many instances I believe that I related to Chris through an earlier kid's part of myself. All this being true, I nonetheless describe my relationship with Christina not as one primarily rooted in kids' culture (see the next section).

When one considers the field notes that were presented in Chapter 2 about my attempting to see the world from Christina's perspective, in the main one can see these as incidents within which I was able to achieve some distance from the prevailing (adult) commonsense or professional logic usually used in interpreting the child's behavior. In each of the ways that these notes documented (whether it be mimicking her, appreciating her use of the rattle, watching her round of life for prolonged periods), I was able to bridge the gap between where "she was at" as a deaf-blind child living at a state hospital and where "I was at" as a young adult graduate student. This turned out to be mutually beneficial in many ways and perhaps, in the sense described in the preceding paragraph, helped Christina be more of a kid than she would otherwise have been.

With regard to Bianca's relation to kids' culture, the situation was more ambiguous. Because she was in her natural home with a sibling, had interactions with many day-care children, and attended a school (albeit a special school), there were opportunities for Bianca to participate in kids' culture. For example, her sister and mother were observed to facilitate play between Bianca and the children receiving day care. At school, there were normal kidlike functions and activities and, though limited, some opportunities to play freely.

Yet while the opportunity was there, Bianca was usually not up to the test of participation. Remember that she was not only very blind, very deaf, and profoundly retarded, she was also non-ambulatory. This made participation in physical/bodily games (*the motif of expression in kids' culture*) impossible for Bianca. In all instances of observed play with other children, Bianca had to be "motored through" (that is, continually assisted during) most of the activity. This was important to do anyway, her mother would remark, because she "had to learn to play."

In several instances I observed neighborhood children attempt to initiate interaction with Bianca unsuccessfully. In two instances she was sitting along on the front lawn when two different little children came up to her and attempted to initiate conversations. In another instance a group of children came to the front lawn and, at their mother's prompting, tried to incorporate Bianca in their play. They were unsuccessful until the mother intervened on Bianca's behalf.

Thus, the impression from Bianca was that she had limited access to kids' culture, and little comprehension of its ways. This was so, even though there were opportunities for her to be with kids and to play with kids in a kidlike way. Bianca's problems sensorially accessing events around her and understanding their meaning were so profound that, even with her opportunities to interact with kids, she could not pick up on their culture (any more than she appeared able to pick up on adult culture). Even though her problem was not that she was surrounded by Itards, because of her severe multiple disabilities considerable thought and effort would have been required to increase her access to kids' culture.

■ VICTOIRE, CHRISTINA, AND BIANCA

What can be learned from the three instances of Victoire, Christina, and Bianca? Can adults ever understand kids? Understand or not, can they facilitate the necessary involvement with kids' culture and with their peers that all youngsters need? Can society ensure that all children will have access to kids' culture in some way?

Obviously the answers to such questions will vary with time, circumstance, and culture. The discussion of these matters in this book has particular pertinence to my own experience with children with disabilities and their families, and it may well not extend in relevance beyond my own circumstance. But given twenty years observation of human services, there appear to be some reasons for optimism that adults and kids will come to understand each other better. This possibility rests upon two facts: one, that most adults have once been members of kids' culture, were acculturated in and participated in it; and two, that genuine cross-cultural contact (if indeed that is what is occurring between kids and adults) is a possible achievement of persons coming from even substantially different cultures.

The stories of Victoire, Christina, and Bianca all share the sadness of children who were not able to participate in kids' culture. Each of these children did have adults who *tried* to understand them in some form or another. The stories ironically show that within all the actors (adults and children) and overwhelming even their differences of culture or disability was a shared hu-

manness, whether explicitly recognized or not. In addition to illustrating certain debilitating effects of exclusion from kids'
culture, these stories also illustrate the terrible things that adults
can do to children, especially children with "problems," when
trying to "help" them. To my own mind there is a striking similar-
ity between Itard's treatment of Victoire and the staff's treatment
of the deaf-blind children on the ward. These children experienced a kind of doublewhammy, missing both kids and loving
adults from their lives. This is something we must help them
avoid in the future.

But more is known today about "inclusion" of children with
disabilities into regular schools and play groups than in 1976,
when the original research with Christina and Bianca was completed. Children with multiple disabilities today are more likely
to experience kids' culture in a real way and ever more likely to
do so as time goes on. So, regarding the question whether adults
can provide all children access to kids' culture, the answer is yes;
if they have the will and resources, the technical know-how is
there. The question of understanding between adults and kids is
more problematic.

Kid-adult interaction needs to be reconceptualized as cross-
cultural contact, or at least as having elements of cross-cultural
contact. The question should then be asked, how is it possible to
succeed in such contacts? how is it possible for adults and kids
to achieve understanding with each other? One answer may lie
in the door to kids' culture that our own youth permanently
leaves open to us. At the risk of sounding silly and kidlike to an
academic adult readership, I suggest that there is a Peter Pan in
each of us, even if he may be very hard to detect and does not
choose to come out and play. "Child is Father of the Man" (as
Wordsworth reminds us). The door to being a kid is there for
most of us, and it gives us direct access to the world of kids, or
at least our own particular version of it.

We adults are aware of the variability in our participation in kids' culture. Sometimes we are very cognizant that we have given up being kids or are no longer able to see things like kids. Sometimes we play at being kids, even manipulating kids by pretending to be acting on their level, while really trying to make them do what we want them to do as adults (that is, we self-consciously "act like children"). At other times the expression of "kidness" in us can be relatively spontaneous and genuine expression of self (we are not acting like children but "finding" ourselves actually being the children). The task for us adults is to recognize these latter opportunities as occasions for mutual enrichment, and to let ourselves get back into the kids way of doing things. We can identify with kids' culture as former kids even if they cannot identify with adult culture as yet-to-be adults. This is a completely asymmetrical arrangement, but one that grounds some real understandings between kids and adults. But it can really "work" in only one direction.

Adult culture currently bears a largely unrecognized and unanalyzed relation to that of kids. It is my firm conviction that by studying kids' culture and understanding it, we stand to improve not only our educational attempts with kids but also our own understanding of our own behavior with them. This will allow us to be more conscious of the adultcentric ways we think about kids and will end some of its negative influence on pedagogy with the young. We can and should begin to appreciate how adultcentric thinking victimizes all who participate in it, regardless of age or size.

This idea has implications for the social scientific community. Most important, the study of kids' culture deserves explicit recognition as a *bona fide* topic of research for the social sciences—one with direct bearing upon our understanding of many of its traditional topics, such as child development, sociology of the family, socialization, sociolinguistics, the sociology of education and special education, and so on. Currently the paradigms employed in our study of such phenomena are not informed of the existence of kids' culture, or even of kids' viewpoints about such affairs, and because of this they await rediscovery in a less adult-centric fashion. One cannot underestimate how important such a rediscovery would be to scientists studying groups and institutions involving children and adults (see Button 1991). Those who are prepared to see and act upon the possibilities posed by an awareness of kids' culture will be able to reenter traditional areas of social scientific inquiry anew and redefine domains of discourse. Thus, the intellectual cognizance of kids' culture is as far-reaching as one can imagine.

The study of kids' culture also holds out tremendous promise to practitioners of the helping professions who are concerned in a hands-on fashion with the development and welfare of children. Whether it be teaching mathematics or understanding and remediating child abuse, an empirical grasp of kids' culture and its relation to adult culture can only be of an immense practical value. This is to say, I see tremendous utility for a science of kids' culture—in human services and in education, for example. In instances where adults have allowed kids to organize their own learning approaches, we have already seen the fruits of this approach. One of the most striking of these is the use of Logo computer language by children. As documented in the book *Mindstorms*, by Seymour Papert (1984), kids are allowed and prompted to use the computer in their own ways to solve their own problems and to use it cooperatively with other kids. Astounding interpersonal and educational outcomes are noted in early experiments with this learning format. While Papert does not base his work explicitly upon kids' culture, he allows it to unfold in the way he supports kids in the learning process.

Politically, the commitment to the study of kids' culture is commitment ot the formal recognition and empowerment of kids. It is important that those with liberating goals who are engaged in the study of kids consider their efforts within the overall history of children. Bearing such a history in mind, it seems highly unlikely that the dialectic between children and adults will ever be resolved, by intellectual efforts or otherwise. But it may be possible through investigations of kids' culture to understand the subordinate perspective and consider it more in our deliberations about kids. It may even be possible for the scientific study of kids' culture to become part of an overall political process aiming at positive changes in quality of life for kids. For example, formal studies of inclusion and exclusion mechanisms of kids' culture might have some bearing on current attempts to include severely disabled children in regular schools and classes. There are many liberating applications for valid knowledge about the organization of kids' culture.

Regarding those youths who fail to participate substantially in kids' or adult culture despite best intentions and efforts—for example, multihandicapped children such as Christina or Bianca, or children with severe chronic illness—there is also reason for hope. I maintain this despite the fact that valid forms of giving help are largely absent for such persons in our society and the fact that we are witnessing a growing intolerance in human services for these types of children. There is even a movement for their euthanasia at birth (Wolfensberger 1981, in press). For those who live at home there is a distinct lack of appropriate services and available expertise. Parents raising children like these are given too little help and often not the help they really need. Yet in spite of these negative circumstances, perhaps even because of them, there is room to hope that a positive basis upon which to interact with such children lies close at hand.

Just as kids can provide us with an opportunity to reenter kids' culture, so the acultural child provides us with an opportunity to appreciate our acultural self, our own aculturality, which is something that every human possesses. Mannoni (1972, 41) writes, "Natural man; savage; ignorant; pupil newly purged with hellebore; what can they represent in their extreme destitution but *subject* separated from *knowledge that lies deep within each of us,* the eternal ignoramus against which autodidact and pedant wage arduous struggle in their different ways."

When I consider my encounter with Christina, my studentship with her, it clearly was not kids' culture about which I was learning. I had always felt that Christina allowed me to reexperience my childhood, but it was not till much later that I understood more what that meant. Among many other gifts, she gave me a legitimate excuse to explore my internal ignoramus, to recontact that part of myself that lay beyond, or was untouched by, society, language, or learning. Through her I was able to find again that thoroughly human state in which all was possibility; an open-ended, undefined, what-you-can-make-of-it, what-it-can-make-of-you world that was both intoxicating and sustaining. It was a world in which there were no lasting achievements, no possessions, and no competition. It was a world of exploring commonly available immediate possibilities—being "masters of the here and now" and exploring music, trampolines, dressing, eating, walking—all novel, open, and without delineable horizons for interpretation. And you never knew what any particular occasion would come to.

Lest I be misunderstood, a kind of magic existed between Christina and me; certainly this was true for me. While I was formally cast in the role of helping Chris to become more of an adult, I could not help feeling that what she was giving me in return was a gift that far outweighed my own efforts. It was a lifelong gift. "If I were to wish for anything, I should not wish for wealth and power but for the passionate sense of the potential, for the eye for which, ever ardent, sees the possible. Pleasure disappoints, possibility never. And what wine is so sparkling, what so fragrant, what so intoxicating, as possibility" (Soren Kierkegaard).

Conclusions

7

■ THIS CHAPTER does not summarize the book's content but rather explains, in general terms, what happened to the children and families I studied in the years since the original research, and briefly discusses implications of this work for some current issues of the disabilities field, such as "inclusion," "quality of life," and "facilitated communication." Implications for disability research more generally are also presented.

■ THE CHILDREN AND THEIR FAMILIES

The disabilities field itself has undergone tremendous changes from the mid-1970s to the early 1990s, probably more so than almost any other human services sector. These changes, fueled by increasing political expressions of people with disabilities and the organizations representing their interests, have been quite progressive, culminating in the passing of the Americans with Disabilities Act in 1990. New, "friendlier" conceptions of disability and new therapies and support systems for persons with disabilities really blossomed during this period, as the lives of persons like Christina became more "normalized" and less "institutional." At the same time, there can be no doubt that tremendous problems still exist for people with disabilities today and that one has to be careful about overly optimistic interpretations of the progressive changes in legislation and philosophy. This is particularly true for people with severe disabilities, whose situation has not changed as dramatically as that of people with less severe disabilities. Still, the overall situation for people with disabilities and their families has substantially improved over the past fifteen years, and many of the ideas presented in this book are far more accepted today than they were when originally conceived. The parents of children with disabilities like those of Bianca or Chris generally stand a far better, if not a good, chance of receiving quality services and supports today than they would have in 1975; of course, their situation is complex and very difficult, whatever services are provided.

Despite these positive changes in the field more generally, the young adults with rubella syndrome (the majority are now twenty-six to twenty-eight years old) continue to experience some of the most difficult life conditions, and their parents continue to struggle with the most basic issues in their children's lives — communication, health, safety, loneliness, stability. These remain parental concerns about their now young-adult children. The problem for this population has not been so much the lack of resources as really not knowing the correct courses of action to take. During the past fifteen years the government spent huge, specifically earmarked amounts of money on the deaf-blind population. These vast sums available to the deaf-blind often did not get used up, because there were insufficient numbers of applications that met federal standards. Generally, service agencies stepped into the deaf-blind arena lightly, or primarily to make a profit, since these adults could (and can be) some of the most difficult "clients" with whom to work, requiring constant and intensive support and services.

Of course not all this population experienced rubella syndrome like Christina's; there was a wide range of severity exhibited in the syndrome. But there are many who never did learn language and still cannot engage unassisted in most basic activities of life. Some of these adults, as they grew from childhood into adulthood, led barren lives filled with neglect, discontinuity of relationships, inadequate or invalid services, violence, self-abuse, and depression. For at least many of these people and their families, the service system by and large failed them in the worst way, sometimes creating more hurt than help, although often with good motivation. For example, when the deinstitutio-nalization movement swept over America and many of young adults with rubella syndrome were moved from state institutions into community residences, these persons experienced a tre-mendous discontinuity of care; often years and years of knowl-edge about a person was lost in a day's move.[1] The person suddenly found him- or herself inexplicably in a new place with new people, none of whom knew each other. There was a big push in the later 1970s to teach the young adults with Rubella syndrome signing. This was, in my view and that of many par-ents, perhaps a well-intentioned initiative but with iatrogenic re-sults.[2] As children, many people with rubella syndrome received terribly inadequate language education, sometimes essentially none. Then, when they became older, larger, more difficult to work with and potentially more dangerous to the service staff, there was a sudden push to teach them formal language. I re-member that in the early 1980s many of the parents were an-gered by this and many of the young adults with rubella syndrome were very upset and frustrated. Whether one believes in the "critical stages" of language acquisition or not (that is, the theory that states that you cannot learn specific aspects of lan-guage unless certain things are taught by certain ages), one can appreciate that learning a foreign language at age twenty-five is far more difficult than learning it at five. Learning one's first for-mal language at twenty-five, if at all possible, is incredibly difficult for any person, but almost unthinkable for a congenitally deaf-blind one.

These same kinds of stories can be told about various areas of these young adults' lives: the system underserving or not serving them as children, and then later their inheriting the problems that this caused. It is a really sad situation, since, as is usual in human services, it is the young adult with deaf-blindness who is seen as "having" the problems, and the role of the service system in making the person the way he or she is, is not usually appreciated. The Christinas of the world came out of state hospitals to places that also largely failed them; inadequately trained staff, high staff turnover, staff abuse, and inadequate supervisory staff are common problems in private and not-for-profit agencies that take care of persons with disabilities, especially in urban areas. The young adults were sometimes transferred from one agency to another; life lacked both stability and continuity. These conditions were powerful influences on people who were already in some ways powerless and open to manipulation by others. Many of the children I knew at the state hospital have become very difficult to deal with as adults—violent, angry, self-abusive, depressed, withdrawn persons that continue to challenge the capacities of even the most sophisticated of our service systems. I have seen some of these "clients" admitted into the psychiatric stabilization-and-care units specifically designed for people with mental retardation who also experience acute mental health problems. A deaf-blind person recently admitted to a local psychiatric unit was one of the most self-mutilated people I had ever seen. Even those with lesser problems are often incredibly difficult to engage in therapy. Almost exclusively, behavior modification is the mode of choice. Successes are usually short-lived, primarily because residential agencies often lack the sophistication and resources to continue consistently with therapy.[3]

Given the above, there are not many agencies that shout with joy when they are asked to consider taking care of a young adult with rubella syndrome. The parents of children like Christina who placed them with residential agencies have had years and years of struggle with these agencies over the conditions of their children's lives. Many of these parents became incredibly frustrated with "the system"; in New York City at least two groups of parents of deaf-and-blind children actually were compelled to start their own service agencies for their children, and even these developed serious problems. In some cases I have heard about, the situation is Pirandellian, like a theater of the absurd in which parents have lost control of their children to agencies of their own making that they no longer trust. Many of the parents who have remained in contact with their children in residential agencies still have their lives very filled up (in both the positive and the negative senses by their children.

Then there are the parents who decided to keep their children with rubella syndrome in the natural home into adulthood. Although this meant a total disruption of the most common family life cycle in our society—that is, where children leave home as young adults and live independently—it was a choice made by many parents. At least some did so because they believed (perhaps rightly) that no one would love and care for their child as well as they. These parents have gotten older, now in their late forties or early fifties, part of the baby-boom generation. They are beginning to confront the eventuality of someone having to take over for them in the care of their children. They worry about an uncertain future. They find themselves having to conduct their own lives and careers while continuing to care for the complex needs of their adult sons and daughters.

Both parents who have placed their children in the service system and those who have kept them at home have learned about the continuing effects of the rubella virus. There have been several reports in recent years out of St. Lukes-Roosevelt Hospital in New York, the Helen Keller National Center, and several Australian agencies about the health problems that these young adults experience as a result of prenatal exposure to rubella. It would appear that the virus continues to affect bodily function in the myriad ways that it affected bodily development. These effects either change or express themselves differently in maturation. This requires very careful health monitoring and interventions, depending upon the individual. The health needs of these persons can be particularly complex, and because of their difficulty in fulfilling the normal requirements in the patient role, they can be very challenging patients to health-care professionsls. Moreover, these changing patterns of health problems were not known in the 1960s and to some degree were not expected by parents. The continued influence of the virus additionally complicates an already complicated situation.

Overall, then, these young adults with rubella syndrome and their parents have persevered through incredibly difficult circumstances of life. Many scars are borne by both the parents and their children. The stories are as individual as the people involved in them, although they often share at least some of the elements I describe above. Finally, in considering the current situation of the parents and children of the rubella epidemic of the 1960s, it is important to note that even among those who were severely affected, like Chris and Bianca, some were able to live happy and productive lives, both in their natural homes and in agencies. Unfortunately, without being able to cite statistics about perceived life satisfaction of young adults with rubella syndrome, it is my distinct impression that the very happy are the rare, although important, exceptions to the rule.

■ FACILITATED COMMUNICATION

Within the past decade the rise of facilitated communication in services for persons with disabilities has been incredible. "Facilitated communication" is not to be confused with "augmentative communication"[4] or "facilitation,"[5] although they sound like and even have something to do with "facilitated communication." Facilitated communication per se is that form of "assisted" communication in which a usually normal adult physically assists a person with a disability to use a typewriter or word processor. The technique was developed in Australia, primarily for children with severe cerebral palsy, and involves supporting the child's hand to type on the keyboard, without directing the typing.[6] The technique was initially so successful in unlocking the inner worlds of the children in Australia that it was quickly exported to Europe and America and employed with a variety of people with disabilities—from the purely physically disabled to those with severe cognitive complication.

Probably the most famous, or infamous, applications of facilitated communication are those that have involved people with autism and people making statements with legal implications (for example, people who were or are being raped or abused). In these latter cases, evidence collected by facilitated communication has been inadmissible in court, largely because disability researchers with a behavioral orientation have discredited the scientific basis for the technique. These professionals believe that it is the facilitator who is directing the communication, either purposefully or in subtle ways of which he or she may be completely unaware. There have been various sorts of scientific "tests" of the technique that are inconclusive in my own view, since different methodologies used to study facilitated communication yield different results. The debate among researchers and clinicians about the use of facilitated communication is active and current.

In the case of persons with autism, the notoriety of facilitated communication, made world famous by Doug Biklen's article in the *Harvard Educational Reivew* and later in the *New York Times Magazine*, has fostered a debate about the nature of autism and particularly the intelligence of persons with that condition. Basically, with the advent of facilitated communication a tremendous number of persons who had never been able to communicate before because of severe "intellectual" deficits began to do so. These young "autists" made statements about the nature of their experience of autism, exhibiting thoughts and reflections that had been regarded, before their facilitated-communication training, as well beyond their capability. There was again a backlash from many professionals who insisted that the introduction of this technique must have been in some way contaminated or invalid, that the students with severe autism that made these statements were simply unable to communicate, or that the students had never been "really autistic." The answer from Biklen and his supporters was that this was a particular form of communication that allowed some deficits of autism (or at least some kinds of autism) to be ameliorated in a way currently not understood. They also claimed that facilitated communication may allow us to redefine this condition completely, since some of the communicational dysfunction that is definitionally part of autism may be modal specific. At the time of this writing the debate for and against facilitated communication is still very active and unresolved, and how this technique will effect our conception of certain disabilities is also still unknown.

While the approach to communication developed in this book does not specifically bear upon facilitated communication, it does provide a direction or frame for thinking about it. The communication system between Chris and me, and Bianca and her mother, was a "lived order" (see Chapter 5) of communication. It had to be appreciated in its historical specificity, as the product of just those two people involved. Bianca, for example, had a tremendous repertoire of communicational acts that were understood by her mother and father but were simply lost to anyone else. Concretely linked to the interaction between progeny and parents, these communications would not even have been visible to an untrained eye (as I remarked in my early tenure in the Smiths' home). Thus, the communication networks I encountered in this research would tend to corroborate the ideas that forms of communication can be *necessarily* dyadic (or triadic) and *only* dyadic. The kinds of tests employed by the behavioral scientists that are used to discredit facilitated communication do not recognize this and therefore, I believe, are not valid ways to assess the facilitated-communication technique. More naturalistic methods, such as those used by the Syracuse group, are much more appropriate. Even these will not ultimately prove or disprove the reality of facilitated communication with many people who are involved, any more than I or the parents could "prove" our communication with Chris or Bianca.

Another implication of these studies for the current debate about facilitated communication is that ordinary language-using people may have difficulty in accounting for how they communicate in extraordinary, non-language-based communicative networks. As noted in Chapter 3, although parents were experts in the communication with their children with rubella syndrome, they were not research scientists and could not prove even an initial, let alone systematic, description of *how* they communicated with their children. It took a scientific outsider, and one trained in a highly rarified form of observation, to put these pieces together. This causes me to have some sympathy for my colleagues who are practicing facilitated communication without being able to prove, or even exactly describe, how it works. These facilitators have the distinct experience that facilitation is "working," but they do not know exactly how or why and sometimes cannot even demonstrate (at least to the satisfaction of a skeptical audience) that it is.

Thus, while we need to be very careful about the use of facilitated communication, especially given its incredibly rapid growth (seemingly without much quality control), and while we do not, and may not for a very long time, understand why and how it works, the experiences of those involved, like the experiences of the parents who "just knew" they could communicate with their alingual children but could not explain how, should be taken with great seriousness. From my personal experience, I would guess that for every problematic and troublesome case of a person engaging in facilitated communication, there are probably ten cases of people benefiting without any apparent fraud or manipulation. Perhaps people using this technique have become converts and a bit zealous in their recommendations and claims, but they are generally good people and completely well intentioned. This is not to say that fraud and manipulation do not occur. I am sure facilitated communication gets misused, and in that regard it joins every other technique in human services that has ever been, or will be, invented.

It is also sensible, given what we know about their lives, that many people with disabilities will have a bad thing or two to say about the world when they are first given an opportunity to do so. That should not be shocking to us and should be taken seriously under any circumstance. On the other hand, the misuse of this probability by others is also not shocking and will also probably continue to occur. This leads me to the general conclusion that facilitated communication is worth pursuing for anyone, but very carefully and cautiously. A long-standing friend, a decent researcher and convert to facilitated communication, said to me recently that she thought Christina might benefit from this training. I objected and registered my disbelief and redescribed Chris to her, but she insisted that Chris still was a candidate and that it would not hurt to try. She told me that I was being a little prejudiced in concluding that such an attempt would not be useful; "You might be right, but you might be very surprised" is what she said to me. Given my own experiences with children with rubella syndrome and the little we know about extraordinary communicators, this attitude seems to be to me a most sensible one to take at this time. I know of too many persons for whom this appears to be a highly successful form of intervention to jump on the bandwagon of hard-nosed scientists who want to stop facilitated communication because they cannot prove it works.

■ QUALITY OF LIFE AND INCLUSION

Two of the watchwords in the disabilities field today are "quality of life" and "inclusion." The former refers to, in many persons' uses (see Goode, in press), an individual's felt and expressed satisfaction with the conditions of his or her life. The latter term denotes a philosophy of full participation in society for people with disabilities. Both terms partake in the new way of looking at people with disabilities and emphasize the quality of their relations with others in society.

In the context of this writing I will not get into a debate about the merits of one term over another. The research reported above, as well as much additional experience in the disability field over the past twenty years, has led me to be suspicious of all philosophies and rhetoric (see especially Wolfensberger 1989). On the hospital ward, one of the staff remarked about "normalization" (the philosophy of service dominant then) that "it is really the same old stuff we used to do given another name."[7] This staff member had the good observational skills to see behind the rhetoric to the actual practices of everyday life, and on that level, she failed to see how "normalization" had made any concrete difference. This is the same way that I look at the emerging philosophies of service in the field of disabilities. No matter how good they are conceptually, politically, morally, or otherwise, they will be misused and cause people harm. Although there needs to be an overt philosophy of service, we need to be very careful about looking critically, thoughtfully, and empathically at the actual conditions of life that people with disabilities and their families experience. This is why qualitative research methods such as those employed in Chapters 2 and 3 are of increasing importance to the field. They can capture in ways stronger than quantitative methods the lived realities of everyday life. When information obtained from inquiries that take seriously the perspectives of people with disabilities and of those who take care of them in face-to-face relations is acted upon in a proactive manner, reality will more likely be brought into line with rhetoric.[8]

■ RESEARCH IN DISABILITIES

I was asked to give a talk in Stockholm in 1990 on the topic of ethnomethodology and disability research. In that talk, entitled "An Ethnomethodological Prospectus for Research with People Who Have Severe Disabilities," I described the particular strengths of approaching topics in disability research "ethnomethodologically." Strictly speaking, there is no "one" ethnomethodological method, only examples or instances of such research. There are, however, ethnomethodological initiatives, approaches, or recurrent themes that can be described and summarized. Here are some of these and their significance to disability research.

The enacted character of social reality. Ethnomethodology is a form of sociology in the "social constructionist" tradition. It emphasizes the study of every social reality and how it is accomplished by societal members. This entails "a transformation of the 'natural' attitude (Husserl [1913] 1962) toward the everyday world; features in everyday life ordinarily treated as given, natural, or real are ethnomethodologically examined as the product of interpretive and interactional 'work'" (Pollner and Goode 1990). The question of the reality of something is suspended in order to examine how it is "addressed, assessed, and used in actions, discourse and reasoning of members" (Pollner and Goode 1990). This approach then allows the observer to see that which is ordinarily taken for granted and to focus upon the construction of reality as work by the members of society. As noted by Marten Soder, a sociologist at the University of Uppsala, Sweden, and others, this perspective has been tremendously lacking in disability research and is probably the most promising approach in many ways today.[9]

The concern for the indigenous and the actor's perspective. Because ethnomethodology is concerned with local perspectives and the work engaged in by people in their everyday lives, it seeks to discover and retrieve these in its data. This is especially important in disability research today, with the increasing emphasis on consumer surveys and consumer-driven program evaluation. Ethnomethodological observation is particularly suited to describing difficult-to-describe worlds, such as Chris's or Bianca's, but also the perspective of parents or caregivers that share everyday life with persons with severe disabilities. If the scientist is interested in the experience of people with disabilities and their families, there is probably no better research approach.

Retrieving paradox and contradiction. Because ethnomethodology requires firsthand knowledge of the events under study, it is able to avoid rationalistic and one-sided accounts of phenomena. The bulk of disability research cannot and does not do this, and this can have dire consequences, considering that people with disabilities and their lives are often filled with paradoxes, discontinuities, and contradictions. Nothing short of a punctilious and self-reflective observational method could have allowed me to conduct the research on Christina's world or on the Smiths' communication within their family.

The person as an accomplished or enacted feature of a setting. Because I do not believe that we have a good descriptive vocabulary for people with disabilities (in fact, people generally), the explicit focus on the way individuals are achieved features of social settings is critical to a science of disability. As mentioned in the text, the whole disability field is predicated on biological and psychological conceptions of disability (themselves achieved features of social settings) and has missed (or purposely avoided) the implications of social constructionism. There are many people with complex disabilities that we understand about as poorly as we do the Christinas and Biancas of the world.

While this is not even a cursory list of the many initiatives that one could describe in ethnomethodology, those listed are ones with particular import to a science of disabilities. Generally, qualitative approaches like phenomenology and ethnomethodology can be used in the study of disability two important ways: exploratory, to generate new ideas and knowledge about disability, and confirmatory, to confirm or disconfirm knowledge about disability generated through other (more traditional) methods. Because much traditional research can be so far from the everyday worlds of people with disabilities and their families, it is extremely important that at least some researchers, if only a small minority, actually engage themselves in these worlds firsthand, and in an observationally critical way.

A final note about research. In disability research and in human research generally, there are a great number of scientists claiming to know a great deal. I am suspicious of anyone who speaks this way. Human scientific research is both very young and all too often very poorly done. Even when it is done well, its results are far from Truth with a capital *T*. There is an incredible hubris in which too many researchers engage, either knowingly to enhance their careers or out of ignorance, but with the same effect. They and the consumers of their knowledge end up looking too uncritically at the things produced by our sciences and taking them too seriously. Without intending this as a postmodern critique of expertism, but more as a methodological comment, I must point out that we researchers really do need to learn some patience and humility in our studies of persons with disability and their families. We need to learn to "listen" to (observe, participate with, talk with) Christina and those who share her life in a deep and reflective way. We need to bring what we learn from them back to our science of disabilities. To have a science of human disability, we have to look beyond the commonsense assumptions built into the words of our language and attempt to suspend the "normal" ways we construct people with disabilities. We need to do more of the kind of research reported in the beginning of this book.

In a book that I hope has presented to the reader many complex and stimulating questions about the nature of language and disability, I want to end with some simple observations in summary of what I have learned in almost twenty years' involvement with people like Christina, Bianca, and their families. Despite all the publicity and marketing of research and knowledge in disability today, none of us, not even people with disabilities themselves, have an adequate grasp on the most basic and profound questions that a science of disability would want to address. Humankind has only reflected on itself for a very short time, historically speaking. The scientific study of disability is but a wink in that short time frame, under one hundred years old. As I see it, there are no real experts in disabilities, or for that matter in any other area of social sciences. Perhaps there are students of disabilities who are more talented than others, but we are all just in the infancy of our science and should reflect on our knowledge accordingly. I distrust those who loudly and fashionably proclaim their expertise; they can be particularly dangerous people.

Among other things, this book lays out several courses of long-term research regarding the social construction of individuals with disability and their families. I believe I have pointed to the existence of many phenomena in disabilities that have received too little or no attention in our writings and thoughts. But I must emphasize that these studies only begin to point to phenomena.[10] They do not systematically explicate "a language of action" or "the body's lexicon" or "routine as a resource in bodily communication" or what have you.[11] In my own view they barely scratch the surface of the problems involved in an adequate description of disabilities. I admit to having a small amount of knowledge about these matters. But I also admit that the single most important thing that these studies have taught me about people like Christina and Bianca is how poorly we understand them and how much more we have to learn about them and from them. Perhaps it is a kind of hubris of my own, but I feel strongly that if Christina and Bianca were here with me now, and if somehow they could understand what I had written on these pages, they would want me to end this book with that thought.

APPENDIX:
ASCERTAINING CHOICE
WITH ALINGUAL, DEAF-BLIND,
AND RETARDED CLIENTS

David Goode | *Michael P. Gaddy*

■ ABSTRACT: A distinguishing feature of the normalization principle is its concern for a client's capability to exercise choice. When dealing with alingual clients, this can prove troublesome. There is no direct way to determine whether such persons are aware of options available to them. Based upon observations of a hospital ward for the alingual deaf-blind-retarded,[1] an observational technique was designed to remedy this difficulty. This technique, a behavior preference-dispreference list, plus an actual example of such a list constructed for a particular resident, is presented. The relation between behavior preferences and choices is also discussed.

■ THE PROBLEM

The principle of normalization (Wolfensberger 1972) is becoming an increasing influence on human services offered to the mentally retarded. Although we should not underestimate the immense benefits that can be provided by this relatively coherent system of servicing principles, the risk of failing to meet its directives in concrete instances of client treatment is present. This is especially true when the persons being serviced are profoundly mentally retarded, marginally educable, and housed in residential institutions. With such persons normalization can easily be used to justify a plethora of practices reflecting the resources and daily routine of hospital life.

There is a basic problem in normalization principles applied to the alingual, congenitally deaf-blind, profoundly retarded individual.[2] The data upon which this writing is based are the result of hundreds of hours of observation, done for a period of twenty consecutive months, on a ward and in other areas of a state hospital. The subject population consisted of ten to sixteen male and female deaf-blind residents who varied in age from four to twenty-four. Many of the children were born with rubella syndrome; all were alingual and exhibited profound developmental, cognitive, and perceptual deficiencies. All residents were, in hospital terminology, low functioning and required assistance in the entire repertoire of self-help skills.

The purpose of the study was to examine the role of client choice in planning curricula for such children. What distinguishes normalization from previous orientations in human servicing, at least in part, is its explicit concern with client choice. Wolfensberger states in *Normalization* (1972, 238), "We should assist the person to become capable of meaningfully choosing for himself among those normative options that are considered moral and those that are not. If a person is capable of *meaningful choice*, he must also risk the consequences" (emphasis added). While this respect for client choice distinguishes a progressive approach in the servicing of retarded clients today, this same concern can prove troublesome for those in charge of planning curricula for the alingual deaf-blind-retarded. Particularly problematic for such persons is the phrase "meaningful choice"—what is "meaningful" to the deaf-blind in their world may not be "meaningful" from within ours. Many deaf-blind children are undoubtedly having meaningful experiences but are unable to communicate them to us. In such cases the danger exists that we function as cultural missionaries—proselytizing our conceptions of the normality and meaningfulness without regard for those of the "natives."

Progress in recognizing choice in the alingual deaf-blind client is made by noting that such persons make choices though our awareness of them is problematic. What is needed is a technology by which such choices can be made available for our inspection. Any technique designed for this purpose will have to be inferential; the deaf-blind-retarded often do not use linguistic symbols, and we, as distinct from the anthropologist in the field, cannot directly translate their inner language. The procedure devised for the study was observational and made use of inferential and empathic capacities. The method has been found to be both simple and useful.

■ THE METHOD

While the client acts in a world that is many ways perceptually and cognitively distant from that of the observer, it is still possible for an observer to make warranted interpretations and categorizations of client behaviors. Both share certain species-specific behaviors and capabilities. For example, the observer is often able to recognize whether a client enjoys an activity (that is, observer and resident can communicate emotionally—through laughter, tears, anger, frustration, and so on). An observer is also able to recognize whether a client seeks or avoids some activity. The resident and observer share a language of action—for example, the observer can understand a client's behavior when the client pulls the observer toward a trampoline, sits by a guitar case, or leads the observer to a door. These shared aspects of the observers and observed provide for the possibility of assembling a list of behavior preferences. Based upon this list of behavior preferences, a client's choices can be inferred (see "Discussion").

Using the following criteria, resident behaviors can be scaled along a five-category preference-dispreference dimension:

1. HIGHLY PREFERRED—behaviors that the resident actively pursues or during which he or she exhibits strong signs of positive affect (excitement, laughter, and so forth).

2. PREFERRED—behaviors during which the resident is cooperative, though he or she does not actively pursue them, and during which he or she shows positive affect.

3. NEUTRAL—behaviors during which the resident seldom displays affect (that is, is passive and disinterested).

4. DISPREFERRED—behaviors that the resident physically tolerates or resists somewhat and during which he or she exhibits negative affect (whimpering, crying, whining, and so forth).

5. HIGHLY DISPREFERRED—behaviors that the resident actively avoids and resists and during which he or she shows strong negative affect (tantrum or rage behavior).

An actual example of a preferred-dispreferred list, completed for a particular nine-year-old female resident is presented.

1. HIGHLY PREFERRED—listening to music; making music (with piano and electronic organ); looking at light box; trampolining; swimming; playground swinging; roughhousing; eating sweet soft foods; (occasionally) taking trips outside institution; (occasionally) being sung to by staff in ear.

2. PREFERRED—bathing; showering; having tongue and teeth played with; rocking (autokinesthetic behavior); licking smooth surfaces (autosomathetic behavior); being left alone to play with small toys; (occasionally) running with staff member; (occasionally) being held by staff or sitting on a staff member's lap.

3. NEUTRAL—classroom activities (such as colored ring stacking or finger painting); language training; (occasionally) trips outside the institution.

4. DISPREFERRED—staff waking her in morning; disruption of hospital routine; being forced to eat hard food (especially meat); being ignored by staff; (occasionally) having hair or teeth brushed; (occasionally) returning to the institution after a visit home.

5. HIGHLY DISPREFERRED—being taken away from a highly preferred activity; being struck by another resident; falling down; being yelled at by a staff member; having temperature taken (rectal); having a nose and throat culture taken; (occasionally) not being taken to a highly preferred activity (for example walking by the music room or trampoline).

Not all the client's behaviors can be unambiguously placed into one or another of the preferred-dispreferred categories. There are many sources of variation (daily mood, maturation, learning, observer bias), but some of these can be controlled. For example, a group familiar with the resident could nominate and vote upon behavior items to be placed on the list; thus, observer bias could be limited. By constructing lists on a regular basis, variation due to maturation and mood shifts should be limited. However, human beings do not act in a completely consistent and predictable way, so one would still expect some degree of ambiguity.

The major advantage in compiling such a list is that written records of the client's assessment of his or her own life is produced; the information is accessible to all who come into a servicing relation with the child. This feature of accessibility is particularly important when dealing with alingual clients. Such persons' preferences and dispreferences often emerge to the staff after long-term and intimate involvement with them. Information built up over long periods should be recorded and made part of the residents' hospital files. Written records ease staff transition and also help implement normalization in a more self-conscious and effective manner. The process of documentation may help to create "conscious rather than unconscious ideologies" in servicing such clients (Wolfensberger 1972, 10). The human services professions have spent a considerable effort in constructing assessment devices to determine how the retarded child's behaviors compare with those of normal youngsters. Both objective and subjective assessment instruments are necessary for the effective implementation of normalization principles.

The information produced by this procedure can be fluid. Clients may be reevaluated on certain of their preferred or dispreferred behaviors. In the example presented, we may wish to extinguish certain forms of self-stimulatory behaviors, even though they are preferred. Or we may wish to emphasize hard-food eating and tooth brushing even though they are dispreferred. On the other hand, it may be found that within the preferred-dispreferred options list certain "normative options" exist and that the client should be assisted in realizing these more effectively. Referring to the example, the resident might be assisted in music making and in performing gross body activities (trampolining, tumbling, roughhouse), since these are all highly preferred, normatively valued options. Or it may be better to avoid disrupting the client's daily routine as much as possible. This is essentially the kind of thing a parent does in socializing normal children, except that we are making the behavior-molding process a more self-conscious enterprise.

■ DISCUSSION

Perhaps the most serious objection that could be raised about our proposal is that preferred behaviors and choices are not synonymous. *To choose* means to select from among options, whereas *to prefer* (at least in our operational definition of it) means only that a particular behavior occurs more or less frequently and has an affective component attached to it by the client. Any procedure designed to get at the subjective content of the client would have to be empathic and inferential. Such procedures are implicitly employed by the staff in their day-to-day contact with the clients, and although there is no direct way to apprehend whether children know if options are available to them (that is, whether their behavior preferences represent true choices), we should make these procedures more self-conscious and through them attempt to consult the deaf-blind clients' assessments of their lives.

At the heart of the issue of choice lies the debate of free will versus determinism. The difference between a preference (as we operationalize it) and a choice is not clear. Much of what we consider to be choice in our lives may represent nothing more than habituation of conditioning. While not having a communicational resource for asking the deaf-blind alingual children what they are aware of further complicates the issue, residents still exhibit choicelike behaviors. For example, given free time in a play area with which they are thoroughly familiar, they regularly seek out one, as opposed to another, available play option. A list of behavior preferences-dispreferences should be used in whatever ways it can to increase our knowledge of residents' subjective evaluations of their own circumstances. We can readily acknowledge that our method may fall short of what one might want ideally. At the same time, we must do the best with what we have.

◼ REFERENCES

Goode, David. 1979. The world of the deaf-blind. In J. Jacobs and H. Schwartz, eds., *Qualitative sociology; A method to the madness.* New York: Free Press.

Wolfensberger, Wolf. 1972. *Normalization: The principle of normalization in human services.* Toronto: National Institute on Mental Retardation, Leonard Crainford.

◼ NOTES

This article, in slightly different form, was originally published in *Mental Retardation* 14 (6): 10–12 (1980), with coauthor Michael P. Gaddy. Goode's participation in this research was supported through PSH Grant no. HD04612 NICHD and no. HD-05540-02, Patterns of Care and the Development of the Retarded, Mental Retardation Study Center, UCLA Medical Center. Gaddy's involvement was performed pursuant to contract no. 300750291 with the Southwest Region Deaf-Blind Center, California State Department of Education, Department of Health, Education, and Welfare. The opinions and conclusions stated in this paper are those of the authors and should not be construed as reflecting the official policies of the California State Department of Health or other governmental agencies.

1. Despite the horrendous language here, the lack of "people-first" language and the term "client," one must remember the context within which this article was published. It was 1975 when it was submitted. The whole idea of children with rubella syndrome having any concept of choice at all was completely radical, even if the language used to describe such persons was not. Although people with disabilities may well be owed a belated apology for such language, I have left it much as it appeared in the original. It was a reflection of the lack of explicit conventions in this regard at the time and can be found in almost all research literature of that era.

2. While the article is written especially with regard to the congenitally deaf-blind-retarded, one could adapt this method to other alingual retarded populations.

NOTES

Chapter 2

This research was supported by PSH Grant no. HD-612 NICHD, the Mental Retardation Research Center, UCLA, and no. HD-05540-02, Patterns of Care and the Development of the Retarded. My special thanks for their assistance in guiding my enterprise go to Robert B. Edgerton, Harold Garfinkel, Melvin Pollner, and Michael Gaddy. My thanks also go to Harold Levine for his editorial assistance. An earlier version of this chapter appeared in *Qualitative Sociology: A Method to the Madness*, ed. J. Jacobs and H. Schwartz (New York: Free Press, 1980).

1. Although extensive description and discussion of the ward is not possible, some brief background on the ward is in order. The ward was located on the grounds of a large state school/hospital for people with mental retardation. For many years this institution had operated as a self-sufficient colony in a rural setting until its transformation into a hospital, with various specialized wards and medical programs. Several thousand people lived there in the early 1970s, although "deinstitutionalization" (the shutting down of large institutions) was already an accepted destiny and policy. (This in fact took over twenty years to accomplish.) The particular ward I observed was specifically for persons with deaf-blindness. Forty to fifty children and adults resided on the ward, in various groups, organized according to age and functional needs. The program in which I was involved as a researcher received federal funding to provide relatively intensive early intervention services to children under thirteen. The person administering this program, Michael Gaddy, was instrumental in providing me with access and continued administrative support during the course of the research. His intensive program involved between ten and fifteen children (the number changed as some "aged out") who received extra staff and profes-

217

sional services (compared to others on the ward who were not in this
program). These children attended school regularly, received occupational, physical, and speech therapy, had extra direct-care staff to help
with basic living skills, and were, if one can conceive of such a thing,
relatively privileged residents of the ward. During the day there might
be four or five people (excluding myself) who were assigned direct-service roles for these fifteen children. The ward itself was a U-shaped,
hacienda-style structure that had living quarters in one leg and dining
facilities in the other, with staff offices in the long section connecting
the two. It was a large and generally dreary structure that resembled the
"Willowbrook" images—the caged windows and institutional furniture;
children lying everywhere in various states of dress, sometimes soiled;
the smell of urine, feces, and disinfectant; the incredible cacophony of
quasi-human sounds. And imposed on this incredibly bizarre and seemingly disorganized place, the veneer of bureaucracy, rationality, and regimentation.

2. This project, as well as the other studies in this book, was done
under the supervision of ethnomethodologists Harold Garfinkel and
Melvin Pollner while I was a graduate student of sociology at UCLA
(1973–80). I am professionally and personally indebted to Professors
Garfinkel and Pollner for the general approach to social research taken
in these studies. In addition to the approach and analysis of social reality taught by Garfinkel and Pollner, I have liberally adapted concepts
and from their work, which are appropriately cited throughout the
chapters. I accept responsibility for my own limitations in interpreting
their ideas. When conscious departures from the ethnomethodological
approach were taken in the research, they are noted in the text.

3. My original field notes contain much detail about the clinical encounters between the children on the ward and various clinical professionals. While some of the professionals at the hospital were not of the
highest caliber (a problem endemic to the low status and relatively poor-
paying disabilities field), many did attempt to provide and adequate di-
agnostic and remedial services. I describe the "ad hoc" clinical procedures used by audiometrists, opthalmologists, dentists, psychologists,
and others. They were not all without humor; the audiometrist was particularly innovative in some of the ways he attempted to capture the

interest of the children in sound, including a sudden and unannounced *1812 Overture* that almost knocked me out of my chair! But the bottom line for these children was that in clinical encounters they could not understand the rationality of the procedures, could not communicate what they were feeling, and generally could not participate in the clinical encounter in any helpful way.

4. By "direct-care workers" I mean workers in the hospital system who were given the title psychiatric technician, a job title with several grades. There were also program supervisers, ward charges, and teachers who interacted with the children on a relatively intimate and long-term basis. Basically, direct-care staff were high school educated and were given some in-service training generally insufficient and inadequate to their work. The jobs were low paying, often attracting young people. Some of the staff were not well qualified; some were even not well intentioned. In my three years of formal association with the ward and the five that followed as a hospital volunteer, I observed how regular abuse in the institution was and how the vast majority of abuse escaped report. In the particular program in which I worked, staff had been given extra training and money because of a federal grant, and thus the program had a slightly better-qualified group of direct-care workers.

5. The sequelae (medical effects) of rubella virus are highly variable. Persons exposed early in fetal development generally developed more severe and numerous sequelae. The pattern of rubella syndrome included sequelae such as the deaf-blindness and mental retardation evidenced by Christina, but might also include organ malformation or malfunction, orthopedic abnormalities, cerebral palsy, dental, endocrine, and other abnormalities. There is even something referred to as rubella hair. Perhaps even more remarkable is that sometimes all these sequelae could be observed in one child.

6. The work of Jean Itard (an eighteenth-century teacher of deaf mutes) with Victoire of Aveyron (a "wolf boy," or child raised in the woods) was, in various ways, quite instructive during the course of my research, even though Chris was a product of a humanly ordered world (home, schools, and hospital), whereas Victoire was not.

7. I say "almost all" because human services employs people evidencing the full spectrum of human frailties, and thus there were abu-

sive and even sadistic personnel on the ward. Some of these persons were discovered and fired. Others were not. The deaf-blind children were easy "marks" for those with such intent. They could be and were tortured and sexually assaulted and had no way of indicating to others what had occurred (and indeed experienced these "abuses" in ways perhaps inconsistent with children in the larger culture). This is a major problem with the adults with rubella syndrome today. In the smaller community residential system, with social visibility much lower than that of state institutions and with much less qualified and less screened staff, one can only wonder what does occur to deaf-blind alingual persons. They continue to remain at extremely high risk for abuse.

8. Huey was a young man of eleven who was legally deaf and blind but who had a real vocabulary of signs that made him very different from the other residents on the ward. After one week there I told the man in charge of the program that Huey did not belong at an institution like this but maybe at an institution for the deaf. He agreed. It took five months to get Huey out of the ward and into another placement. In the meantime we became buddies, based upon our mutual interest in martial arts (he in boxing—probably taught by his dad—and I in tai chi and karate). Huey was a good-looking and bright kid who was also very angry. Almost unbelievably, he took a bite out of an oak table top once and loosened a couple of teeth. He had, understandably, a lot of anger in him. I identified with Huey and liked him very much.

9. At the risk of being pedantic, I must point out that it is a general truth about direct care that the direct-care giver must separate out in some way his or her own feelings from those of the person being helped. Further, there needs to be a valuation of the feelings and position in the world of the person to be helped if help is ever to succeed. Without such a separation and valuation it is very likely that harm will be the result of the helping relationship, regardless of intent.

10. I do not want to dismiss this problem at all lightly, and in the end I do not think I can make a strong claim that I was ever able to describe Chris's point of view on things. A comment written to me in a letter by Jim Swan of Buffalo University is instructive in this regard. He writes, "Another dimension of this all-important matter of negotiating the distance between you is your very deliberate analysis of your own

writing about her—of just how it does and does not (can not) really describe her point of view. For all we know, you come awfully close, and maybe that's the best we can hope for. I'm certainly glad that you were not persuaded by the impossibility of the task; besides, once you begin to think it over, it becomes apparent that all writing is impossible in just this way—the object inevitably slides out from behind the words." He then provides an epigram from a book by Thomas Caramagno, *Flight of the mind,* that "evokes the problem quite nicely if Christina were to speak":

> I am not the one you think I was
> Rather, yonder you have
> With your pens given me another being
> And another breath with your life . . .
>
> You have praised the image of
> Your very own idea
> And being yours, it well deserves
> Your very own applause.

> —Sor Juana Ines de la Cruz (Mexico, 1651–95)

I cannot tell you that if Christina were able to speak, this is not what she would say of my efforts; it is a "for all we know" sort of thing.

11. "Fault-finding procedures" is a phrase suggested by Harold Garfinkel (personal communication, 1974). I have adopted the phrase (not Garfinkel's sense of it) to refer to a structure of practical reasoning in which the deaf-blind-retarded are found to be faulted with respect to some setting-occasioned normative criterion of action. While the specific flaws located vary from setting to setting (for example, a child can be found to be an incompetent eater at lunch, or an incompetent test subject for normal audiometric examination procedures, or an incompetent ambulator in walking from the ward to the classroom, and so on), the *form* of the reasoning—that is, the judging of the child as deficient with respect to a normative criterion of behavior or action—is invariant from setting to setting. The ethnography of the ward indicated that the staff (and other normals) also engaged in "asset-finding procedures" that, in a fashion similar to the faulting practices, find the child competent with respect to some "normal" behavioral capacity. Both asset and fault finding are suggested as possible basic structures of practical rea-

soning in that all settings are seen to produce "their case of local heroes and villains" (Melvin Pollner, personal communication, 1975).

12. Toward the end of my stay on the ward, the staff began to resent my presence and complained that my playing with Chris was interfering with her programming. I feel that at least part of this resentment stemmed from my relatively enviable position—that is, I could play with Chris and not be responsible for her training and maintenance (instead of the normal staff's position of having to be responsible for training many children). When staff were allowed simply to play with the residents, both staff and residents seemed to enjoy themselves a great deal. "Play" was that time in hospital routine when the normative rules and goals for interacting with the children could be suspended and the staff were afforded the opportunity to experience the residents in nonideologically defined activity. Play activity, for the sake of itself, transcended the institutional goals of remediation and provided for the staff a time when they could "meet the residents on their own grounds."

13. This text, designed to deal with issues of field method and procedure, focuses almost exclusively upon the interactional strategies used in collecting ethnographic *data*. Conspicuously absent are analyses of these procedures—that is, conclusions about how my involvement with the deaf-blind allowed me to produce findings about the nature of human intersubjectivity. At least two modes of analysis are suggested in my concluding remarks. One of these, the concept of intersubjectivity as human praxis, is explicated in some detail in Chapters 3 and 4.

14. Several years before any theoretical or academic writing appeared about this research, the administrator of the deaf-blind program and I wrote an article and aimed at direct-care staff working with children born deaf-blind. In 1976, this article was published in the largest applied research journal in the field, *mental Retardation*, and provided direct-care staff with a concrete protocol to locate "client choices" made by such children (Goode and Gaddy, 1976). A copy of this original article constitutes the appendix following Chapter 7. The article proposed that choices of all types are routinely made by these children and that it is possible to observe these choices. It presents a typology to arrange these choices according to a continuum of preference, from highly disliked to highly preferred. In addition to this publication, I proved a couple of

training sessions and research presentations at the hospital in order to explain the "practical" results of my work. Put succinctly, the results of these efforts were disappointing. The article appeared, but with little reaction from the professional community. (Despite its title and placement in so large a journal and the tremendous emphasis on choice making today, it remains largely uncited.)

15. Other reasons this article fell on deaf professional ears included bureaucratic tendencies to resist change and decentralization of power and decision making; the social-organizational imperatives of power and authority described by Erving Goffman, Stanley Milgram, Philip Zimbardo, and others; and the inability of American culture to sustain the idea that persons without testable intelligence are nonetheless intelligent in their own right.

16. An interesting parallel exists between how I treated Christina and how parents observed by W. D. Winnecott in the 1950s prompted their children to establish what he called "transitional objects and spaces." Transitional objects were those objects the infants used to appropriate into their experience the "not-me-ness" of the world and to quell the attendant anxiety of this experience. Using Winnecottian terminology, I could say that what I was about with Christina was facilitating her access to objects and experiences of the outside world. In this sense, the comment made by Jim Swan (an English professor at the University of Buffalo) about my relationship with Chris—"D. G. acts like a Winnecottian mother"—is basically correct. There were important differences also, which included the serial character of my relationship with Chris and the relative self-consciousness of my acting as a "superplaymate," or facilitator to external experience.

17. Christina's life after the termination of my formal research involvement on the ward had three distinct periods. First, there was a period of about four years during which I visited her at least several times a year. While her life was not without incident during this period, her quality of life at the hospital basically improved because of the reorganization of the state care system. Her ward was significantly improved physically and made to look much more homelike. This process continued on through the 1980s, although I was no longer in California and was able to visit only every few years. She eventually shared a room on

the ward with two other deaf-and-blind persons, had many personal possessions (including an electric organ that she was permitted to play recreationally, even though it drove the staff crazy). The homelike atmosphere on the ward was partially due to some staff who did stay on for many years and who became committed to the residents and particularly attached to Chris. While Chris made no significant academic progress, and indeed has never learned language of any type, she did mature as a human being. By fourteen she had stopped her incontinence; she became physically stronger and had incidents of bad behavior during adolescence—but what adolescent does not? In 1986, as a young adult, she was generally liked as a resident. Of course by 1986 she also had become almost totally blind in both eyes because of postsurgical scarification. She was far more blind and more disabled than when I had met her in 1968. In 1988 Christina had an emergency gastrectomy and almost died. There was massive ulceration and bleeding of the stomach, the origin of which was never determined but was speculated to be either rubella syndrome, diet, habit, stress, genetics, or a combination of any of the above factors. When I visited her in April of that year, it was one of the most difficult experiences of my life to share with Chris her attempts to communicate to me what had happened to her—her feelings were overwhelmingly powerful, breaking me down completely, so that at one point we were two hysterical people sobbing on one another, walking arm in arm. It was just terrible and is difficult to write about even now, almost five years after the visit. That, together with her recovery and the change of lifestyle required by a gastrectomy, is the second period in Chris's life since I left the ward. Finally, there is a third period about which I know very little, and that began with her placement in a community program. This occurred a couple of years ago, as was mandated by the California State law requiring the closing of state-run hospitals for persons with mental retardations. Both Chris's mom and I had our worries about how such a switch of environment would affect Chris. But I have not heard recently from Christina's mother and cannot tell the reader about this new chapter of life for Chris. Ideally, we can hope that the community facility in which she resides is able to provide her with more appropriate and individual supports. Perhaps she will get to interact with others in the community and become a part of that community. But there are also risks in this new arrangement, and it is more than likely Christina will experience some of these as well.

■ CHAPTER 3

Material from this chapter originally appeared under the title "On Understanding Without Words: Communication Between an Alingual Deaf-Blind Child and Her Parents," *Journal of Human Studies* 13 (1990): 1–37. My participation in the research was supported by PSH Grant No. HD04612 NICHD and No. HD-05540-02, Patterns of Care and the Development of the Retarded, Mental Retardation Research Center, UCLA Medical Center. I gratefully acknowledge the contributions of various readers of previous versions of this chapter, including Harold Garfinkel, Melvin Pollner, George Psathas, Robert Emerson, Warren TenHouten, Robert Edgerton, Larry Irvin, George Singer, Nancy Mandell, Donald Sutherland, and Sylvia Bercovici.

1. While still relatively small, interest in qualitative disability research is definitely growing. The most recent reader in qualitative research on disabilities is *Interpreting Disability: A Qualitative Reader*, ed. P. Ferguson, D. Ferguson, and S. Taylor (New York: Teachers College Press, 1992). Because of the presence of Steven Taylor and Bob Bogdan at Syracuse University, there is much interest and activity in this area at the Center for Human Policy. That center published a special report on qualitative methods and disability policy and is currently trying to publish a directory of ethnographic researchers in disability research. Readers interested in contacting the network of currently practicing ethnographic/qualitative researchers in disability may write Pam Walker, Research Associate, The Center for Human Policy, 200 Huntington Hall, Syracuse University, Syracuse, New York 13244-2340.

2. I exclude here forms of social science research that deal particularly and exclusively with statistical and actuarial matters such as demography.

3. The relationship and communication between Tanya and her sister is not part of the data of this chapter. These topics, while fascinating in their own right, were more difficult to observe and to get information about than I felt was trustable. Although Tanya was very respectful and helpful to me during this research and tried to answer whatever ques-

tions I asked her to the best of her ability, there were certain topics and certain questions that she was not very comfortable with and about which she would provide cryptic (though not necessarily intentionally deceitful) answers. Studying Tanya and Bianca would involve an excursion into kids' culture (see Chapter 6) and complex epistemological issues that this chapter, with its focus on parental communication, need not entertain.

4. A biography of Bianca, though interesting in its own right, is not possible within the space of this book. It may be important to point out that the Smiths had been very devoted to their daughter, and especially in the beginning of her life, Barbara had provided her own form of early intervention and sustained care that probably allowed Bianca to beat the medical predictions of her early death—that and, as Barbara described it, Bianca's stubborn and tough nature. When I met Bianca, she was just thirteen, and the Smiths had been taking care of her, save for her stays in the hospital, every day for the past thirteen years. They had literally never been away from her and had formed what might be called a "hyperintimate" relationship with her. They knew her so well, and she they, that there was an additional element of rapport probably not found in parent relationships with nonhandicapped thirteen-year-old daughters.

5. Bianca attended a large segregated school for children with severe disabilities that serviced children from several communities. There were over a hundred children in the school, and they had an enormous range of physical, psychological, and emotional disabilities. In Bianca's classroom, one that was run on a "contingency management" philosophy that imposed a clear behavioral sequence on both students and teachers in terms of shaping behavior, there were usually eight to ten children with a master teacher, assistant teacher, and one or two classroom aids. The students tended to be younger than Bianca and did not appear to have one "kind" of disability. What these students shared is that they were regarded as particularly difficult to work with, and Steve, the master teacher in the class, was regarded as one of the better teachers in the school. Even so, Bianca's physical and sensory handicaps made it impossible for her to compete for attention with the other students, and she often was ignored for long periods. The class curriculum

devoted time to academic skills, daily living skills, social interaction, physical development, and recreation. The school provided professional therapy (physical, occupational, speech, and language), which entailed removing the children from the class and taking them to special thera-peutic clinics on the school grounds. The school was a relatively happy place, and certainly it was one of the better schools of its type that I had seen in the area. This is not to say it was ideal, or even good, but rather that it was the "cream of the crap." Even two teachers and two aids were nowhere near sufficient to teach the eight to ten children in the class I observed, although it was better than most staff-student ratios. Thus, while not a bad school, it did not appear to be giving Bianca the services she really needed educationally, and she had not progressed in the cur-riculum.

6. I describe the organizational basis for human identity most fully in Goode 1984. These remarks stem from Garfinkel's contribution that all people are "organizationally incarnate"—that is, they participate in and depend upon an immediate socially organized situation within which their actions are interpreted and granted meaning. As with Chris-tina, it is this context, rather than the particular concrete traits, behav-iors, or competencies that determines the person's identity. Human service organizations have specific motives and relevancies for partici-pants to construct identity in specific and concrete ways. Because home and institutional settings vary considerably in organization, the identi-ties afforded individuals within these settings can vary accordingly.

7. One notable exception to this is the writing of "parent-profes-sionals," which testifies eloquently to the system's treatment of such parental claim.

8. This needs to be explicated and qualified a bit. The motivated and corrective feature of this work is somewhat in contradistinction to "ethnomethodological indifference" as presented in various books by ethnomethodologists. That principle asserts the analyst's ultimate disin-terest in any practical matter whatsoever regarding analysis. Analysis under such a conception can be seen as a process of dis-interesting oneself, in the phenomenological sense. The analytic part of this work was done under such a principle; that is, I studied communication with Bianca as a worldly matter of its own right and with its own structures

and idiosyncracies, without regard for the political or professional (or, for that matter, any) implications of the descriptions of communicative praxis. At least this was the conscious methodological principle that was employed.

9. This reference is to the medieval play in which individual characteristics of the characters are unavailable. The characters literally stand for all men or anyman.

10. In discovering this, I was also aware that access to this communication between Barbara and Bianca allowed me to observe a relationship somewhat similar to that I had with Christina, though I was on the outside now. When I listened to Barbara begin to speak about her communication with Bianca, I immediately recognized in some of what she was describing my own communication with Chris. An attempt to integrate the observations about these two studies is made in Chapter 4. No specific comparison will be undertaken in this chapter.

11. In this respect the family related to communication with Bianca much as other families related to communication with normal children. "Communication" was never a theme until its breakdown made it an issue. Also, the family conducted their inquiry within an overall frame that never questioned that Bianca was an active, intelligent person trying to communicate through a very deficient body. To family members she was "fully present" (in their interaction) (see discussion of Merleau-Ponty in Chapter 4).

12. I have referred to the differences between knowing of the doing and knowing of the saying by using the term "praktognosic" to refer to the former and "production accounts" to refer to the latter. Although ethnomethodology correctly asserts a certain isomorphism between accounts of activities and their actual worldly production, they are not at all identical phenomena. "Praktognosic" refers to a kind of knowing through doing (praxis) and was first used by the German neurologist Adolf Grünbaum in his *Aphasie und Motorik,* as cited by Merleau-Ponty (1962, 140). Garfinkel characterizes this usage as a "cognate version" of the praxiological conception of social action espoused by his program of ethnomethodology (personal communication, 1979).

13. Lived order is the ethnomethodological treatment of what Durkheim (1938) described as "social facts." From the ethnomethodological

perspective, Durkheim's analysis is one-sided, describing well the orderly features of societal action that are reproduced over and over again by societal members, but missing in an important way the creativeness of these members in being able to produce social facts with "just these people, in just this place, at just this time, under just such conditions." The Durkheimian conception of social facts was the underpinning of functionalist sociology, which is an equally one-sided fashion portrayed societal members, in Garfinkel's language, as "cultural dopes"—rule followers and reproducers of social structures imposed upon them by society. The term "lived order" reinjects the incredible capacity and creativity of social members, not as puppets being manipulated by the puppet master, but as authors and creators of their own world.

14. This is an observation of ethnomethodologists and language pragmatists, that what is not said, silence, the unspoken, may define group membership even more strongly than what is said. This observation bears upon the existence of routine in the Smith household in that routines were often treated as assumed and unmentioned matters, as facts of family life available to family members.

15. One reaction some readers have had to this description is that it can be read symptomatically, as an expression of an extremely tolerant family that accedes to the every wish of their daughter out of guilt or some other compensatory motivation. There is some validity to this observation; parents did indulge Bianca in some ways to an apparently extreme degree. But this was not an unconscious matter for them but, as far as I could tell, an overt matter of policy. They had decided to allow Bianca as much power over her world as they could support in their home. And they were consistent in this, I think, even when it was not exactly in their own interests—for example, when they tolerated Bianca's physical aggression against them.

16. Another aspect to this failure to teach sign was the parents' belief after years of trying, that Bianca would never learn anything but a very small number of signs (under ten) and probably without consistency or generalization of use. This impression, right or wrong, is the same one that I had of Christina after trying to teach her signs for three years. There was a sense that this was a waste of time with both Bianca and Christina.

17. These remarks can only begin to describe the complex social phenomenology of family space. The most general articulated version of social space is found in the work of Alfred Schutz (see, for example, Schutz 1970). A number of his concepts are directly relevant to an inclusive understanding of the spatialization of family life. His approach to social observation, his conception of the reciprocity of perspectives, of the world within sight, the manipulable world, and his notion of in-group and out-group perspectives are only some of the material that could profitably be explored in an explication of family space. Schutz's paradigmatic studies remind us powerfully of just how little is known of the empirical regularities of everyday existence. The same work allows us to appreciate just how sketchy this current treatment of family space is. This treatment of the topic merely points to the existence of shared spatial knowledge in the Smiths and is not an explication of it.

18. Children with rubella syndrome display a very wide range of facial emotions (see Eibl-Eibsfeldt 1973), tending to corroborate a non-learning theory of facial displays of emotion. They apparently possess what Ekman and Friesen (1971) call inborn "facial affect programs."

19. Many of the children with rubella syndrome have become adults. Many still do not use language and rely upon others to interpret the meaning of their actions. Because of turnover and system instability of various sorts, these adults often lack any person who knows them at all well. This social situation renders them far less communicative than they could be.

20. There are many reasons for parents' inability to formulate their practices with children like Bianca into words. The fact of the matter is, no one, parents or otherwise, has published a study of family communication in this detail and with the deconstruction of family communication praxis as its aim. But it is particularly sensible that no parent has ever written such an article about his or her own child. Many parents recognize themselves in these descriptions. They have their own versions of the lived order of communication with their own deaf-blind children. But to transform the minutiae and orderliness of life with one's child into a research topic and to publish the details of such research is a serious decision, perhaps a decision to thematize that which best remains unanalyzed and not formally named. Doing and knowing reflex-

ively about doing are not necessarily resonate activities, and perhaps this too plays a role in parents not sharing with us the details of these kinds of communicative networks.

21. I maintain this not on the basis of systematic observation or collection of information but on the basis of letters from various individuals over the years who, having read the account of communicating with Bianca, have written to say that they have observed similar phenomena with their relatives.

22. There is a basic value issue in this statement that should not be left implicit. This has to do with the general way one should or should not think about people with severe disability. A good friend of mine with a disability said that it made him nervous when people were too interested in disability or thought that people with disability saw things very differently from other people. He emphasized the commonalities that all persons have and the variety of experience found in all people with or without disabilities. Interpreting the difference or sameness of people like Bianca or Chris is a very interesting issue and requires, I think, recognition of both simultaneously. Such matters are more open to empirical discovery than policy.

23. These professional models, learned during graduate training, make professionals in some sense stupider about communication than they would be just as human beings. In one instance I observed a psychologist interviewing a friend of mine (Bobby) with mental retardation and Down syndrome. He had a very severe apraxia that made his speech almost unintelligible to a nonfriend. During the half-hour interview this psychologist was not able to understand anything my friend said. At no time did it occur to her that one remedy to her predicament might have been to ask me or the other person in the room whether we understood what Bobby had said, which it turns out we had. When I gave this woman a ride to her sister's house later that afternoon and her one-and-a-half-year-old niece came up to her and said, "Ta ta tee la ater" (or something to this effect), my psychologist friend was quick to turn to her sister and ask what the child had said, essentially doing the obvious and commonsensical thing. It was this same commonsensical thing that her professional training prohibited her from acting upon in the interview with Bobby. Professionals can thus be trained out of natural competence.

■ CHAPTER 4

Portions of this chapter were originally presented at the International Association for the Education of the Deaf-Blind meetings in Orebro, Sweden, August 4, 1991; and other portions were prepared for the International Institute for Ethnomethodology and Conversational Analysis, Boston, Massachusetts, August 13, 1992. Lindsey Churchill provided a reading of the 1992 version of this chapter.

1. Oliver Sacks's remarkable work, a major contribution to the understanding of sign language and deaf culture, is not clear on the necessity of language for human society and humanness. On the one hand, we find the statement I have quoted, which in principle endorses the functional indispensibility of language for humanness and human relations. On the other hand, the book contains clinical material about several alingual people who appear to have been able to achieve a great deal of participation and intersubjectivity in their everyday lives. I pointed out this contradiction to Sacks, who verbally acknowledged it. The reader should not take this critical remark as a condemnation of Sacks's book in general, since the book is, as most of his work, outstanding.

2. On the basis of the relationships described in this book, in which shared formal language did not play a significant role in the achievement of society, I would have to disagree with this statement. On the other hand, I would agree with the idea that "society without communication is not possible." The question is to what degree language represents the primary and most important form of human communication. Merleau-Ponty, in his *Phenomenology of Perception*, warns us not to fall victim to the "ruse of language." It is possible to read his distrust of emphasizing the role of language in constituting the human life world as grounds for my own observations and motivation for pursuing the studies of deaf-blind, alingual persons. These relationships essentially convinced me of Merleau-Ponty's proposition. It also is important to clarify the role of formal language in these studies. The ward and the home were indeed social forms structured around language activities and descriptions. The relationships between staff and children were linguistically organized, in a nonintersubjective sense, where the staff, the dominant class of the ward, enforced in knowing and unknowing ways

the structures of the everyday world that came with their mother tongue. The childen were forced to comply with the vision of the mother tongue as it was represented by the speaking, seeing, and hearing staff. These understandings seemed to be extrinsic to the children's ways of looking at the world as nonformal-language users. Thus, when I write of the ward as a society without language, I do not mean that language did not exist on the ward. Instead, I am pointing to the relationships between deaf, blind, alingual children and seeing, hearing, speaking adults that were achieved without the common resource of shared formal language. I mean to point to the possibility of concerted forms of work without formal language as a resource.

3. "Animal behavior aims at an animal setting (*Umwelt*) and centres of resistance (*Widerstand*). . . . Human behaviour opens on a world (*Welt*) and upon an object (*Gegenstand*) beyond the tools which it makes for itself, and one may even treat one's own body as an object. . . . Human life 'understands' not only a certain definite environment, but an infinite number of possible environments, and it understands itself because it is thrown into a natural world." Although the terms *Welt* and *Umwelt* are not used consistently in the text, they are meant to point to two aspects of the human life world (*Lebensfeld*): one, the relatively given perceptual and motor machinery of human bodies (our animal inheritance as it were), and the other, the socially produced institutions, objects, languages, cultures, and the rest, that distinguish human life from that of most other animals.

4. The term *Umwelt* was originally popularized by the comparative psychologist Jacob von Uexkull in the beginning of this century. See especially his essay "A Stroll Through the Worlds of Animals and Men," in C. Schiller and K. Lashley, eds., *Instinctive Behavior* (New York: International Press, 1934). This is a particularly interesting and innovative essay that examines the way the perceptions and actions of species are geared into a world particular to its biological organization.

5. The essay "Sociogenic Brain Damage," by Ashley Montague, is a treatment of the effects of social class and culture on the organic development of the brain. It has long been known in the neurosciences that nutrition and stimulation/activity have an impact upon the postnatal development of brain tissues and functions. Montague suggests the rela-

tion between poor nutrition and activity in the lower classes and the incidence of developmental neuropathology in children. Thus, the claim of self-constitution of biological capabilities can be taken literally in this case.

6. Take, for example, Merleau-Ponty's description of "knowledge of place," in which knowledge is reduced to a kind of mute coexistence that cannot be conveyed communicationally (1962, 105). See also the discussion below of the concept of praktognosia, a way of access to the world and object that again cannot be formalized or spoken in so many words.

7. Merleau-Ponty writes, "Our view of man will remain superficial so long as we fail to go back to that origin, so long as we fail to find beneath the chatter of words, the primordial silence, and as long as we do not describe the action which breaks this silence" (1962, 184). In a way, the current discussion of what was known in common by children and adults in these studies points to the existence of powerful forms of "mutual sharing," not formulated as such, that were anterior to language per se. These could be called "silent" forms of intersubjectivity. On the other hand, Merleau-Ponty argues that because of the way understanding human gesture occurs without formal comprehension or analysis, but as an act or spectacle in the world, it is not clear that these silent understandings are not in some way communicated. Certainly they are part of our life world and come with or are present beneath every communication. They are part of the unexplicated grounds for action and understanding.

8. Merleau-Ponty points repeatedly to various forms of bodily knowledge and specifically the body as it is used in everyday life (not the body "as an idea"). Of particular interest regarding deaf-blind children is the idea that "the body is borne towards tactile experience by all of its surfaces and all its organs simultaneously, and carries with it a certain typical structure of the tactile 'world' " (317). The structure of a tactile world is a kind of bodily knowledge that is shared by adults and children vulgarly.

9. It is possible to include other kinds of bodily expressions as items in the lexicon—for example, posture or pose. In the discussion of the history of art it was once remarked that the painting of a back can reveal

the station, emotional disposition, and character of the person represented. In this sense, the posture of an individual can also serve as indexical expression in the conversation of the body. It is also important to think of this lexicon, not as discrete building blocks, like a dictionary, for example, but as ways of relating to a world and as silent understandings given by the body.

10. In his essay "On Multiple Realities" Schutz (1973) describes several modalities of reality (everyday reality, dreaming, phantasm, the world of science) experienced by humans. The world of everyday reality is seen by him as the "paramount reality," by which he means that all others are experienced as deviations from this reality and that consciousness within them eventually return to this everyday reality. The remarks made within this chapter do not address the meaning or occurrence of other realities for the adults and children in the studies.

11. In Harvery Sacks's essay "on Sociological Description" (*Berkeley Journal of Sociology*, 1963) the first explication of the conversational machinery can be found. The person-defining character of this machinery, that a person is that being (member) who as conversationalist does, is, and thinks what the machinery of conversation requires, is also a major contribution of that essay. Many of the structures/processes/happenings of the conversational machine have been documented by conversational analysts; see especially the work of Emmanuel Schegloff. I think that there may be parallels between the conversation with our bodies, such as those that occur in the above studies, and the conversation with language (for example, taking turns).

12. The interpretation of pathological behaviors and their reinterpretation as socially meaningful ways of participation in institutions (the rationality of action in institutions) is available on the one hand in formal institutional studies such as that of Stanton and Schwartz (*The Mental Hospital*), David Rosenhan ("On Being Sane in Insane Places"), and Braginsky, Braginsky, and Ring (*Methods of Madness*). The interpretation of pathological behavior as meaningful social participation in informal institutions such as the family may be found especially in the work of Laing and Esterson (*Sanity, Madness, and the Family*) and Jules Henry (*Pathways to Madness*). In various ways these studies depict the participation in "projects" of persons "working" together. Such a revelation of the context of action reveals its sensibility.

13. For purposes of this discussion I am reordering the elements of Garfinkel's definition in a way that allows me to deal with the easier parts of it first and the more difficult later. Thus, the numbering of definitional components in this writing does not correspond with that found in Garfinkel's article.

14. Interestingly, when such resources are taken or absent from the interaction, the use of these bodily expressions becomes easier to see. In the case of persons from whom language has been taken through accident, stroke, or other trauma, the use of these bodily expressions includes the substitution of bodily expressions for words (nodding one's head to indicate agreement), akin to signing, as well as the use of the body to express messages similar to the ways Christina and Bianca did. (For example, see Davies and Meehan's 1978 work on head trauma victims.) The study of communicative interaction between parents and neonates would also reveal these kinds of phenomena.

15. Another objectivity of the first order in this study was the rubella virus and its effect upon these children. In some sense the "facticity" of the virus, whatever the societal reaction to it, gave these studies an unusual character for ethnomethodology. As opposed to the construction of nebulous visual phenomena in a lab or demonstrations on a blackboard, these observations were of something that had an empirical resting point, the "ultimate reality" of the effects of rubella on these children.

16. It is also true that these studies have been used to advise special educators and others about their work with deaf-blind children. This obvious lack of "indifference" is in no way in contradiction to ethnomethodological indifference, although some people have interpreted it in this way. Such an interpretation mistakes a methodological recommendation related to the conduct of "ethnomethodological inquiry" for an ethical principle forbidding action in some other form of activity (for example, "trying to make things better"). The activity of analysis and that of training special educators are not identical; whether or not research is insightful and uncovers aspects of, in this case, professional reality that are interesting and useful to professionals, there is no ethnomethodological argument for or against such work.

17. Oliver Sacks quoted Mary McCarthy's remark about Hannah

Arendt's writings that they were "both astounding and obvious," and then proceeded to say that "this is equally true of [mine]." I accept that characterization of my work, insofar as that work tries to make obvious that which might only have been known in the praktognosic sense described in Chapter 3. This makes many of the results of analysis *obvious* in the sense that one is reminded that one "knew" that already, *astounding* in that one did not at all know that one knew that.

◼ CHAPTER 5

Parts of this chapter appeared in an earlier unpublished paper written in 1983 and revised in 1988. A paper upon which this chapter is based was written for use at the seminar "Video I Kvalitativ, Paedagogisk Forskning" (Video in qualitative pedagogical research), September 28–October 2, 1992, Sonderborg, Denmark.

1. This exercise was a simplified version of one used by Garfinkel in the late 1970s in an undergraduate course on sociological theory at UCLA. I served as graduate assistant for this course one quarter and learned the exercise from him at that time.

2. A final category, "a phone ringing itself," will not be included in this discussion of Garfinkel's exercise.

3. Student recorded Garfinkel's office phone and mine, for which they had previously arranged, thereby contributing yet another kind of phone call (that is, a phone summoning someone else, but as a simulation). One student recorded a phone call off of the introduction to her favorite television show (the *Rockford Files*).

4. Members knowledge of taking turns is praktognosic—that is, a knowledge that is available in the doing, but not in the saying.

5. If readers are inclined to dismiss this example as either trivial or poor methodology, I should point out that this particular example was selected (I believe) partly because it mirrors exactly the kind of methods employed by the "objectivists" in sociology, those who would only measure behavior by some preconceived theory and encoding device and who subsume every research problem to their methodology (this has led persons in sociology to be experts in methods rather than in problems). Garfinkel is well aware of how misfitted this method is to an explication of the lived orders under investigation; he is not a bad methodologist

but rather tries to display in a metaphorical fashion how some of his colleagues study the lived orders of everyday life. It is a demonstration.

6. The term "normal science" refers to the most commonly found science. Thus, in the case of scientific studies of families with retarded members, at the time of my research there were no qualitative or naturalistic observation studies of families that had been published in the research literature, and thus normal science consisted overwhelmingly in the procedures of clinical interviews, questionnaires, and scales.

7. This is one of those phenomena that blatantly points to itself as being the "opposite of what it appears to be," to paraphrase the rock singer Harry Chapin.

8. As a person married for many years I found myself very equivocal in responding to these items. "Sometimes" was by far the most common response I had, because almost all the statements that I read had been true at one time or another, and many of them did not seem related to how I perceived my own sexual satisfaction.

9. The whole idea of social researchers constructing scales to precisely measure something before they have made any attempts systematically to describe it *in situ*, as it is actually manifest in particular instances and situations, is a paradox or absurdity of the quantificationist methodological practice. As Garfinkel put it in class one time, "The problem with scientists is not that they do not know enough about what they are interested in; it is that they know too much." I have chosen to label the use of the procedure I am discussing here a variant of meaurement madness in American social science research.

10. It is at this point where social and human services researchers begin talking about the limits of the predictive ability of their method or about the inherent complexity of prediction or about the very limited knowledge that we have amassed thus far (of course requiring more research!).

11. To the degree this is true, social researchers have turned their graduate students away from "problems of world constitution," as Habermas puts it.

12. Garfinkel found some pleasure in this anecdote. When my father took me to UNIVAC in the mid-1950s, there were signs on everyone's desk in all sorts of foreign languages. When I asked someone what all

the signs meant, the man showing my father and me around said, "They all mean the same thing . . . crap in, crap out." The remark parallels the recommendations of the phone exercise.

13. To select this article I turned to the most reputable research journal in the field at the time (1983) and started searching from its most recent edition backward until an article on the topic of family response to disability was found. *The American Journal of Mental Deficiency* (today *The American Journal of Mental Retardation*) was a peer-review journal with a highly sophisticated editorial staff.

14. Since Waisbren was apparently in no way aware of ethnomethodology or the concept of a lived order, it is not intended by this explication that she ought to have been so aware. The archaeological use of her work, as an object of a historical situation, is not intended as criticism of her capacities as a research scientist, then or now.

15. Such observations may or may not have been done informally. If they were, they were not reported as part of the article and were obviously not considered as data relevant to the analysis.

16. Interviews of parents may be very useful as sensitizing devices to researchers or, as described herein, as techniques to elicit parents' thoughts and reflections about their situations. This knowledge is not identical with the structures and processes of the lived orders that they produce with their children.

17. This notion of assumed isomorphism is similar to the hermeneuticists' "copy" or "correspondence" theory of reality building in science.

18. Reflections about one's everyday life—for example, in a casual conversation, at a physician's office, in a researcher's office, and so forth—are common matters of discourse and easily observed. Their content is not unrelated to the actualities of everyday life. Reflections and accounts of one's everyday life as part of the arrangements and affairs of everyday life are also strongly related to the organization and production of those affairs. However, in both cases it would be epistemologically naive to assume that the "production accounts" are in any way isomorphic with the actual, observable production and recognition of everyday life. Garfinkel remarked, "It is saying an awful lot to claim that somebody knows what he or she is doing" (personal communication, 1978). On the other hand, ethnomethodologists believe that the reflec-

tions (accounts) of members engaged in the activities of everyday life are essential elements in the structuring and production of those activities.

19. I have discussed the reactivity of this method in the case study in Chapter 3. Basically, in a home setting any method would have its own form of reactivity. I judged this procedure to be far better that actually taking notes while in the home. This also allowed for more spontaneous and normal reactions on my part.

20. In his most famous film, Kurosawa leaves his audience with four contradictory interpretations of a murder-rape without resolving which was the "correct one."

21. There are approaches to fieldwork, most notably "grounded theory," that attempt to separate out individual subjectivity in data analysis and gathering. They may enhance reliability of observations through intersubjective checking of interpretation, but they do not solve the essential problem of flattening epistemology into methodology; that is, they are not ethnomethodological.

22. As a fieldwork supervisor for this student. I was always impressed by her sensitivities as an observer and how these were often very different from my own. In the summary of her first visit to a setting in which little babies with severe disabilities were educated, Roxanne said, "They didn't smell right. Not like babies. Sour. I wanted to undress them, wash them, and powder them right away, so they would smell right." As a non-olfactory-oriented male, I would never have made so beautiful and revealing an observation.

23. My purpose here is not to demonstrate this phenomenon to the reader, who is invited to reread Chapter 3 for details.

24. That is, "just" these notes, written at just this time, with just such teachers instructing me, recorded on just this tape recorder, and so forth. The "justs" of the data production.

25. It is in some ways a real pity that this lengthy dissertation was never actually written. It was rejected by all involved as entirely impractical and beyond the physical capabilities of the author or the readers. It would indeed have been all that, but had it been written, it might have stood as one of the most profound answers to the question, What can be learned from a single case?

26. There is, and has been for some scholars for a very long time, no

such knowable thing as "the Smiths in themselves." Given the interpretable character of what one sees and reports about any lived order, it is not possible to decide what are true or objective features of any particular construction, since any criterion of objectivity is based on someone else's construction of that lived order. What are pertinent or not pertinent aspects of the lived order to report upon is nothing but a practical matter. Views about what are part and not part of the lived order under investigation are embedded in the data-production procedures themselves and are not usually matters for direct observation and inspection. As Grunwald ([1924?] 1970) argued, part of what is taken to be "reality" in any scientific study is not open to empirical demonstration and is accepted on the basis of unexamined beliefs, or faith.

27. The anthropological concepts of emic (native's) knowledge and etic (anthropologist's) knowledge may also be used to characterize ethnographic data.

28. This study was done under the clinical supervision of Gary Kielhofner, chair of the Occupational Therapy Program at UCLA's Neuropsychiatric Institute, and under the academic supervision of Melvin Pollner, an ethnomethodologist at the Department of Sociology, UCLA.

29. In ethnomethodology a common type of project that would be "purely" videotape based would be conversational analysis. Frequently tape data is employed by persons who have not participated either in the conversation or the taping of it. In this case they rely solely upon videotape as the source of data.

30. This phrase parallels that used by Karl Mannheim (1936) in characterizing his approach to causation ("It is no accident that . . .") and truthfulness (one attains a "deeper understanding" of some issue). These phrases are particularly vague and weak, by which Mannheim points to his own uneasiness with saying that something caused something else or that one has access to the truth of a situation. Similarly, I am neither clear nor hard in my claims about the relation of my notes to the lived order.

31. In actual practice the collection of videotape data is often very tiring and demanding for the researcher. He or she must attend to the formal problems and demands of getting videotape data while acting as participant-observer. After a day's shooting with "the clients," as they

were then called, people would return exhausted, and it was all that could be done to rewind the tape, label it, and put it on the shelf (and often not even all these were done). The viewing and cataloguing of taped material was a constant and difficult task that required incessant bugging to get people to do it. While working with videotape can be fun, sad, profound, and so forth, it can also be difficult, boring, and tedious.

32. I labeled each critical incident by a name such as "Privacy Lost," "The Interrogation Tape," or "Being on the Inside on the Outside."

33. There were no locks on the doors of the facility in which these persons lived. Therefore any situation was potentially public. Thus, and consistent with this same fact of institutional life, persons would routinely come to the door in their underwear and often would clothe only after they saw it was researchers from the project (they saw it bothered us and so would cover up for us). One time I knocked at the door of the two sisters, was told to come in, and found them in bed naked with a man! When I swung the door closed, I was told to "come on in, Dave. Don't worry. No problem."

34. The clinical misassessment of Bobby's everyday communicative competencies closely parallels that of Bianca's, having the same underlying epistemology and unexamined correspondence assumed to exist between the results of formal clinical procedure and the everyday behaviors exhibited by the person.

35. It is interesting how, when reconstructing the details of the utterances, the transcriber gains access to a world that may be quite different from that experienced by participants (that is, quite different from the emic perspective about those affairs). For example, were you to ask the project members if they understood Bobby during the conversation, they would have said, Almost not at all. The project staff were as amazed at the tape and transcription and the accompanying transformation of Bobby's identity as I was. But in point of fact, the utterance-by-utterance transcription revealed that various statements made by Bobby were understood and that a variety of strategies existed to deal with Bobby's problematically perceived utterances. Even though project staff thought they did not understand Bobby, they did so much more than they thought. Linguistic strategies and reactions to Bobby's utterances could be demonstrated in detail in the transcript, whatever the self-impression

that project members had about their participation in the conversation. A similar phenomenon was noted on another piece of tape, an intake interview with Bobby, after which the psychologist said, "I did not understand a single world he said." In fact, a careful inspection of the transcription revealed that she had understood much of what Bobby had said. Both these tapes reveal the demonstrable difference, through video transcription, between what persons think they do and what they actually do.

36. The distinction between syntactics and semantics, form and content, medium and message, is ultimately synthetic and arbitrary in that every phenomenon displays one and the other, as do our conversations and reflections about phenomena.

37. Art once remarked to me that he had chosen Bobby as his special friend. Since there were over one hundred residents, many of whom were mentally ill, some of whom were attractive women and men, I think that Bobby probably had to work very hard competing with these more competent and attractive others to win Art over as his special friend.

■ CHAPTER 6

A version of this chapter was originally published in 1986 in *The Journal of Human Studies* 9:83–106. The author's involvement with the original data collection for this study was supported in the grants cited in Chapter 2.

1. For a more complete list of observational sociologists working on child and child-adult issues, see Waksler 1991. The bibliography to that volume is fairly complete.

2. Associated with this view of development is that of education as basically and most importantly preparation for adult life; it does not have much merit in and of itself. Hence there have been no studies of quality of school life in educational research (see Hegarty, in press).

3. In Chapter 2 this view, as it applied specifically to language development, was discussed; there the scientific and commonsense wisdom was that not to have formal symbolic language was not to be fully human.

4. Indeed, adultcentric thinking is a particular form of ethnocentric-

ism that occurs within a particular culture or even subculture. It is a unique form of ethnocentricism in that all its proponents were once members of the culture they now misconstrue and even fail to see entirely.

5. Another really excellent example of this is Frederick Weisman's film *High School.* In this unedited film shot in an American high school during the Vietnam War, Weisman displays (as I see it) virtual physical domination of high school students by authority, the insensitivity of authority to reason, the arbitrariness of authority, the arbitrariness of the categories adult and child, and many other aspects of child-adult interaction in high schools that are not productive, if not counterproductive, to the general social welfare. The film is really fascinatingly horrifying, as many of Weisman's films are.

6. While Garfinkel (personal communication, 1979) noted that there is a definite faulting to how we view "children"—and this certainly is portrayed in the adult view of children described above—there is also a certain nostalgia in our writings about "childhood and children," as found in Wordsworth's poem above. Our writings about the young are not at all free of heavy emotional investments that we (adults) really do need to face and understand better.

7. Likewise, adultness, seeing and acting upon the world in ways consistent with the official version of adults, is not guaranteed by virtue of having matured biologically and is not barred to the young.

8. The film *L'enfant sauvage,* directed by and starring the late french director/actor Francois Truffault, is a beautiful rendition of the Itard-Victoire story with a few cinematic liberties and excellent acting.

■ CHAPTER 7

1. There were attempts to control for this in the transfer of all "clients" out of state institutions. When this control took the form of written records and documentation (that is, the new agency staff was expected to "learn" the client through the documentation that came along with him or her), the process was often a failure. The other method used by some state agencies was to transfer clients into state-run community facilities and transfer the institutional staff along with them. This, according to internal evaluation documents in New York State, for exam-

ple, appears to have been more successful in achieving a satisfactory adaptation to the community by clients but brought its own problems (namely, that the institutional patterns of care and support followed the staff out of the institution). But for all too many people with rubella syndrome, leaving the institution meant leaving everything behind: their friends, caretakers, and identities. And they all too often found themselves completely alone in an entirely new world. They were forced to make this radical break, and many I knew found it entirely negative and traumatic.

2. Iatrogenesis is a Greek word meaning literally "physician-caused illness." I am using it here loosely to refer to "human-services-caused problems."

3. This is true for most persons with mental retardation who experience acute mental health problems and is not unique at all to persons who are deaf and blind.

4. This term refers to the use of technology, broadly conceived, to enhance communication of individuals. Augmentative communication can involve the use of voice/language synthesizers, computers, typewriters, communication clocks, cards, signs—almost any device or system that can be used to enhance someone's ability to communicate. The approach to communication taken most recently by this group, largely consisting of speech and language pathologists, is consistent with that taken in this book. Indeed, these were the first professionals in the field of disabilities to see the value of the work on Bianca, and they invited me to report the results of the research at national meetings. There is currently a *Journal of Augmentative Communication* published by Lyle Lloyd at Purdue University. There is also an interdisciplinary and inter-organizational group called the National Joint Committee for the Communicative Needs of Persons with Severe Disabilities (an ad hoc group associated with the American Speech and Hearing Association) that comprises speech and language professionals with beliefs and policies about communication that are consistent with those expressed in this book. They should see this book as providing empirical evidence for their perspective.

5. In the field of developmental disabilities, this term is taken to refer to the practices used when trying to help a person with a cognitive,

emotional, or physical disability participate more fully in interaction. Thus, facilitators help those with disabilities to participate in meetings, social gatherings, or other situations where the help of an assistant might be useful.

6. Although I have not personally been trained in facilitated communication, I have observed it and spoken with many professionals who have become facilitators. The technique involves a series of preparatory training exercises for those without formal language mastery.

7. Out of respect for the originator of this philosophy, still very such discussed and in use today, Neils Eric Bank-Mikkelson, and students of his concept Bengt Nirje and Wolf Wolfensberger, I should point out that the problem that existed at the hospital was in the poor interpretation and application of their work. The misuses and perversions associated with the concept of normalization caused Wolfensberger in 1983 to rename his version of the concept "social role valorization."

8. Thus, many states—New York, Colorado, and Oregon, to name but a few—are employing what are called consumer-based, or consumer-driven, service evaluations. These consumer evaluations employ some form of systematic data gathering, usually questionnaires and interviews, to assess the opinions of consumers about their services. These systems tend to be difficult to design and manage. Because the data they produce often conflict with bureaucratic forces and regulations, they can produce tensions in the system. One's interpretation of this as a good or a bad development is primarily political. These kinds of systems are growing with the advent of the era of self-advocacy in the field of disabilities.

9. See especially Soder's keynote address at the Quality of Life research session at the international Association for the Scientific Study of Mental Deficiency, Dublin, August 1988.

10. In characterizing these studies here, I am including all the materials cited in the reference section that I have written about the deaf-blind to date. There is a small but growing observational literature (not all of which directs itslef to the social construction of disability and to the critical description of persons with disability in a social context).

11. It is fitting that the last note to this work be based upon a conversation with a parent of a child who had never developed language (and

who died tragically at a young age). In a train station in Esberg, Denmark, in 1990 I sat with Frank Ulmer, a psychologist who is also the parent to whom I refer. We had spent several days together, and he had shared with me his own experiences communicating with his son, similar to those reported in my work with Chris and Bianca. The Ulmers had had their own "lived order" of nonformal language communication. At the station, with only twenty minutes until I was to depart, we madly plotted out the systematic research that could be done to document how the body has its own lexicon and form of making meaning in the structures of everyday existence. We scribbled on a napkin and realized the project was a considerable, if not a noble, undertaking. We would collect data more systematically on communication in households like his or the Smiths, and we would begin to build up categories and structures from the data—a kind of "grounded theory" approach that makes sense in moving beyond the initial exploratory work offered in Chapters 2 and 3. This note, then, is an invitation to other researchers to follow up on these studies and to continue to observe *in situ* communicational networks not primarily based upon shared formal language. We may be able, one day, actually to write the language of the body and to know it in a more comprehensive and critical way.

REFERENCES

Aries, Phillip. 1962. *Centuries of childhood: A social history of family life.* New York: Alfred A. Knopf.

Bar-Hillel, Y. 1954. Indexical expressions. *Mind* 63:359–39.

Benthall, Jonathan, and Ted Polhemus. 1975. *The body as a medium of expression.* New York: E. P. Dutton.

Bettelheim, Bruno. 1959. Feral and autistic children. *American Journal of Sociology* 64 (5): 455–67.

Birdwhistell, R. L. 1960. Kinesics and communication. In E. Carpenter and M. McLuhan, eds., *Exploration in communication.* Boston: Beacon Press.

Bogdan, Robert, and Steven Taylor. 1989. Relationships with severely disabled people: The social construction of humanness. *Social Problems* 36 (2): 131–44.

Bordieu, Pierre, and L.J.D. Wacquant. 1992. *An invitation to reflexive sociology.* Chicago: University of Chicago Press.

Braginsky, B. M., D. B. Braginsky, and Kenneth Ring. 1969. *Methods of madness: The mental hospital as a last resort.* New York: Holt, Rinehart & Winston.

Button, Graham, ed. 1991. *Ethnomethodology and the human sciences.* Cambridge: Cambridge University Press.

Cicourel, A. V. 1964. *Methods and measurement in sociology.* New York: Free Press.

———. 1974. *Cognitive sociology: Language and meaning in social interaction.* New York: Free Press.

Cicourel, A. V., K. H. Jennings, K. C. Leiter, Robert Mackay, Hugh Mehan, and D. Roth. 1974. *Language use and school performance.* New York: Academic Press.

Clarke, Michael. 1975. Survival in the field: Implications of personal experience in fieldwork. *Theory and Society* 2 (spring): 95–123.

Davies, Philip, and Hugh Mehan. 1978. Professional and family understanding of impaired communication. Unpublished paper, Oxford Rehabilitation Research Unit.

de Fornel, Michel. 1991. Voir un evenment: Comptes rendus de perception et semantique des situations. *Raisons practiques* 2:97–122.

Durkheim, Emile. 1938. *The rules of sociological method.* Chicago: University of Chicago Press.

Eibl-Eibsfeldt, Iranaus. 1973. The expressive behavior of the deaf-blind born. In M. V. Cranach and I. Vine, eds., *Social communication and movement.* London: Academic Press.

Ekman, P. E., and W. V. Friesen. 1971. Constants across cultures in face and emotion. *Journal of Personality and Psychiatry* 17 (2): 24–29.

Garfinkel, Harold. 1967. *Studies in ethnomethodology.* Englewood Cliffs, N.J.: Prentice-Hall.

———. 1991. Respecification: Evidence for locally produced, naturally accountable phenomena of order, logic, reason, meaning, method, etc. in and as the essential haecceity of immortal ordinary society (I)—an announcement of studies. In Graham Button, ed., *Ethnomethodology and the human sciences.* Cambridge: Cambridge University Press.

Garfinkel, Harold, and Harvey Sacks. 1970. On formal structures of practical action. In J. C. McKinney and E. Tiryakian, eds., *Theoretical sociology.* East Norwalk, Conn.: Appleton-Century-Crofts.

Glassner, Barry. 1976. Kid society. *Urban Education* 11 (1): 5–21.

Goffman, Erving. 1961. *Asylums.* New York: Anchor Books.

Goode, David. 1974a. Some aspects of interaction among congenitally deaf-blind and normal persons. Working paper no. 1, Mental Retardation Research Center, UCLA Medical Center.

———. 1974b. What shall we do with the rubella children? Unpublished paper, Mental Retardation Research Center, UCLA Medical Center.

———. 1975a. Some aspects of embodied activity on a deaf-blind ward in a state hospital. Unpublished paper, Mental Retardation Research Center, UCLA Medical Center.

———. 1975b. Towards the grounds for achieving intersubjectivity: An initial report from a ward for the congenitally deaf-blind, retarded. Department of Sociology and Mental Retardation Research Center, UCLA.

———. 1979. The world of the deaf-blind. In J. Jacobs and H. Schwartz, eds., *Qualitative sociology: A method to the madness*. New York: Free Press.

———. 1980a. Behavioral sculpting. In J. Jacobs, ed., *Phenomenological approaches to mental retardation*. New York: C. C. Thomas.

———. 1980b. Deaf-blind: An examination of extraordinary communication and its significance to the sociology of knowledge. Ph.D. diss., UCLA, 1980. Abstract in *Dissertation Abstracts International*. Ann Arbor, Mich.

———. 1983. Who is Bobby? In G. Kielhofner, ed., *Health through occupation*. Philadelphia: F. A. Davis.

———. 1984. Socially produced identities and the problem of competence among the retarded. In S. Tomlinson and L. Barton, eds., *Special education and social values*. London: Croom-Helm.

———. 1985. Stigma management as a family affair. *Journal of Family Relations*.

———. 1986. Kids, culture, and innocents. *Journal of Human Studies* 9:83–106.

———. 1988. What's wrong with the way we study families with retarded members? Paper presented at the annual meeting of the Academy on Mental Retardation.

———. 1990. On understanding without words: Communication between an alingual deaf-blind child and her parents. *Journal of Human Studies* 13:1–37.

———, ed. In press. *Quality of life for persons with disabilities: International perspectives and issues*. Cambridge: Brookline Books.

Goode, David, and Michael P. Gaddy. 1976. Ascertaining choice with alingual deaf-blind and retarded clients. *Mental Retardation* 14 (6): 10–12.

Goode, David, and Francis Waksler. 1990. The missing who of social interaction: Situational identity and fault-finding with an alingual deaf-blind child. In Nancy Mandel, ed., *Sociological studies of child development*. Greenwich, Conn.: JAI Press.

Grunwald, Ernst. [1924] 1970. Systematic analysis. In J. E. Curtis and J. W. Petras, eds., *The sociology of knowledge: A reader*. New York.

Habermas, Jürgen. 1971. *Knowledge and human interests*. Trans. Jeremy Shapiro. Boston: Beacon Press.

Hegarty, Seamus. In press. Quality of life at school. In David Goode, ed., *Quality of life for persons with disabilities: International perspectives and issues*. Cambridge: Brookline Books.

Henry, Jules. 1965. *Pathways to madness*. New York: Vintage.

Husserl, Edmund. [1913] 1962. *Ideas: General introduction to pure phenomenology*. Trans. W. R. Boyce Gison. New York: Collier.

Itard, Jean-Marc Gaspard. [1801] 1972. Of the first developments of the young savage of Aveyron. In L. Maison, ed., *Wolf children and the problem of human nature*. New York: New Left Books.

Kendon, Alfred. 1967. Some functions of gaze direction in social interaction. *Acta Psychologica* 26:22–63.

Konrad, Gyorgy. 1974. *The caseworker*. New York: Harcourt Brace Jovanovich.

Kupferberg, Tuli. 1983. Kiddie porn. *High Times*. January.

Laing, R. D., and A. Esterson, 1964. *Sanity, madness, and the family*. London: Tavistock.

Lewis, M., W. E. McLean, W. Bryson-Brockmann, R. Arendt, B. Beck, P. S. Fidler, and A. A. Baumeister. 1984. Time series analysis of stereotyped movements: The relationship of body-rocking to cardiac activity. *American Journal of Mental Deficiency* 89 (3): 287–94.

Lynch, Michael. 1991. Method: Measurement—ordinary and scientific measurement as ethnomethodological phenomena. In Graham Button, ed., *Ethnomethodology and the human sciences*. Cambridge: Cambridge University Press.

Mackay, Robert. 1974. Conceptions of children and models of socialization. In R. Turner, ed., *Ethnomethodology*. Markham, Ont.: Penguin Books. First published in H. P. Dreitzel, ed., *Recent Sociology No. 5*. New York: Macmillan.

Malson, Lucien. 1972. *Wolf children and the problem of human nature*. New York: New Left Books.

Mandel, Nancy, ed. 1990. *Sociological studies of child development*. Vol. 3. Greenwich, Conn.: JAI Press.

Mannheim, Karl. 1936. *Ideology and utopia*. New York: International Library of Psychology, Philosophy, and Scientific Method.

Mannoni, Octavio. 1972. Itard and his savage. *New Left Review* 74 (July/August).

Mao Tse-tung. 1971. On contradiction. In *Selected readings from the works of Mao Tse-tung.* Peking: Foreign Language Press.

McNeill, M. C., E. A. Polloway, and J. D. Smith. 1984. Feral and isolated children: Historical review and analysis. In Adrian Ashman and Ronald Laura, eds., *Education and training of the mentally retarded.* New York: Nichols Publishing.

Merleau-Ponty, Maurice. 1962. *The phenomenology of perception.* London: Routledge & Kegan Paul.

Opie, Iona, and Peter Opie. 1959. *The lore and language of schoolchildren.* London: Oxford University Press.

Papert, Seymour. 1984. *Mindstorms.* New York: Basic Books.

Polhemus, Ted. 1974. *The body reader: Social aspects of the human body.* London: Penguin Books.

Pollner, Melvin, and David Goode. 1990. Ethnomethodology and person-centering practices. *Person-Centered Review* 5 (2): 203–20.

Poole, Roger. 1975. Objective sign and subjective meaning. In Jonathan Benthall and Ted Polhemus, eds., *The body as a medium of expression.* New York: E. P. Dutton.

Robbins, Nan. 1963. *Auditory training in the Perkins deaf-blind department.* Perkins School Publication no. 23.

Rosenhan, David. 1973. On being sane in insane places. *Science* 179 (January).

Sacks, Harvey. 1963. On sociological description. *Berkeley Journal of Sociology* 13:1–17.

———. 1974. On the analyzability of stories by children. In Roy Turner, ed., *Ethnomethodology.* Markham, Ont.: Penguin Books.

Sacks, Harvey, E. A. Schegloff, and G. Jefferson. 1974. A simplest systematics for the organization of turn taking in conversation. *Language* 50 (4): 696–735.

Sacks, Oliver. 1989. *Seeing voices.* Berkeley and Los Angeles: University of California Press.

Sartre, Jean-Paul. 1956. *Being and nothingness.* New York: Philosophical Library.

Schutz, Alfred. 1970. *On phenomenology and social relations.* Chicago: University of Chicago Press.

————. 1973. *Collected papers. Vol. 1, The problem of social reality.* The Hague: Martinus Nijhoff.

Schwartz, Howard. 1978. Data, who needs it? *Analytic Sociology* 1 (2).

Stanton, Alfred, and Morris Schwartz. 1954. *The mental hospital.* New York: Basic Books.

van Dijk, Jan. 1968. Movement and communication with rubella children. Paper presented at the annual general meeting of the National Association for Deaf/Blind and Rubella Children, The Netherlands.

von Uexhall, Jacob. 1934. A stroll through the worlds of animals and men. In C. Schiller and K. Lashley, eds., *Instinctive behavior.* New York: International University Press.

Waisbren, Susan. 1980. Parents' reactions after the birth of a developmentally disabled child. *American Journal of Mental Deficiency* 84 (4): 345–51.

Waksler, Francis, ed. 1991. *Studying social worlds of children.* London: Falmer Press.

Watzlawick, Paul. 1973. *The pragmatics of human communication.* New York: W. W. Norton.

Whorf, Benjamin Lee. 1956. Language, thought, and reality. In J. B. Carroll, ed., *Selected writing of Benjamin Lee Whorf.* New York: Wiley.

Wikler, L., and Melvin Pollner. 1985. The social construction of unreality: A case study of a family's attribution of competence to a severely retarded child. *Family Process* 24 (2): 241–54.

Wolfensberger, Wolf. 1981. The extermination of handicapped persons in World War II Germany. *Mental Retardation* 19 (1): 1–17.

————. 1989. Human services policies: The rhetoric versus the reality. In Len Barton, ed., *Disability and dependency.* London: Falmer Press.

————. In press. Quality of life: A useless term we should hang up. In David Goode, ed., *Quality of life for persons with disabilities: International perspectives and issues.* Cambridge: Brookline Books.

INDEX